BEYOND WITHIN

SRI CHINMOY

BEYOND WITHIN

A Philosophy for the Inner Life

SRI CHINMOY

Printed by:
Agni Press, 84-47 Parsons Blvd.,
Jamaica, N.Y. 11432

CONTENTS

Sri Chinmoy

INTRODUCTION

i

Beyond Within is a title to be read in two ways. Used as a noun the word "Beyond" suggests that within each of us there is an experience of "the Beyond," an awareness of ourselves as limitless, extensive: transcending the narrow frame of self-conception which marks our ordinary life. Used as a preposition, "Beyond" suggests that we do not remain within, but go beyond the within to manifest in the world the fruits of our inner experience. The title is intended in both senses.

In so reading the title, however, we may foster the illusion that the realization of the Beyond within us and the manifestation of that awareness in the outer world are separable. We may, if we choose, distinguish inhaling from exhaling, but breathing is an act where both are required. So with inner realization and outer manifestation: they are always in relation to one another. The more we realize of our true nature in our inward soundings, the more we will enact that awareness in all our relations with the world.

We select the word "Beyond" from Sri Chinmoy's writings because in whatever grammatical sense we take it, the word represents the *dynamism* of his spiritual vision. The process of inner experience is not a reaching of some final state, but rather the engagement in an ever-widening experience of oneness; and the process of transforming ourselves and the world we encounter in daily life is also ceaseless. "Beyond," then, is not a place, but the conception of a process and a capacity, and neither has an end.

The empirical mind rebels at this. Mind rejects infinity. Mind doubts the vision of "Beyond Within," for what Sri Chinmoy calls the "unlit mind" is happy only with measurement, analysis, and limitation. Mind cannot seize upon the flow. For this reason our mind will find itself quarrelling with much of what this book contains. And so be it; may that quarrel be the beginning and continuing experience of our openness to growth. Sri Chinmoy must use words when he talks to us, but he is speaking, like the pipers on Keats' Grecian urn, to our inner ear. Sri Chinmoy calls this inner ear the spiritual "heart"; the heart is his designation not so much for a place in us as an intuitive capacity which experiences what the analytic mind can only piece out or cannot grasp at all. Sri Chinmoy writes as a poet, appealing always to something quicker and more subtle than our reasoning mind.

"Heart?" mind asks; "heart pumps blood; heart is a muscle." Yet what is it we point to when, asked to say, "This is me," we find ourselves tapping with two fingers on the center of our chest? Who is the "I" located here? And what is the capacity in us that responds to the feeling of peace, beauty, love or compassion and *knows* the authenticity of such experiences?

Here, then, in the heart center is our starting place with Sri Chinmoy, either as readers of his writing or as those who experience his presence in meditation. For many of us the heart center may seem an unfamiliar area of self-awareness, if not a new mode of knowing ourselves and the world. "Mode?" mind queries; "What is the mode you speak of?" Heart answers, "This mode is love."

The "Beyond" within us is the experience of love within us—a love without end; we go beyond our "Within" to love the world and all living beings without attachment to them as objects. This love, which can see past preference or taste, which can love the enemy and the friend, is what Sri Chinmoy calls "divine love" in contrast with "human love." And what is this love? In fact it is a dawning awareness that the world without is the same nature as the love within us. Within and without grow to be one; or rather the process of inner awareness ripens into the realization that inner and outer were always one. The separation is not the final reality; for "reality," as Sri Chinmoy will use the word, describes our experience that all is One, One Consciousness comprehended as divine love. The "real world" is not something external to ourselves, pleasing or brutal; reality is the experience of living in the expanding consciousness of an identifying love. "Love your neighbor as yourself" because your neighbor is yourself.

As a title, then, *Beyond Within* indicates a respiration of awareness and action as true to our whole nature as breathing to our body. And as necessary.

The essays, poems, discourses, stories, songs and aphorisms gathered in this book represent only a fraction of what Sri Chinmoy has poured out since he came to the United States from India in 1964. His gifts are hardly confined to the written or spoken word. For those who accept him as a spiritual teacher, the primary experience of him is the silence of meditation. Silence is the language of the Beyond, and the printed words in this book can best fulfil themselves by reaching our heart center and sending us into that silence. The consecutive and apparently discursive movement of the book need impose no obligation on the reader, for there is no argument here, and the whole will be found everywhere in the parts.

The book is arranged in the hope that the reader will look up often and easily into the space of silence surrounding the writing. Its design is more musical than logical. It is a book to be opened and listened to; to be read as long as there is a consenting disposition. The book comes as a friend who does not argue or persuade. If this book contains a version of the truth which has been with us and within us from the beginning, then it addresses us, as that truth always has, asking to be welcomed, not contested. We are invited to read familiarly and to let the words lead us *beyond within*.

ii

To indicate as we have that *Beyond Within* may be opened at any place is not to suggest that this body of Sri Chinmoy's writing is without form. Sri Chinmoy is not a systematic philosopher, and we may be most comfortable at first dipping into his work to read as we might a poet, for momentary insight and inspiration. But in the remainder of this introduction we will sketch the outline of a unified vision which informs every part of Sri Chinmoy's utterance and has shaped the sequence of selections this anthology contains. It must be said, however, that this introduction is no more than a map of the stars, and in identifying constellations we may at times be imposing our own patterns upon a more fluid reality.

It will be useful to begin with Sri Chinmoy's conception of mind. We were using that word earlier to define an aspect of our cognitive process which calculates, names, judges, and measures the world. To this mind Sri Chinmoy applies various qualifying terms, the "physical mind" or the "unlit mind." Without any modifier, "mind" is implicitly being measured against what he calls the "illumined mind."

This distinction between "mind" and "illumined mind" derives from an awareness that we appear to have two mental modes of comprehending the world. The mode of the "physical mind," at its most refined, is scientific in the strict sense of the word, creating order out of the empirical flux. But it depends for its functioning on the separation of the self from the other. Mind works busily with its images, constructions, versions and memories of the world attempting always to reduce the mystery of being to verifiable laws. Useful and creative as are these various forms of mental analysis, they can never by themselves fully account for the richness of our human experience.

The "illumined mind," on the other hand, is in essence this very same mind but responding to and irradiated by the intuitive knowledge and vision of what we have termed the heart center. From the heart's point of view, the "unlit mind" is like a child insisting on its own stubborn ways, far from fully matured. Sri

Chinmoy is not denigrating mind, but rather suggesting that mind — with all its capacities for construction and analysis — still functions far from its potential; the "unlit mind" is simply in the dark. The heart, with its capacity to experience reality through identification rather than separation, is the source of illumination. Illumination is the experience of oneness.

"Mind," then, is "illumined" when it accepts the heart's light, when it develops its capacities to respond to the promptings from a more intuitive center of human consciousness. The "illumined mind" recognizes the world to be its own nature, for its knowledge is identification, oneness. No longer perceived only in its physical aspect, the world is known as fundamentally composed of consciousness. The world is alive, not sentient in some simple sense, but, as Sri Chinmoy writes, "Consciousness on various levels and consciousness enjoying itself in varied manifestations." To experience the world as consciousness is to realize identity, for we see we are the *same* as that. The feeling of identity is borne in upon our minds, in Sri Chinmoy's terms, as "Peace, Light and Bliss." It is toward such a feeling, such a realization, that the spiritual seeker moves: this is the goal, though not the end. The chapter of this book called "The Goal of Goals " is a description of this illumined state.

Oneness is the goal, but what we know in that experience is that oneness is dynamic. We realize the inexhaustible nature of consciousness, its endlessness of forms, its independence of all forms; we discover, as Sri Chinmoy expresses it, that oneness is "an ever-transcending, ever-manifesting, and ever-fulfilling Beyond." At the top of illumination, then, there is a vision and feeling of the very nature of the cosmos, of life itself, Sri

Chinmoy's writings issue from such a height to tell us that we may know the cosmos and its living beings as "God's dream," as he puts it, infinitely and eternally evolving beyond itself, and yet in every dimension of the process harmonious and perfect, and that we, far from being flotsam on this vastness, are one with it. It is all God—in Sri Chinmoy's terms, the "Supreme"—and all the Supreme is alive in us. What Sri Chinmoy calls our "Immortality" is our awareness of this oneness as ourselves.

Most of us are indeed a long way from such a height of vision—a long way in terms of our awareness, but not in time or space, for Sri Chinmoy assures us that the experience is already ours, though unrecognized. One reason that we do not realize our oneness consciously is due to the authority of our physical mind, and our failure fully to attune our awareness to the heart's mode of knowing. Yet whenever we experience beauty, tranquility, understanding or compassion and sense in ourselves a sudden opening of energy and awareness, we come into touch with a capacity in us that is always there yet only fitfully claims our full attention. Such experiences may hint to us that illumination is already ours; we need only to see as we have always been able to see, and to free ourselves from what limits and divides.

This apparent riddle—that we are illumined yet unaware of that illumination—expresses itself in another distinction in Sri Chinmoy's writing that may at first appear puzzling. He talks about "Perfection" and "perfect Perfection." The latter would appear to be a redundancy, except only by such a phrase can we embrace the paradoxical truth that we are "perfect" and at the same time in ignorance of our perfection. "Perfect

Perfection" is the *conscious* awareness of oneness. In what Sri Chinmoy calls our "ignorance" we perceive the universe to be a multiplicity of objects, apparently interrelated by laws our science still gropes to articulate. In our most painful moments of "ignorance" the unlit mind looks out into an absurd and chaotic night. Imprisoned in the separating ego of the mind, we may be overcome by a sense of despair. But then, by some grace of insight, we have also known the universe to be no warring multiplicity of complex forces at all, but a single whole — whole as a thought or as a feeling. At such moments our sense of the universe is irradiated by a glimpse of oneness in whose light we see that the chaotic movement of relative objects is and has been no other than the interplay of the One with Itself, self-evolved, self-delighting, self-confirmed. The universe so experienced Sri Chinmoy calls "The Absolute Supreme." By virtue of such a realization we see that what we had taken to be imperfect was always perfect. It was "Perfection" as we slept; it is "perfect Perfection" when we awaken.

To our "mind," then, the "Goal of Goals" appears a long way off. Though the goal, being within us, is not separated from us in space or time, yet the process of coming to our full awakening may conveniently express itself in temporal and spatial terms. We may talk, as Sri Chinmoy does, about our "path" to that goal; we may refer to the apparent time it takes to achieve illumination. We may even talk about achieving what we already possess. For the seeker's mind such terms are relevant and inevitable; in our perception, now, there is indeed a path to be taken. But the journey is full of hints of its own fulfilment, and its end is not a termination, but an ever-increasing joy in the process of itself.

Where, we may inquire, does this "spiritual path" begin? The beginning lies in the moment of what Sri Chinmoy calls "inspiration." Inspiration is nothing we can will for ourselves, and thus all seekers — no matter what their path — have in common an implicit conception of Grace. Grace is, on one level, our experience that there is a source of energy or insight, remedy, clarity, or guidance beyond ourselves. Inspiration, the breath of this Grace, does not obey our will. Under the influence of inspiration we discover an ability to function that is quite different from the ordinary: what we had always accomplished by applied intentions and hesitant trial, we now effect not as doers but as instruments. Inspiration leads us; in our obedience to it we perform something that delights us but which, paradoxically, we cannot really take credit for performing.

Inspiration may touch us at any time. It may come to us as a mild euphoria that mysteriously lightens a routine. It may come to the practiser of a craft or art who will, for the spell of its duration, recognize and relish its presence like a dearest friend. In any of us who have felt it — and who can say they have not? — inspiration leaves us always with a longing, great or small, to feel its presence again. For where inspiration comes to us, there we are most alive, most ourselves, though puzzlingly least ourselves as well. For the spiritual seeker, inspiration is the hint of oneness. Its effect is to kindle a longing, and Sri Chinmoy terms that longing "aspiration." Aspiration, the willed dedication of the seeker to know God or Truth, to reach the "Goal," is the dynamic center of Sri Chinmoy's teaching. Only by understanding its nature and function can we appreciate how the entire spiritual journey depends on the presence and continual growth in the seeker of aspiration.

Aspiration is openness to divine inspiration, the very process of opening. It is our source of energy, yet it is also energy of the Source. The Source, Sri Chinmoy calls the "Supreme," "God," or "Truth." Just as the seed planted by the oak is its own self, so the seed planted by the Supreme is aspiration—of His very same nature, capable of fullest growth, yet still embryonic. Aspiration, then, is another form of the Goal itself. For if the Goal is truly the "ever-transcending Beyond"—truly endless—then aspiration must also be endless. Aspiration is ultimately identified as the human face, upturned, of the Supreme Himself manifesting as the human individual. By aspiration's light we will see that the Goal and the path are one and the same.

Aspiration, then, is longing *and* belonging. Only to the physical mind are we separated from God, from each other. To the heart, aspiration is the feeling of the divine inspiration in us, the flash of oneness. The heart cries for a fuller experience of this oneness, for more light, even as it sends the light it has into the physical mind. Feeling the heart's inspiration, the physical mind glimpses that illumination which will finally be its own when it fully accepts the heart's light. But what, we may ask, is this light which enters the heart? What is its source? It is, Sri Chinmoy says, "the light of the soul."

Thus aspiration, most exactly understood, is the energy of the soul. The soul is the center of our eternal and dynamic consciousness which is ultimately one with the infinite consciousness of the Supreme. We do not perceive the soul with our minds; we know the soul by the heart. The heart center is the window through which the soul sends its energy into our awareness and activities. We experience that energy as inspiration which seems to come to us, but actually comes *from* us, from a source in us that is both within and beyond the within. Until our direct illumination in the soul occurs, however, we will experience the soul as a veiled influence, as the light of the sun is known even though the sky is overcast.

In order for us to have a direct perception of the soul and to realize our identity in it, the entire physical and emotional being must be transformed. We have seen the reluctance of the mind to accept the light the heart has access to. The mind remains reluctant because it listens, not to the heart, but to what Sri Chinmoy calls the "vital." The vital is the emotional web of impulses, cravings, desires, appetites, ambitions, fantasies and dreams. The vital is constantly sending signals to the mind: acquire that, taste that, accomplish that, fear that, demand that, cling to that, reject that. To the extent that the mind obeys the vital, it experiences a bewildering round of frustrations, false starts and unfinished undertakings. Happiness seems to elude: peace is never attained.

Yet the vital can be our ally, for if we can harness its restless energy to our own longing for the Truth, then we have joined a powerful force in ourselves with our aspiration. As the heart's competitor, the vital will make us feel a painful division between a higher and a lower self. But in collaboration the vital force becomes what Sri Chinmoy calls "the progressive vital"; and he sees it as indispensable to our spiritual growth.

The transformation of the vital does not occur overnight, any more than does the illumination of the mind. The mind we saw was illumined by the heart; the heart by the soul; the soul by itself, for in its oneness with the

Supreme it is self-effulgent consciousness, pure joy. As the soul passes its light to the receptive heart, and the heart transmits this light of love to the physical mind, so the mind takes its illumination and shares it with its younger brother, the vital. It gives the vital a taste of the true joy which the vital had sought under various frustrating disguises. The mind may guide the vital to a higher and purer perception of its own fulfilment. The vital then is wooed, not destroyed. The transformation of our nature takes place not by reasoning or willpower, but by opening ourselves increasingly to the light of the soul.

iii

We have now to consider in what ways the spiritual seeker, like the artist, practises a discipline which provides a form for inspiration, a discipline through which the transformation is accomplished. We have seen that in essence it is aspiration that energizes our spiritual journey and percolates through all our being. To any and all the ways in which we cultivate aspiration, draw from it and permit its force to transform in our lives, Sri Chinmoy applies the word "meditation." Though that word may suggest a particular form of physical and mental discipline — and we will examine directly how Sri Chinmoy uses the word precisely in this sense — the meditative life is the entire life of the spiritual seeker, the life of aspiration.

Meditation is also, most surely, a formal practice which is, like petitionless prayer, a concerted attempt to experience directly the heart and the soul at rest in God.

The musician practises an instrument; the archer the bow; the spiritual seeker practises a form of meditation. And just as each music teacher has a technique to which a student is apprenticed, so each spiritual teacher has a style of guiding a student to a full awareness of "perfect Perfection." The analogy bears extension, for properly understood the aim of the music teacher is to release the apprentice through the act of playing into the realms of music. By whatever transmission of skill and insight, the teacher hopes finally to see the student fully independent. The same is true of the spiritual teacher, whom Sri Chinmoy most often calls the "guru." The guru's hope for the disciple is that he achieve the Master's own height. Indeed, since the true guru comes in a state of full realisation of soul, the Master *is* the disciple as he will one day recognize himself. That self-realization, and the total freedom it confers, comes only from the most willing and dedicated apprenticeship.

The practice and process of meditation, as a form which Sri Chinmoy teaches, may be most readily understood if we parallel two triads of terms central to his writing: one triad is "Concentration-Meditation-Contemplation," and the other is "Love-Devotion-Surrender." Let us begin with the first members of each: Love and Concentration.

Loving concentration (the term is our shorthand, not Sri Chinmoy's) may designate for us the beginning phase of a process finally to be fulfilled in the experience of our conscious oneness with God, the Supreme. Love, it will be noted, is a feeling; concentration an activity. Loving concentration brings together the two: the action by which a seeker centers awareness on a source or living symbol of love. That source or symbol may be a *mantra* (a word-vibration that draws the mind to more subtle levels of awareness) ; it may be a candle flame, a flower, the photograph of a beloved face, or a spiritual aphorism. But the process of concentration is definitely not thinking, but rather entering into the object of concentration. Mind does not force itself into concentration, nor need it repress thought. Sri Chinmoy sees necessary only the turning—or tuning—of the awareness to the heart center for there to be initiated a slow and natural intensification of concentration, a one-pointedness in which awareness does not bear down upon an object so much as open itself to feel the impulses of a loving presence, the heart center.

As this process of calm attention intensifies—and it does so automatically, for one naturally welcomes the collected joy that comes from the heart center—we experience a kind of transition from the feeling of love to the feeling of devotion, from the activity of concentration to the activity of meditation. There is no clear border line, for devotion as a feeling is only an intensification of love; meditation as an activity is only an expansion of concentration.

We all know the ways in which concentration expands. The magnifying glass is an optical example of this process. But who has not spontaneously concentrated upon a single object or vivid memory until there was felt a falling away of present boundaries? What we hold under regard seems imperceptibly to enlarge until peripheries melt. The part becomes the whole, expanding to fill our consciousness. When what we are concentrating upon is, in fact, an image, impulse, or vibration of love, then not only does it appear to enlarge, but the feeling intensifies by degrees until the tug of love becomes the steady holding pull of devotion. Concentration is the narrow stream; meditation is the widening river.

The experience of meditative devotion evolves naturally, then, from loving concentration. It may surface momentarily in the mind that the seeker is no longer the doer, but is being drawn inward by the heart and to it. *We* are no longer meditating, wilfully exerting ourselves, but riding easily on an expanding feeling: there is great stillness, a brightening all through our awareness, a feeling of joy. There is no longer a sense of effort, only a fullness and poise. We seem to have lifted above the mind with its busy calculation; we experience ourselves beyond its shrill activity, its ego-centered insistence on "me," "me," "me."

Sri Chinmoy has called meditation "the transcendence of ego." We are now in a position to understand more clearly what he means by this, and how that transcendence takes place. Concentration began as a directed act of attention initiated by the ego, but as we expand into meditation, the awareness of a directing ego diminishes. We still have the experience of individuality, but self-awareness shifts from the figure to the ground. The ego, which by its nature separates, is inundated by a more expansive and inclusive awareness. Individuality still remains to register and to enjoy this deeper awareness, but the feelings of this expansion cannot be shaped in ego's terms or won by ego's efforts.

In the slow motion of meditation, time, bodily functions—breathing and heartbeat—alter as if we were in deep rest. In meditative devotion the whole being feels its stillness as a wide calm, feels its capacity to know as an expansive receptivity, its joy as a plenitude. Only remotely aware of the physical self of time and space, the illumining mind, irradiated by the heart, has transcended its discrete modality to float like a wisp of cloud in a serene sky.

Before we go on to describe the culmination of this experience in contemplative surrender, we need to remind ourselves that the process we are surveying extends over months or years and depends to a large degree on transformations occurring in the seeker's life outside of formal meditation. The daily life of an aspirant is sufficiently filled with frustration, doubt, confusion and fear to make the perfect experience of meditative devotion an occasional one at first. Aspiration is still green, and the individual still disperses its powerful centering potential. As the effects of loving concentration begin to integrate our whole being, energy and awareness are liberated which flow into our aspiration and facilitate the transformation of the vital and the mind. Love purifies, and as our aspiration opens us steadily to the influence of love wherever we meet it, our capacity to love and to enter into our love also develops. Our moments of quiet sitting — these glimpsing realisations of our soul's life — influence our outward activity, "manifest," as Sri Chinmoy would say, in our daily work.

In meeting and overcoming the inner and outer obstacles to our spiritual growth, the presence of a spiritual guide is of great value. If we had to compress into a single word his counsel for dealing with the stubbornness of ourselves, that word would be the compound: "self-acceptance." The clearest indication we have of our spiritual progress is in the growth of our capacity to accept ourselves, to accept not only the light in ourselves, but also the darkness and the limitation. Only self-acceptance permits self-awareness. We cannot begin to open into love until we love ourselves. This self-acceptance becomes the basis for our capacity to understand and love our fellow human beings.

The spiritual guide serves here because he is our clearest experience of this acceptance and love. What we feel from the guru — and what constitutes the bond between us — is that he accepts us completely as we are right now. We are forgiven the things we cannot yet accept in ourselves and the rejections we inwardly cherish. We are known for what we are going through and are helped to go on. The treatment may be firm or gentle, always unpredictable, but it is, like the sun, total, and under its influence we will slowly flourish. The growth we experience in the light of the guru is being increasingly liberated to our own capacity for self-love. That self-love, purified of egotism, makes us feel increasingly in touch with our whole selves, increasingly able to be ourselves.

Thus one of the tributaries that expand our capacity for meditative devotion is self-acceptance. To the extent that self-acceptance frees energy in us, turns us away from the fatigue of inner contention and doubt, there is more strength in our aspiration. Thus the fullness of meditative devotion corresponds to our sense of a great fullness in ourselves, and that fullness again finds its manifestation in our daily lives, our human relationships. It is out of this plenitude that we rise to the third level of our triad, where on the plane of feeling, devotion becomes surrender, and on the plane of inner action, meditation passes into contemplation.

It needs to be stressed here that our metaphor of levels, stages or planes is misleading. The spectrum would be a more appropriate image. The terms "Love-Devotion-Surrender" and "Concentration-Meditation-Contemplation" are intensifying bands in a continuum of experience. From the highest point of view that experience may be felt as a fluid movement of awareness out of an initial sense of narrow, isolated individuality to a full identification with the Divine Reality, the Absolute Supreme. Even this full identification is not the end of our spiritual path but a new beginning, the process of which we will consider in Part iv of this introduction.

There comes, then, in the expanding experience of meditative devotion another transition, this one to surrendered contemplation, when we undergo a merging of our self-awareness into what we have been meditating upon. We might put it that we enter totally into the heart center and discover that the heart center is a chamber without walls. It is indeed a center of consciousness, but we now realise that the ultimate consciousness is not only within the heart but beyond it. And going beyond, we become one with the Ultimate, no longer involved in the dualism of self and other. As Sri Chinmoy puts it, "Lover and Beloved become One."

Such an experience depends on our letting go, permitting our awareness to detach itself from its habitual locus in time and space, to flow out upon a sea of light, to be everywhere pervasive. This letting go Sri Chinmoy calls "surrender." It would be a moment of utter terror, but that feeling is not of terror but of ultimate assurance.

On the brink of this surrender there is indeed a great fear in the physical, vital and mental beings, for surrender seems a departure into an unknown from which there appears no way of return, no self—as we have always used that word to describe our human individuality — to return to. Under the influence of a spiritual teacher, totally identified with our aspiration, we finally go beyond the high margin of meditative devotion into the Divine Reality itself. It is indeed a kind of dying; it is also the moment when we are made *new*. For in that experience we recover, rather than discover, our souls. ✳ We know ourselves to be, as Sri Chinmoy puts it, "unique manifestations of God's Reality ... like petals of the lotus, each with its own beauty and perfection." Thus the experience of contemplative surrender is our birth into identity.

In that birth we experience the nature of the Supreme, at once the formless light *and* the luminous forms. Ceaselessly the Supreme flickers into form, yet always transcends the forms He distils. We realise our own mysterious poise, our singleness *and* our oneness, gliding beyond the dualities, even of life and death, into the flow of light which knows neither beginning, middle, nor end. We achieve what Sri Chinmoy calls our "divine individuality," our essential identity as beings endowed with the capacity to know both the infinitely various "petals of the lotus" and the spirit's perfect freedom from all forms. The dance of light may coalesce as "The Supreme," the Godhead, as the ultimate and inclusive form of all forms, generative and implicit; yet too we may experience the flow without form, the "Absolute Supreme," centered everywhere, but unbounded and eternally Beyond.

As we indicated earlier, the experience reached in contemplative surrender of oneness with the Divine Reality is not the final stage of the seeker's path. There is one further triad, the first stage of which we achieve through our birth into "divine individuality." Sri Chinmoy calls this birth "Realisation," and the two stages of growth which follow are identified as "Revelation" and "Manifestation."

The process of "Realisation," which we have traced in the previous section, is explored in and through the practice of meditation. Were we to leave the seeker here, we would leave ourselves with an image of one withdrawn from the so-called everyday world in a state of complete self-fulfilment. In marking a further movement of the realised seeker through two stages of transformed relation to that everyday world, Sri Chinmoy addresses himself to a central question: What is the bearing of meditation upon the needs of humanity? The chapter of the anthology entitled "Serving the World" contains a number of ways he takes up this question.

At an early point in our discussion we noted that Sri Chinmoy views inner realisation and outer manifestation as going hand in hand. Sri Chinmoy states this not so much as a requirement but as a fact: inner transformation will, perforce, be expressed in outer action. Consequently, when the inner experience is as momentous as Realisation, our sense of ourselves in relation to the world will be equally transformed. For as we now experience the ground of oneness shared by all human beings and conditions of life, we now greet all experience with new capacities of vision and awareness. This ground of oneness permits what Sri Chinmoy calls "compassion" — our awareness of the Supreme in all beings; and "concern" — the enactment of that awareness in our interchanges with others. Compassion and concern are qualities central to Sri Chinmoy's path.

The dawning of our compassionate identification with others is "Revelation." What the illumined mind now experiences, it reveals. What it recognises in itself is revealed to it as latent in others. The seeker becomes a revelation to others of what he or she has realised, while others become a revelation to the seeker of the living truth that resides at the heart, and as the center, of all being.

Revelation is the showing forth of divine love and joy, a sunniness of our nature which warms and illuminates, and is independent of the boons or privations of circumstances. In the seeker this light is revealed as "humility." Humility is no conscious diffidence in a personality, but rather the capacity of the soul to regard its equality with all beings, the spontaneous honouring of the Supreme in ourselves and in others. Sri Chinmoy most often refers to the sense of humility as "gratitude." As our experiences in meditation deepen, as the immersion of the seeker in contemplative surrender continues, humility grows, and the seeker feels himself guided by an intuitive voice which comes from within.

Sri Chinmoy calls that voice the "Inner Pilot." Our relation to that guiding presence in us transforms our inner contemplative surrender into an outer attentiveness and obedience to what the soul needs for its fulfilment and for the fulfilment of others. Our "divine individuality," in Sri Chinmoy's sense of the term, involves more than the individuation of infinite consciousness into form; each divine individual has a "mission," asserts Sri Chinmoy, which begins in realising his or her conscious oneness with the Supreme and is then enacted in the obedience or surrender of the individual to what Sri Chinmoy calls the "Will of the Supreme." Each soul has, in its successive incarnations, different experiences to undergo and perform. Ultimately the divine individual has a single momentous work or duty: to participate, with other spiritually awakened beings, in what Sri Chinmoy calls "the transformation of the earth-consciousness." By this he means the process of bringing all humanity to a total and conscious realisation of its true nature. The particular mode of working for that transformation, however, is different from soul to soul. All forms of obedience or surrender to the Will of the Supreme, to the "Inner Pilot," constitute the field of our "Manifestation."

This obedience, or what Sri Chinmoy may call "duty," is not our doing what is expected of us by society, but our surrender to the task of the soul to manifest and to transform. We seek to become what Sri Chinmoy calls "perfect instruments of the Will of the Supreme," where perfection depends on the purity of surrender. The more complete and perpetual the surrender to the Supreme, the more freely the soul may "bring down," as Sri Chinmoy expresses it, "Peace," "Light," "Delight," "Compassion," "Love," "Concern" and "Power" from the Supreme. In our Realisation human life becomes divine life. In our manifestation the divine life takes a human form.

No separation any longer exists between who we experience ourselves to be when we sit in meditation and
who we experience ourselves to be in our daily activity.
In surrender we integrate all aspects of our being—
body, vital, mind, and heart—into the soul's identity
and purpose. In the service of our soul we experience the
full poise of our divine humanity. Life is meditation.
Meditation is service.

v

The danger of a formulation such as we have under-
taken is twofold. It may oversimplify or schematize experiences which are more fluid and richer than its cate-
gories. And it may call too much attention to the struc-
tures rather than to the life that animates them. It is
best to regard our patterns as provisional and to see
through them, in our reading of this anthology, the living relation of elements in harmony. This book can
open for us a world, a vision, in which what we had
thought to be separate is seen to be fused. We should
not assume that any given sentence or entry is dependent
upon a highly articulated philosophical system that still
eludes us. We do not read the poet needing to know all
his work before enjoying a single poem. No more here
do the parts hinge upon the whole for either their
meaning or their power, but contain the whole
implicitly.

The most common grammatical form in Sri Chinmoy's
writing is what we might recognize as an equation. For
example, "Consciousness is Reality," or "Fulfilment is

voluntary sacrifice." In such sentences, Sri Chinmoy not only joins but makes equivalent terms which we might think differ in meaning. The mind, encountering such equations, slides by all too easily, finding no grist for its analytical mill. Thus a casual or critical reading of Sri Chinmoy may yield a sense of either abstractness or childlike simplicity. However, the sentence "Consciousness is Reality" is a *perception*, not an abstract equation. And just as an image in a poem is a perception to stimulate the reader's imagination, here these spiritual images in Sri Chinmoy's writings, often bare of embellishments, require for their understanding an act of reading that is, in effect, meditative. If we hold such images in a silent mind, or allow them to resonate in an aspiring heart, the meaning of the words will be released, not by any process of analysis, but by an intuitive glimpsing into the level of awareness which inspired the utterance and on which it is true. Thus we often encounter in Sri Chinmoy's writings an apparently philosophical prose style actually operating in a meditative mode. Each sentence may become for the reader a living image of reality, not simply a thought about it. To experience the revelatory power of the image, we must let thought be still. The intention in the writing is never to puzzle, but to elicit our illumination; if we pause long enough in silence to let Sri Chinmoy's images unfold in patient reflection, we may find ourselves smiling at their directness and momentarily arrested by the depth revealed.

Finally it may be said that the variety of writing contained in this anthology corresponds to a variety of situations, attitudes and audiences. In this book are many voices — playful, lyrical, discursive, colloquial, impersonal and personal—and many were evoked by seekers to whose spiritual needs Sri Chinmoy was speaking or writing. Thus we may find that *we* are in this book, in some mood, perplexity, or sincere desire for enlightenment. We can come to these pages with the most practical and specific questions about the spiritual life and hear an answer. His lines—any one of them—may suddenly open like a casement and reveal dimension after dimension of spiritual significance. The purpose of Sri Chinmoy's writings—as with the revelatory wisdom literature of all cultures—is to awaken and refine in us a spiritual aspiration that will lead us as seekers *beyond within*.

vi

Some of Sri Chinmoy's students and I conceived of this anthology while I was teaching a course about Sri Chinmoy at the University of Connecticut at Storrs in the spring term of 1973. We found much of what we wanted the students to read was out of print or difficult to reproduce, and so over the summer we selected material and composed the book called *Beyond Within: Writings on the Journey of the Soul.* I used that handmade mimeographed edition in my second year of teaching a course at the University. After the fall term at Connecticut, we revised and rearranged the book. That revision is this anthology, *Beyond Within: A Philosophy for the Inner Life.*

* * *

Sri Chinmoy has often called the Supreme our Guru and his Guru. We gratefully dedicate this book to that Supreme, Source and Goal, Beyond and Within.

* * *

Brihaspati
(Peter Pitzele)

April 1974
New York, New York

INVOCATION

Supreme, Supreme, Supreme, Supreme!
I bow to Thee, I bow.
My life Thy golden plough;
My journey's Goal Thy soulful Dream.
Supreme, Supreme, Supreme, Supreme!
I bow to Thee, I bow.

Supreme, I am Thy glowing Grace.
My world Thy Feet of Light,
My breath Thy Vision's kite.
Thou art one Truth, one Life, one Face.
Supreme, Supreme, Supreme, Supreme!
I bow to Thee, I bow.

CONSCIOUSNESS

CONSCIOUSNESS

CONSCIOUSNESS-LIGHT

Consciousness is the spark of life which connects each one of us with the Universal Life. It is the thread that puts us in tune with the universe. If you want to fly into the Transcendental, you need the thread of consciousness.

Consciousness is a spark that lets us enter into the Light. It is our consciousness which connects us with God. It is the link between God and man, between Heaven and earth.

In the physical world the mother tells the child who his father is. In the spiritual world our aspiration tells us who God is. Who is God? God is an infinite Consciousness. He is also the Self-illumining Light. There is no human being who does not have within him this infinite Consciousness and this Self-illumining Light.

Our Goal is within us. To reach that Goal we have to enter into the spiritual life. In the spiritual life the thing that is most needed is consciousness. Without this, everything is a barren desert. When we enter into a dark place, we take a flashlight or some other light in order to know where we are going. If we want to know about our unlit life, we have to take the help of consciousness.

Man, in his outer life or his outer achievements, is very limited. But the same man, when he enters into the inmost recesses of his heart, feels that there is something which is constantly trying to expand itself. This is consciousness. This consciousness links him with the highest Absolute.

Consciousness is our real teacher, our dear friend and our sure slave. As a slave, consciousness carries our teeming ignorance to God. As a friend, consciousness tells us what the supreme Knowledge is. As a teacher, consciousness reveals to us the undeniable truth that today's imperfect and unfulfilled man is tomorrow's perfect and fulfilled God.

Consciousness sings. It sings the song of universal Oneness. Consciousness plays. It plays the game of cosmic Manifestation. Consciousness dances. It dances with God's fulfilling Vision within and God's fulfilled Reality without. Consciousness acts. It acts through man's crying, climbing and surrendering aspiration, and God's descending, protecting and illumining Compassion.

When consciousness is all activity, it bows to God the Mother, its Source. When consciousness is all silence, it bows to God the Father, its Source. From the Mother it gets the mightiest Power to make the supreme sacrifice for the unconscious earth. From the Father it gets the highest Light to illumine the unlit earth. Consciousness itself is at once Light and Power. As Light, it identifies with the pure inspiration and deep aspiration of our inner world. As Power, it exercises its divine sovereignty over the darkest bondage and the wildest ignorance of our outer world.

The consciousness that the unaspiring body uses is called the hopeful consciousness. The consciousness that the unyielding vital uses is known as the hurtful consciousness. The consciousness that the uncompromising mind uses is called the doubtful consciousness. The consciousness that the uncovering heart uses is called the truthful consciousness. The consciousness that the unlimited soul uses is called the fruitful consciousness.

Aum Anandamayee Chaitanyamayee Satyamayee Parame

"O Mother Absolute of Existence-Consciousness-Delight!" This triple consciousness is the longest length, farthest breadth and deepest depth. The longest length is Infinity. The farthest breadth is Eternity. The deepest depth is Immortality. When consciousness lives in Existence, humanity devotedly receives what Divinity soulfully offers. When consciousness lives inside its own domain, humanity and Divinity lovingly yet surprisingly share each other's experience. When consciousness lives in Delight, humanity is realised and transformed and Divinity is manifested and fulfilled.

Blind is he who does not see the Consciousness-light. Deaf is he who does not obey the Consciousness-right. Poor is he who cannot eat the Consciousness-fruit. Foolish is he who denies the existence of the Consciousness-sea.

* * *

Question: Are consciousness and thought the same?

Sri Chinmoy: No, let us take consciousness as a table and thoughts as flies. The flies are constantly sitting on the table, or seeking and flying from one place to another. The table will not be permanently affected, but it has to be cleaned. Now, how do you clean your consciousness? You clean it with your heart's light.

Question: Can the mind help us to maintain a high level of consciousness?

Sri Chinmoy: No, the mind can never help us maintain a high level of consciousness. If the mind is searching and crying, it can help raise the level of consciousness. But the mind cannot help us maintain a high level of consciousness. Only the light of the soul has the capacity to do that. The soul has given this capacity to the heart also, and the heart can do it on behalf of the soul. If the soul itself helps us, then our consciousness remains perfect. But if the help comes from the heart, which is not yet fully illumined, then our consciousness does not remain on the same high level. Nevertheless, the heart has far more capacity than the mind to help us maintain a high level of consciousness.

Question: How can someone new to meditation tell whether his consciousness is rising, steady or falling?

Sri Chinmoy: Someone new to meditation can easily tell whether his consciousness is rising, steady or falling.

If he feels purity inside his heart, inside his entire being, then his consciousness is steady. If he feels sincerity, then his consciousness is rising. But if he becomes a victim to doubt concerning what he is feeling or observing, then his consciousness is falling.

Question: How can we raise our consciousness when we feel threatened by negative forces?

Sri Chinmoy: When we are threatened by negative forces we have to feel that we have the strongest friend within us, and that friend is the soul. Let us take shelter under the wings of the soul. Let us invoke the soul and pray for its guidance. If we call on this friend, naturally he will fight against the negative forces on our behalf; the soul will save us, protect us, illumine us and perfect us.

Question: Should one realise or reach the highest consciousness before mingling with unaspiring people?

Sri Chinmoy: First you have to realise the Highest. Then only can you dare to mix with unaspiring people. When you mix with unaspiring people, it is as if you are going to visit a mental hospital. Unless you yourself are very powerful, you will also be affected.

If you are aspiring, you need not reach the Highest in order to help other aspiring people. While you yourself are going high, very high, you can help your younger brothers who are aspiring but have not yet climbed as high as you. But it is stupidity for you to try to help people who are not aspiring at all. You will not be able to change their nature because they do not want to change.

To a seeker who is still unrealised God usually says, "You aspire, and while you are climbing up, if you see that somebody is a little behind you, then help him, inspire him, guide him so that he can also come up to the place where you are. But do not mix with unaspiring people, for if you do, then you will never aspire. If you don't aspire, then how will you realise Me?"

So let us be wise. First let us reach some height and mix with those who are aspiring. Then when we reach the Highest, if it is God's Will we can mix with those who are unaspiring.

Question: What is inconscience?

Sri Chinmoy: Inconscience is a state of consciousness where there is no light, not even a streak of light.

Question: When you talk of mineral, plant, human and divine consciousness, what exactly do these terms mean?

Sri Chinmoy: In mineral consciousness there is practically no light, and in plant consciousness there is only a streak of light. Limited light is or may be in human consciousness. But human consciousness is capable of housing unlimited light, as is the case with very advanced seekers. Finally, the divine Consciousness embodies boundless, infinite Light.

Question: Is there an ultimate consciousness or can consciousness always be transcended?

Sri Chinmoy: From the strict spiritual point of view nothing is ultimate. Everything is transcending. The Supreme Himself is constantly transcending His highest Height. The Supreme is He who is singing the Song of Self-transcendence all the time.

We call something ultimate according to our present realisation. What is ultimate today need not and cannot be ultimate tomorrow. Today's goal is tomorrow's starting point. There is no ultimate reality. The ultimate reality is for today, for today's present achievement. But tomorrow we can climb up and surpass the reality which we yesterday considered as the ultimate. Today's ultimate consciousness has to be transcended by tomorrow's more intense aspiration.

Question: What is the relationship between the soul and consciousness?

Sri Chinmoy: The soul may be taken as a piece of ice, and consciousness as water.

Question: What is the relationship between consciousness and realisation?

Sri Chinmoy: Consciousness is like a plain green field and realisation is like the topmost peak of Mt. Everest. The field is directly connected to the mountain and the foot of the mountain is directly connected to the top of the mountain. But consciousness and realisation are both part of the same unbroken flow of universal Consciousness.

Question: What is the relationship between intuition and consciousness?

Sri Chinmoy: Intuition is the arrow and consciousness is the bow. When the arrow is released, it enters into the target. If there is no bow, the arrow cannot play its role, and vice versa. Both are indispensable.

Question: Is it possible that the soul is in any way connected with what we call consciousness?

Sri Chinmoy: Consciousness is always connected with the soul. But what we in the human life call consciousness is not real consciousness at all; it is a mere feeling. When we perceive something subtle which we cannot define, we call this awareness of ours consciousness; this is actually not real consciousness at all. It is, rather, very subtle desire. We enter into it, and immediately we feel that it is our consciousness. But real consciousness is the Light which connects Heaven and earth. Heaven itself is in our consciousness.

Consciousness and the soul can never be separated, whereas the body can easily be separated from the soul and also from consciousness. When we use the term 'physical consciousness', we are referring to the finite consciousness. It is a portion of the infinite Consciousness which has entered into the gross physical and is now possessed and utilised by the physical itself. The same can also occur with the vital consciousness and the mental consciousness. But the divine consciousness is a vast unity which houses silence and power. When it houses silence, it houses its own true form. When it houses power, it manifests its inner reality.

The soul, which is eternal, and consciousness, which is infinite, go together. They have a common source, which is life, eternal life. The soul has eternal life and consciousness also has eternal life. They complement each other. The soul expresses its divinity through consciousness, and consciousness expresses its all-pervading silence through the soul.

Question: Sometimes I awake in the morning feeling a very high state of elation and unity, but I am not conscious of what has taken place. Does any work take place at night on the spiritual plane that we are not aware of?

Sri Chinmoy: You are partially aware of this work. If you had not been aware of it at some point, then you could not have told me about it right now. You are not aware of it on the mental plane, but there are many other planes of consciousness. When you actually have the experience, your soul is aware of it.

Consciousness is like a ladder. You can go up or down the various rungs. Right now there is no link between the rung where you are now and the rung where you had the experience. If you remain in the physical consciousness, which most human beings do during the day, then the experience that you had in the inner world cannot function properly. The physical consciousness does not have free access to that particular plane of consciousness where you had the experience. The physical consciousness must have divine light; then only can it have free access to all planes of consciousness.

During sleep, when the soul moves from one plane to another, it is like a free bird. If the physical consciousness wants to know what the soul is doing twenty-four hours a day, then it has to be moulded and guided by the soul's light. In your case, you were conscious at the time of your soul's experience, but afterwards you could not remember it because you are not aware of all these planes of consciousness that exist between the soul's region and the physical consciousness.

Question: What is the difference between human consciousness and divine consciousness?

Sri Chinmoy: Human consciousness is made up primarily of limitation, imperfection, bondage and ignorance. This consciousness wants to remain here on earth. It gets joy in the finite: in family, in society, in earthly affairs. Divine consciousness is made up of Peace, Bliss, divine Power and so forth. Its nature is to expand constantly. Human consciousness feels there is nothing more important than earthly pleasure. Divine consciousness feels there is nothing more important and significant than heavenly Joy and Bliss on earth. Human consciousness tries to convince us that we are nowhere near Truth or fulfilment. It tries to make us feel that God is somewhere else, millions of miles away from us.

But divine consciousness makes us feel that God is right here, inside each life-breath, inside each heartbeat, inside everyone and everything around us.

Human consciousness makes us feel that we can exist without God. When it is in deep ignorance, human consciousness feels that there is no necessity for God. We see millions and billions of people who do not pray or meditate. They feel, "If God exists, well and good; if He does not exist, we don't lose anything." Although they may use the term 'God' in season and out of season, they do not care for the reality, the existence of God, either in Heaven or in their day-to-day earthly lives.

But the divine consciousness is not at all like that. Even the limited divine consciousness that we have makes us feel that at every moment there is a supreme necessity for God. It makes us feel that we are on earth precisely because He exists. And when we cherish divine thoughts, the divine consciousness makes us feel it is He who is inspiring us to cherish these divine ideas. In everything the divine consciousness makes us feel there is a divine purpose, divine aim, divine ideal, divine goal. In ordinary human consciousness there is no purpose, no positive goal; it is only a mad elephant running amuck.

In the divine consciousness there is always a goal, and this goal is always transcending itself. Today we regard one thing as our goal, but when we reach the threshold of our goal, immediately we are inspired to go beyond that goal. That goal becomes a stepping-stone to a higher goal. This happens because God is constantly transcending Himself. God is limitless and infinite, but even His own Infinity He is transcending. Since God is always making progress, we also are making progress when we are in the divine consciousness. In the divine consciousness everything is constantly expanding and growing into higher and more fulfilling Light.

* * *

THE HUMAN PSYCHE

THE BODY

MY BODY

O my body, you are a gift of the Supreme. Potentiality inexhaustible you have deep within you. To misunderstand you means to misunderstand the chosen instrument of God.

You must not, you cannot conquer the length and breadth of the world with your physical strength. Offer your growing heart to the hearts far and near. Offer your glowing soul to the souls around, below, above. Then alone you become the conqueror and possessor of God's entire universe.

O my body, invoke your soul always to lead you. Invoke! Never shall the monotony of the uneventful life plague you. With lightning speed yours shall be the ceaseless march . . . upward to the highest, inward to the inmost, forward to the farthest.

Sing! Sing the song of bliss in Immortality. Breathe! Breathe in the breath of consciousness in Immortality. Live! Live the life of existence in Immortality.

Death? Die you must not. For your death will be a great loss to humanity and by far a greater loss to Divinity. Fight, O my body! Fight with ignorance to the bitter end. Never allow ignorance to envelop you, your outer cloak. Your struggling efforts shall be crowned with success.

O body of mine, fare you well for Eternity. May each earthly year of yours have a trillion fulfilling years.

God the eternal Dreamer is dreaming in you, through you, with you. God the eternal Reality is living for you, with you and in you.

* * *

Before realisation, the body, by virtue of its very existence on earth, helps the soul unconsciously. After realisation, the body serves the soul, not only consciously, but also unconditionally.

* * *

Man the desiring body-consciousness is the only wall that stands between man's inmost cry and God's mightiest Compassion.

* * *

A Yogi is not in the body. He is not of the body. But he is for the body—for the transformation of the body and for the perfection of the body.

* * *

BODY AND SOUL

We may call the body a temple. Inside the temple is the shrine, the heart. Within the shrine is the deity, the soul. Now, let us speak only of the soul and the body. Body and soul are like a house and its owner. The soul is the owner and the body is the house. The soul and the body are complementary. Without the soul, without the owner, the house is useless. The soul works inside the body, as well as with the body, through the body and for the body-consciousness. Again, without the body, the soul will have no place to live. It will not be able to manifest its qualities on earth. When the owner is there and the body is in perfect condition, then the message of the soul can be revealed and fulfilled.

We have to know what the soul can offer us and what the body can offer us. The soul can offer us realisation; the body can offer us manifestation. For its manifestation, the soul needs the body. For its realisation, the body needs the soul. The body offers its capacity in service; the soul offers its capacity in meditation. In this way they go together perfectly.

The earth is the field of realisation and, at the same time, the field of manifestation. God-realisation can be achieved only here on earth, and not in other spheres, not in other worlds or on other planets. Those who care for God-realisation have to accept a human body and come into this world. Again, it is only on earth and through the physical body that the soul can manifest its own divinity, which is infinite Peace, infinite Light, infinite Bliss. The body needs the soul; the soul needs the body. For the realisation of the highest

Truth, the body needs the soul; for the manifestation of the highest and deepest Truth, the soul needs the body.

If the soul does not try to inspire and illumine the body, the body will remain blind, ignorant, obscure and impure. And without the body's cooperation the soul will remain unmanifested, almost useless. Often we see that the soul is crying for realisation and manifestation through the body, but the body is not responding to it. The body may be physically strong, but if it is not aspiring for the inner light and truth which the soul can offer it, then the soul cannot fulfil itself.

Body and soul are not inseparable but complementary. The soul can exist without the body, although it cannot manifest itself. The body cannot exist for more than a few hours without the soul. For their total mutual fulfilment, body and soul need each other.

* * *

Question: I have difficulty sitting in the lotus position.

Sri Chinmoy: It is not necessary at all. The only thing you should do is to keep the back straight. Some people recline on a chair or slump over, but this is not good. The lotus position is good because it keeps the body quiet. But many people remain in the lotus position for three or four hours and their mind is still roaming, while somebody else may sit on a chair with his mind calm and quiet. The main thing is to keep the back erect and the mind without thoughts.

Question: I find that when I eat meat I cannot medi-tate very well; I feel restless. But if I don't eat meat, I feel very weak.

Sri Chinmoy: You know very well that animals are restless, aggressive, destructive and unevolved. We have transcended the animal consciousness to some extent, and we have come out of the animal kingdom. We are only one step ahead on the ladder of evolution, but the difference between an animal and a human being is very vast. Now, when you eat something, naturally you will absorb the qualities of that thing. What you have within you will unavoidably manifest itself outwardly in some way. When you eat meat, the immediate result is rest-less, aggressive and destructive impulses and thoughts, and lowering of the consciousness.

It is not true, however, that if you do not eat meat you will lose strength, power or energy. There are mil-lions of people on earth who do not eat meat, but who are physically very strong and healthy. You may say that your constitution is different from theirs, but I wish to say that in God's creation there is something called inner food. What is this food? It is Peace, Light and Bliss and all other divine, fulfilling qualities. When you aspire properly, meditate properly, you will be able to draw this inner food into your body. It may take quite a number of years for you to attain this degree of inner proficiency, but in the meantime try to go deep within and see what actually gives you most of your strength. I have known people to claim it is meat that gives them strength, but when they go deep within, they discover that it is their own feeling and idea about meat that is giving them strength. You can change that idea and feel that it is not meat but the spiritual energy pervading your body that gives you strength. That energy comes from meditation and aspiration as well as from proper nourishment. The strength you get from aspiration and meditation is infinitely more powerful than the strength you get from meat and fish, so these things can easily be omitted from your diet.

You are practising meditation most sincerely and most devotedly. What you have to do is get rid of the idea that meat gives you strength. That idea is so deeply rooted in your mind that now you cannot separate yourself from it. But the moment you are totally freed from that idea, you will see that it is not principally meat that gives you strength; it is wholesome food in general as well as the proper mental attitude and spiritual aspiration.

Question: Please tell me if we are in better contact with the Divine when we are fasting, drinking only juice and water. Does fasting help us to realise God?

Sri Chinmoy: When you drink juice you are not fasting. Many people say, "Early in the morning I drink a cup of coffee, and at noon I have a glass of juice, and in the evening only a glass of milk." This is their idea of fasting. But to me that is not fasting. In true fasting, you can only have pure water and nothing else.

If you decide to fast, you have to know why you are doing it. If you feel that by fasting you will realise God, it is foolishness. The real name of God is Delight and Joy. If your Father is all Joy, will He ask you to torture yourself in order to come to Him? God is the possessor of boundless Joy, and we know that He is also infinitely compassionate. He gave you the body—it is His body—and if you start torturing His body, will He be pleased? Never! If you start fasting for God-realisation, God will say that you are walking on the wrong path.

But fasting can help us reduce weight, cure some of our physical ailments and purify our nerves and mind. Very often we eat unwholesome food, and the poor body needs some rest and purification. Also, when we look at undivine people and things, their vibrations enter into us from the atmosphere and affect our physical body—the skin, the muscles, the nerves. If we want to fast one day a month to purify our system, it is advisable. We need purity to appreciate God's existence on earth. It is in purity—pure thoughts, pure deeds, pure consciousness—that God abides. Fasting can help us to a great extent in self-purification. But this is only the first step; fasting alone will not give us God-realisation.

So for purification you can try fasting—drinking only water—once a month. Now, I am speaking from the spiritual point of view. I know nothing about your physical constitution. If you are strong and healthy you can fast; otherwise, it is not advisable. But even if you don't fast, if you are a sincere seeker you can, once a week, reduce the amount of food you take. This can be done especially on Sundays, when you do not have to be very active. On Sunday most people get up late in the morning, so they can easily forget about breakfast. At lunch time they can say, "Every day I eat. If today I eat a little less, it will not hurt me at all." Then in the evening, at dinner, they can say, "At lunch time I did not eat the usual amount, and it did me no harm. I am still quite energetic. Why not do the same now?" So once a week, on Sundays especially, if you can lighten your meals, it will help you enormously. And you need not undergo a severe, torturing fast, which real spiritual figures do not recommend.

Question: If we are tired or sick, should we sleep more?

Sri Chinmoy: If we are very tired or sick we should sleep according to our body's necessity, but not according to our body's demands; for the body, being unconscious and ignorant, may demand more sleep than it really needs.

Question: What are the predominant qualities of the body, vital and mind?

Sri Chinmoy: The unlit physical likes to remain idle. The very nature of the physical is to be inactive. The unlit vital is aggressive. It likes to show off its power. And the unlit mind doubts and suspects everybody and everything.

If we accept the spiritual life, the body has to be active. Even if it runs in the wrong direction at first, at least there should be some movement. The body has to be energetic, but not restless. Otherwise, although the physical body itself may not sleep twenty-four hours a day, the body-consciousness will be sleeping. An aspiring body is an active and energetic body. We are fast asleep when we are not aspiring.

The vital has to become dynamic instead of aggressive. It should try to energise and inspire others, instead of trying to control or destroy others. It should say to others, "Don't waste your precious time. Get up and do something for yourself or for humanity."

The clear, pure, divine mind, the mind which is illumined by the soul's light, will become vast. It will say, "I cannot be bound by anything; I will not suspect anybody. I will not belittle anybody. On the contrary, I shall expand my own consciousness and help others to expand their consciousness."

If we practise the spiritual life, we get this kind of active body, dynamic vital and illumined mind. If we do not accept the spiritual life, we have to be satisfied with a body which is fast asleep, with a vital which is aggressive and destructive and with a mind which is limited and which wants to doubt, criticise and suspect itself and the world.

* * *

My soul's owner is Divinity.
My heart's owner is sincerity.
My mind's owner is clarity.
My vital's owner is capacity.
My body's owner is purity.

* * *

DON'T THINK, DON'T SLEEP

When he was a child,
One day
  His father said to him:
    "Don't think, my child.
    God never thinks."
Since then, he never cared
To learn the art of thinking.

When he was a child,
One day
  His mother said to him:
    "Don't sleep, my child,
    God never sleeps."
Since then, he never cared
To learn the art of sleeping.

* * *

VISION-SKIES

    The body
Loves to be swayed by the wind of emotion.
    The vital
Loves the prickings of desire.
    The mind
Loves the confines of the finite.
    The heart
Loves to be in the galaxy of saints.
    The soul
Loves the life of unhorizoned vision-skies.

* * *

TRANSFORMATION, TRANSCENDENCE AND BEYOND

His body,
A picture of austerity.
His vital,
A picture of humility.
His mind,
A picture of serenity.
His heart,
A picture of purity.
His soul,
A picture of nobility.
His Goal,
A picture of Reality.
And he himself
Is the picture of yesterday's transformation,
Today's transcendence
And tomorrow's Perfection-Beyond.

* * *

My sleeping body I offer to my God's Compassion.
My dreaming body I offer to my God's Love.
My crying body I offer to my God's Concern.

* * *

THE VITAL

MY VITAL

O my vital, my first choice falls on you. Without your dynamic and stupendous inner urge, nothing can be embodied, nothing can be revealed here on earth.

O my vital, when you fall fast asleep, my mind's undying frustration grips my outer existence; my body's helpless surrender to the prince of gloom poisons my inner existence.

Man's most powerful imagination fails to fathom you, your depth. Man's far-flung, brightest wisdom fails to determine you, your breadth.

Yours is the indomitable courage that springs from the fountain of boundless emotion. Kill not your emotion. Never! Emotion killed within, fulfilment starved without. Emotion divinely fed within, God the eternal Delight revealed without.

O my vital, you know no tomorrow. You want to be born, you want to grow and fulfil yourself in the immediacy of today. With the infinite Blessings of the Supreme, on you march across the path of Infinity's bloom, Eternity's glow and Immortality's lustre.

Your life is green, the ever-aspiring and ever-growing green. Your breath is blue, the ever-encompassing and ever-transforming blue.

O vital of mine, in you is humanity's glowing hope. With you is Divinity's reverberating clarion.

The vital either embodies divine dynamism or hostile aggression. When the aspirant brings the soul's light to the fore, the hostile aggression changes into the divine dynamism and the divine dynamism is transformed into the all-fulfilling supreme Reality.

* * *

THEIR OPINIONS DIFFER

The mind says:
Love is sex.

The vital says:
Sex is love.

The heart says:
Love is love.

The body says:
There is no such thing as love.

The soul says:
There is nothing but love.

* * *

Question: How can we tell if our love is vital or pure?

Sri Chinmoy: You can easily tell whether your love is vital or pure. When your love is vital, there is a conscious demand, or at least an unconscious expectation from the love you offer to others. When your love is pure or spiritual, there is no demand, no expectation. There is only the sweetest feeling of spontaneous oneness with the human being or beings concerned.

Question: Is it possible to prevent oneself from giving off impure vital love and to substitute the heart's pure love for it? How can we consciously give pure love?

Sri Chinmoy: It is not only possible, but absolutely necessary, to prevent oneself from giving off impure vital love. Otherwise, one will have to constantly wrestle with the gigantic forces of ignorance. One has to use love, not to bind or possess the world, but to free and widen one's own consciousness and the consciousness of the world. But one must not try to substitute the heart's pure love for the impure vital love. What one must do is to bring the heart's purifying and transforming love into the impure vital. The vital, as such, is not bad at all. When the vital is controlled, purified and transformed, it becomes a most significant instrument of God.

You want to know how you can consciously give pure love to others. You can consciously give pure love to others if you feel that you are giving a portion of your life-breath when you talk to others or think of others. And this life-breath you are offering just because you feel that you and the rest of the world are totally and inseparably one. Where there is oneness, it is all pure love.

* * *

THE TRANSCENDENCE OF SEX

Do not try to suppress sex. With your inner wisdom, inner experience and inner light, sex can be transcended, and it *has* to be. But by fighting, struggling and suppressing it, sex cannot be conquered. The easiest way to transcend something is to pay no attention to it, to feel that it is unnecessary. If you think that it is necessary, then it comes to tempt you, and you will feel that you are caught.

If you want to conquer your desires, there is only one thing to do. You have to pay more attention to the light, in a positive way. But not by hook or by crook! If you try to subdue your vital urges in any kind of repressive way, then you will never be able to conquer this physical need. You have to open yourself toward the light and reach or feel the light within you. By thinking constantly of your desires, vital, sex life, you will never be able to conquer them. It is impossible. Even if you want to think of them with a view to conquering them, you are making a mistake. But think of the other things—light, joy—which you need and which you actually want. Through concentration and meditation you can have inner joy and inner light. You will try to bring them into your gross physical, and your physical being will also feel divine joy and divine light. At that time the life of destructive pleasure will leave you and the life of fulfilling joy will embrace you.

* * *

Question: I have read some place that when one uses sexual energy he is using up some spiritual energy at the same time. Is this true? If so, what can be done if one wants to lead a spiritual life?

Sri Chinmoy: What you have read is absolutely true. Animal human life and divine God-life do not and cannot go together. To attain the highest Truth the seeker needs total purification and transformation of his lower vital. If one wants to have real joy, everlasting joy, then he has to transcend the need of sex. If the seeker wants to be inundated with boundless Peace, Light and Bliss, then he has to eventually transcend this physical need. Otherwise, the transcendental Peace, Light and Bliss will remain a far cry for him.

But you cannot realise God overnight. It is impossible! You do not get your Master's degree in a day, or even in a year. It may require twenty years of study to achieve. And God-realisation is a far more difficult subject. It requires many incarnations of aspiration and spiritual discipline for anyone to realise God. In each lifetime the possibility of your God-realisation depends on both your present aspiration and your previous spiritual life.

If you tell a beginner that he will have to give up his lower vital life, his sex life, all at once, he will say, "Impossible! How can I do that?" If he has to do it all at once, he will never enter into the spiritual life. But slowly and steadily he can make headway towards his Goal. If he tries to run too fast and does not have the capacity, he will simply drop in the field. He will lose what limited aspiration he has.

Transforming one's sex life is like give up a bad habit, but for many people it is more difficult and it takes a longer time. Suppose somebody drinks a lot. If he drinks six or seven times a day, let him first come to realise the fact that this is something harmful for his God-realisation. Then let him try to drink less. If he drinks six times a day, let him change to five times. After a while, let him drink four times a day. Then, after a while longer, let him drink three times a day. Gradually, let him diminish his desire for alcohol.

In our ordinary human life we have many weaknesses. If we try to conquer them all at once, the body will resist and break down. The body will revolt, and we shall be torn to pieces. We have to have a real inner will, the soul's will, to conquer our desires slowly and steadily. Gradually we have to diminish our need for sex on the strength of our aspiration. There will be a tug-of-war between aspiration and the gross physical desire, and slowly our nature will be purified.

On the strength of our inner urge, we have to run towards the Light. Then we will see that there is a great difference between pleasure and joy. Pleasure is always followed by frustration, and frustration is inevitably followed by destruction. But joy is followed by more joy and abundant joy, and in joy we get real fulfilment.

If one enters into the spiritual life and says, "Today I shall conquer all my lower propensities," he is just fooling himself. Tomorrow his physical mind will torture him with doubts. His impure and cruel vital will try to punish him in every way. He will be frustrated, and inside his frustration his own destruction will loom large. The lower vital life must be transformed completely before God-realisation can take place, but I advise my students to do it gradually and with sincere determination.

Question: How can we expand our heart and have more of its divine qualities in our daily actions and our relationships with people?

Sri Chinmoy: The spiritual life is not the life of indifference. However, one has to have discrimination when dealing with the world. If you give of your heart to everyone, irrespective of who the person is, then people may exploit you. If a thief wants to buy tools to steal with, and if someone with a magnanimous heart gives him the money without questioning what kind of person he is or why he wants the money, who will be partially responsible for the thief's future thefts? The man who gave him the money. A spiritual person may have a truly wide heart, but to utilise his heart's qualities with wisdom is more important than to cry for the enlargement of the heart.

God has already given our heart many divine qualities, but we do not use them and thus we slow down our spiritual growth. Very few people, I must say, know what the spiritual heart really is. What we mistake for the heart is actually the emotional vital. This moment we want to give everything to someone, but the next moment we want to keep everything for ourselves. This moment, for no reason, I am ready to give everything to you, and the next moment, again for no reason, I am ready to take your life away. This kind of feeling does not come from the heart at all. It is the play of our demanding and unlit vital.

If our vital is trying to play the role of the heart, it will try to dominate others or make them feel that they need us badly because we have wisdom or light, whereas they do not. But the very existence of the heart is based on identification. Identification is light. The spiritual heart can identify only with light and delight, for it gets continuous light and delight from the soul. We may identify with someone's sorrow, but what we are actually identifying ourselves with is the light inside that sorrow. Inside pain, inside suffering, inside darkness itself, there is light. Ultimately, the heart is identifying with the light within. If we cry every day for our own inner light, then we will see that the heart is bound to expand. But if we want to expand the heart without light, we will merely expand our ignorance. Only when we cry for the Highest will our heart really expand.

We must realise that the vital, which is deceiving and exploiting us, must be put aside. Very often forces from the impure vital, below the navel, enter into our heart and cause us to suffer. Purification of the vital is absolutely necessary if the vital wants to act divinely, together with the heart. Otherwise, the heart will have to play its part alone. So please be careful in dealing with humanity, that you do not offer the false light of the demanding and possessive vital. In the name of concern, we very often offer worries, anxieties, impurities and so forth.

It is not at all difficult to bring forward the heart's good qualities such as sympathy and concern. We can bring forward these good qualities through our aspiration. We are aspiring for God, who undoubtedly has more Concern, Affection and all other qualities of the heart than we have. Our sincere aspiration can bring these qualities down from God.

Question: Whenever I see a beautiful woman, sex thoughts enter my mind. I try to destroy them, but they persist.

Sri Chinmoy: There are two ways to solve this problem. As soon as you see a beautiful woman, just try to concentrate and lift her up with your will so that, like a kite, she is flying. The other way, the easiest way, is when you see a woman to look only at her feet. Indian *sadhus* say to look only at the feet, not at the eyes, not at the face. Look only at the feet if you want immediate release from temptation. Look at the feet and then try with your whole consciousness to go deep within yourself. This takes only a second. Either lift this woman up or look at her feet. Then immediately lower vital thoughts will be controlled. Many have done it and have been very successful. There was a great Indian *avatar* named Sri Chaitanya. He used to tell all his disciples, "Even if it is your mother, don't look at her eyes; just look at her feet."

But these methods are only for beginners. A day will come when you will have to look at women with your eyes open and, with your inner experiences, with your own inner realisation, go beyond the feeling of man and woman. There is only one universal Consciousness; there is no masculine, no feminine. There is only one Consciousness flowing in two different forms. This feeling can be developed only along with our own inner development. It is a very advanced state. Right now perhaps we don't even feel oneness with our limbs. If I can throw a shotput farther with my right hand than with my left hand, I give more importance to my right hand and I ignore my left hand. I have seen many athletes who curse their left hand because they need the help of the left hand even though it is not as powerful as the right. If we cannot feel oneness even with our own two hands, how can we be one with another person? With aspiration and with our inner spiritual development the whole creation becomes ours. At that time there is no difficulty.

Question: For what purpose is the union between man and woman?

Sri Chinmoy: When union takes place between a man and a woman, each one gives a significant or insignificant meaning to the action. But in the highest, deepest spiritual life, when the realisation of oneness with all humanity is coming to the fore, this ordinary human union does not serve any purpose. One can have physical relations with someone hundreds of times, but the real union, the inner union, does not take place. Only when we can establish our soul's union with a person will we be fulfilled. When we can liberate ourselves from the meshes of ignorance, and when we can realise the entire earth as our own, when we feel that all of mankind is our very own, then only can we have proper union. Physical union is no union in comparison to the all-pervading union of spiritual oneness which we can have.

I am telling you all this from the strict spiritual point of view. We have to reach a certain level before we can reject the ordinary human relation. Many times disciples in India come to their Master and say that there is no joy in human union. These very students then enter into deeper spiritual life and get the highest joy and purest delight from inner union with their Supreme Beloved.

Delight and pleasure are two different things. If one cares for the inner spiritual life, one will get delight. If one cares for the ordinary human life, one will get pleasure. Pleasure is bound to be followed by frustration because in pleasure there is no permanent fulfilment. But delight itself is all-fulfilling. This delight we get only in the spiritual union with the Divine, with our inner being. We have to know what we want. If we want pleasure, the union between man and woman is enough for a while. But if we want delight, which is the nectar of Immortality, the immortal Bliss, then we have to launch into the path of spirituality and establish the supernal union between man and God.

Question: Can you please speak about marriage with regard to the spiritual life?

Sri Chinmoy: Since each soul is a divine portion of God, marriage can be something very spiritual. When both husband and wife are with the same Guru and have utmost faith in the Guru, then they can make very fast progress together. Because they have faith in the Guru, he brings down the Supreme Power to help them, guide them and mould them, and they also help each other. But in many marriages we see that the husband is spiritual and the wife is unspiritual, or vice versa. When this happens, both are caught in a tug-of-war. One cannot make satisfactory inner progress, and the other cannot make satisfactory outer progress.

Marriage is not necessary in some cases. Those who

have gone through family life and have found it a life of misery and frustration should not repeat the same mistake. But those who are young and inexperienced, who want to have a bridge between the inner world and the outer world, will not be making a mistake if they enter into married life with the proper spiritual partner. If inner necessity demands, at any moment they can give up that tie. Everything depends on whether God wants the individuals to get married or if He wants them to remain unmarried. No unmarried person should feel superior to the married ones. God can take them to Him fast, very fast, through married life as well as through unmarried life.

Question: What is a vital demand?

Sri Chinmoy: Usually a vital demand is a desire that comes from a very low plane of consciousness. This plane is unlit, impure, frightening and threatening. It tempts us to lead a very undivine and corrupted life. Those who lead this kind of life should feel that their hour has not yet struck. Further, a vital demand is always destructive. It does not embody any light and, at the same time, it does not care for light.

Question: Is there any difference between emotion and the vital?

Sri Chinmoy: Emotion and the vital are two different things. You can say that the vital is the house and in that house emotion is the tenant. The most predominant emotion is the vital emotion. But emotion can also be in the body, in the mind and in the heart. Emotion in the body usually degrades our consciousness. Emotion in the impure heart blinds and binds us, while emotion in the pure heart illumines us and liberates us. In the mind there is some emotion, but the mind is by nature dry, and it does not have the exuberant or uncontrolled childlike or childish emotion of the vital. When we say, "He is an emotional fellow," we are referring to his undisciplined and unillumined vital emotion. This emotion usually originates in the two centres below the navel centre.

If there is no effort to transform the vital emotional life into the purest spiritual life, then all your spiritual activities will be a kind of self-deception, and in self-deception there is no God-realisation. Many so-called aspirants feel that they can deceive their spiritual Master. But God has given the true spiritual Masters a third eye which is fully open. They are always aware of the aspirants' imperfections and shortcomings.

If you can transform your vital emotions into divine joy, this divine emotion is not bad. When you use your emotions for enjoyment or self-indulgence, then you are ruining your inner life. But if you use emotion for inner determination, for self-liberation, then emotion is the strongest power in you. Please use it in this way, as your inner assistant.

Question: How can I express love and manifest love in the physical world?

Sri Chinmoy: If you want to express and manifest divine love in the physical world, you have to use your spiritual will power. This will power is not aggressive; it is all surrender. On the strength of your conscious oneness with the Supreme's Will, you will be able to bring forward your spiritual will power. When it is sanctioned by the Supreme, automatically and spontaneously you will have a way to use your divine will power to express love for humanity. When you really possess this divine will power, then even in your unconscious movements your pure love will radiate. Those around you will undoubtedly feel the divine love and get the utmost benefit from your divine presence.

Also, you can express and manifest love in the physical world through your pure meditation. When you are in your deepest meditation, try to feel your purest love. Then think of the person that you love. By concentrating on him you can inject your pure divine love into him. By looking at a person with the eyes of your soul, you can manifest love in the physical world.

* * *

ONCE MORE DO COME

Once more do come and appear before me.
Around me is all darkness and the flow of tears.
Once more do come and appear before me.
This heart of mine is now the garland of surrender.
Once more do come and appear before me.
This restless, wild, indomitable, dark vital breath
of mine will be silent.
Once more do come and appear before me.
Do give me the right to worship You, You alone.

* * *

YOU MUST TEACH

Only one body,
You must teach it.

Only one vital,
You must guide it.

Only one mind,
You must perfect it.

Only one heart,
You must use it.

Only one soul,
You must treasure it.

Only one Goal,
You must become it.

THE MIND

THE PHYSICAL MIND AND
THE SPIRITUAL MIND

There are two types of mind: the human or physical mind and the spiritual mind. The physical mind is enmeshed in the gross physical consciousness; therefore, it does not and cannot see the proper truth in its own world. The spiritual mind, which is the illumined or illumining mind, has the capacity to stay in the aspiring heart; therefore, it sees the higher truth, the truth of the ever-transcending Beyond, and aspires to grow into this truth.

The human mind does not like to remain in the human consciousness. Yet this same human mind is afraid of the infinite Vast. When vastness wants to appear before the physical mind, the physical mind is horror-struck. Further, it looks at its own insufficiency, its own limited capacity, and says, "How is it possible? I am so weak; I am so impotent; I am so insignificant. How can the vastness accept me as its very own?"

First it is afraid of vastness, then it doubts. It doubts

the very existence of vastness. Then, by God's infinite Grace, fear leaves the mind and doubt leaves the mind. Alas, now jealousy comes in. The mind looks around and sees that there is some fulfilment in the vastness, whereas in its own existence there is no fulfilment, there is no joy. So jealousy starts. Fear, doubt and jealousy — these three undivine forces — attack the mind and make it meaningless, helpless and hopeless in our upward journey. When the mind is attacked by fear, doubt and jealousy, something else consciously and deliberately enters and feeds the mind, and that is ego. With ego starts the beginning of our spiritual end.

The human mind cares for aesthetic beauty, for poise and balance. The human mind is searching for Truth, for Light, for Reality. But unfortunately, it wants to see the highest Truth in its own limited way. It does not want to transcend itself in order to reach the ultimate Truth. Furthermore, the physical mind wants to examine the highest Truth, which is absurd.

The paramount importance of the human mind has, until now, been undeniable. The human mind separated us from the animal kingdom through the process of cosmic evolution. Had there been no awakening of the human mind, the conscious human life could not have blossomed out of the animal kingdom. But now the animal in us has played its role. The human in us, the unaspiring human in us, will complete its role soon. The divine in us has begun, or will soon begin, its role.

The spiritual mind gets illumination from the soul with the help of the heart. And in the process of its own inner illumination, it wants to go far, far beyond the domain of reason in order to see, feel and grow into the ultimate, transcendental Truth.

* * *

MY MIND

O my mind, no earthly chain can fetter you. You are always on the wing. No human thought can control you. You are forever on the move.

O my mind, hard is it for you to believe in my soul's constant fulfilment. And hard is it for me to believe that you are doomed to be the eternal victim of venomous doubts. Alas! You have forgotten. You have forgotten the golden secret: To remain in the Silence-Room is to open the Fulfilment-Door.

O my mind, vast are your responsibilities. You have to please your superiors: heart and soul. Only with your warmest admiration will you be able to conquer the heart. Only with your deepest faith will you be able to conquer the soul. You have also to satisfy your subordinates: the body and the vital. Only with your pure concern will you be able to make the body smile. Only with your genuine encouragement will you be able to help the vital run unmistakably toward good and not pleasure.

O my mind, I need you desperately, either to abide in you or to go beyond you. You see and thus protect the physical in me. You serve and thus reveal the spiritual beyond me.

O my mind, cast aside your long-treasured arid reason. Welcome the ever-virgin faith. Possess the naked sword of conscience. Far above the storms of fear you are destined to climb. Stay no more in self-created, somber shadows of death. Don the golden robes of simplicity, sincerity and purity. Permit not the gales of disbelief to extinguish your inner mounting flame. Yours is the arrow of concentration. Yours is the soil of lightning intuition. Yours is the unhorizoned peace.

Behold the Supreme! He crowns you, O mind of mine, with the laurel of His infinite Bounty.

* * *

Question: When I try to think out a problem and plan a course of action, I find myself unable to make up my mind. Why is this?

Sri Chinmoy: When people use the mind, they constantly suffer from one thing: confusion. They go on thinking and thinking, and the moment they think that they have arrived at the truth, they discover that it is not truth at all, but just more confusion. The difficulty is this: when we think of someone or something, we form a positive conception which we think is absolutely true. But the next moment doubt comes and changes our mind. This moment you will think that I am a nice man. The next moment you will think that I am a bad man. Then after that you will think something else. Eventually you will see that there is no end to your questions and there is no solution.

Each time we think, we are lost. Thinking is done in the mind, but the mind is not yet liberated. Only the soul is liberated. Our problem is that we want to be liberated by thinking. But the mind itself is still in the prison cell of darkness, confusion and bondage, so how can we expect liberation from the mind?

When we plan, we very often are frustrated because we do not see the truth right from the beginning. We plan to do something because we feel that if we do it we will achieve a certain goal. But between planning and executing, different ideas and different ideals enter into us and create confusion for us. Then our planning goes on and on forever, and we never enter into the world of action because our plans are never complete or certain. There is a yawning gap between our mental plan and the action itself.

But if we have an inner will, soul's will, which has come to us from meditation, then the action is no sooner conceived of than it is done. At that time there is no difference between our inner will and our outer action. When we enter into the totally dark, obscure, unlit room of action with our mental plans, it is like carrying a candle. But when we enter the room with our soul's light, the room is flooded with illumination.

Right now we are labouring with our mind. The mind says, "I have to achieve something. I have to think about how I can execute my plan." But God does not do that. God sees the past, present and future at a glance. When we are one with God, when—by constant aspiration—we identify ourselves with God's Consciousness, then whatever we do will be done spontaneously. We will not utilise the mind but will always act from our own inner consciousness, with our intuitive faculty. And when we develop that intuitive faculty, we can easily act without having a plan. At each moment the possibility of the total manifestation that is going to take place will materialise right in front of us.

Now we think that within, let us say, ten or twenty days some possibility may materialise concerning our hopes and aspirations. But when we are one with God's Consciousness, it is more than a possibility. It is an inevitability, an immediate achievement. The vision and the fulfilment go together. In the ordinary human consciousness the vision is one thing and the fulfilment is something else. But when we are one with God's Consciousness, the vision and the fulfilment are inseparable.

Question: About the vision and its fulfilment, how do you know that you are having the right 'vision'?

Sri Chinmoy: Are you referring to yourself or are you speaking generally? If it is yourself, I can tell you easily. I know that in your meditation there are times when you go very deep, and your inner voice tells you, on the spur of the moment, that something has already been done. Your mind does not come and impose its ideas on that voice, saying, "If you do this, perhaps it will be a mistake; don't do that, or something may happen in the future; if you do it . . . and if you don't do it . . . etc." The mind does not interfere. You can rest assured that when you get this kind of vision in your deep meditation, it is correct and it will spontaneously bring its own fulfilment.

Every day when we start our day, we build our own world. We make decisions. We think that things have to be done in a certain way: "I have to deal with this man in this way. I have to say this. I have to do this. I have to give this." Everything is "I, I, I." But instead of all this planning, if we can make our minds absolutely calm and silent, we can know God's Will. This silence is not the silence of a dead body; it is the dynamic, progressive silence of receptivity.

Through total silence and the ever-increasing receptivity of the mind, God's Will can be known. When the human mind works powerfully, the divine Will cannot work. God's Will works only when the human mind does not work. When the mind becomes a pure vessel, the Supreme can pour into it His infinite Peace, Light and Bliss.

We are constantly building and breaking our mental house. But instead of making and breaking the house at our sweet will, if we can empty our mind, make it calm and quiet, then God can build His Temple or His Palace in us in His own Way. And when He has built His Abode within us, He will say, "I have built this for you and Me to reside in together. I have built it, but it is not Mine alone. It is also yours. Come in."

So the easiest way for us to know God's Will is to become the instrument and not the doer. If we become only the instrument for carrying out God's plans, God's Will will act in and through us. God does the acting, and He is the action. He is everything. We only observe.

Question: Some people say that we should always listen to the voice of reason. Can you comment on this?

Sri Chinmoy: In the beginning many things may help us, but later they may become obstacles. Desire was a helper when it raised us out of the world of lethargy. But it became a hindrance when we wanted to enter into the world of spirituality. Developing the reasoning mind is necessary for those who do not have any brain at all, who will not be able to grasp any truth, who are little better than animals in their understanding. But once we have some mental capacity, we must begin to transcend our servitude to the mind by bringing down the Grace, Peace and Light from above to illumine the mind. We have to go farther, deeper and higher than the world of reason—far beyond the reasoning or intellectual mind.

The reasoning mind has to be transformed into a dedicated instrument of the Supreme.

The reasoning mind is really an obstacle for an aspirant. Using the mind becomes a limitation because the mind cannot grasp the Infinite. If we live in the mind, we will constantly try to circumscribe the Truth; we will never be able to see the Truth in its proper form. Only if we live in the soul will we be able to embrace the Truth as a whole. Beyond reason is Truth. Beyond the boundaries of the reasoning mind are Truth, Reality and Infinity. Reason has very limited Light, whereas what we want and need has infinite Light. When infinite Light dawns, reason is broken into pieces.

Question: Is it desirable to bring to our conscious mind things from our subconscious?

Sri Chinmoy: There are many things in our subconscious mind which need not and should not come to the surface. In the subconscious there is obscurity, there is impurity, there is negation. These things should be purified, transformed and perfected from within without being brought into the physical or conscious mind. It is better not to disturb the subconscious mind at all.

Question: But orthodox psychology states that the subconscious has to be brought to the fore and illumined.

Sri Chinmoy: Here you are making a mistake. If you bring down the Light from above or bring forward your soul's light, automatically the subconscious will be illumined. At that time the subconscious will enter naturally into the conscious plane. But if you try to bring forward the subconscious without illumining it first, you will only create more problems for yourself.

Question: Is there a spiritual method of self-analysis?

Sri Chinmoy: No, there is not. The psychological kind of self-analysis, from the highest point of view, is wrong. In self-analysis we use the physical mind to try to examine our obscure past and our subconscious. In self-analysis we say, "I have done the right thing," or "I have done the wrong thing." There is always a positive and negative. But we have to go beyond positive and negative. In the Upanishads it is said that we have to accept ignorance and knowledge and then go beyond both to where all is divine wisdom. When we adopt self-analysis, one moment we are in knowledge and the next moment we are in ignorance. We are constantly identifying ourselves with knowledge or ignorance and with our mental doubt. But when we enter into deep spiritual meditation, when we are far along in the spiritual life, we are above ignorance and knowledge. We only cry for infinite Peace, infinite Light and infinite Bliss.

If the seeker is constantly examining himself with his mind, there will always be a strong pull from the negative forces in the mind. Like a magnet they will pull us, even though with our mind we are trying to discard whatever we think is wrong. The difficulty is that we do not use the soul's light to strengthen our will power in self-analysis. When one means to do the right thing, that does not mean that he will be able to do it. The lower propensities and the wrong forces have tremendous power and this power comes in the form of temptation. If we give way to this temptation we are totally lost.

If a spiritual person wants to reach the realm of highest Peace and infinite Light, where there is no temptation, he has to go beyond mental analysis. He has to aspire. If, however, one has not accepted the spiritual life, it is better for that person to use self-analysis than to act like a wild animal. For him it is good, to some extent. If he does not use his power of self-analysis, for him there will be absolutely no difference between light and darkness. But if you want the quickest and most convincing way to transform your nature into a divine nature, you have to aspire. Aspiration is the only ultimate solution to the problems of human limitation.

Question: What is the best way to prevent wrong thoughts from attacking us?

Sri Chinmoy: The thoughts that we have to control are the thoughts that are not productive, the thoughts that are damaging, the thoughts that are destructive, the thoughts that are silly, the thoughts that are negative. These thoughts can come from outside and enter into us; or they may already be inside us and merely come forward. The thoughts that come from outside are easier to control than the thoughts that are already inside. If an undivine thought comes from outside, we have to feel that we have a shield all around us or right in front of us as a protection, especially in front of the forehead. If we feel that our forehead is something vulnerable, delicate, exposed, then we will always be a victim to wrong thoughts. But the moment we consciously make ourselves feel that this forehead is a shield, a solid wall, then wrong thoughts cannot come in. We have to make ourselves feel consciously that we are protected by a solid wall or a fort with many soldiers inside. We have to be constantly vigilant and, when an attack of wrong forces comes, we have to know that we have inside us soldiers stronger than they are. The strongest soldiers are our purity, our sincerity, our aspiration and our eagerness for God. These divine soldiers inside us will be on their guard the moment a wrong thought comes, and they will serve as bodyguards to us.

The thoughts that are already inside us creating problems are more difficult to throw out, but we can do it. We can do it through extension of our consciousness. We have a body, and inside this body are wrong forces that have taken the form of thoughts. What we have to do is extend our physical consciousness through conscious effort and aspiration, as we extend an elastic band, until we feel that our whole body is extended to Infinity and has become just a white sheet of infinitely extended consciousness. If we can do this, we will see that our consciousness is all purity.

Each pure thought, each pure drop of consciousness, is like poison to impurity or to wrong thoughts in us. We are afraid of impure thoughts, but impure thoughts are more afraid of our purity. What often happens to us is that we identify ourselves with our impure thoughts and not with our pure thoughts. But the moment our physical existence can identify with purity, when we can say, "This pure

thought represents me," then impurity inside us immediately dies. Wrong thoughts are inside us just because
we identify ourselves with these thoughts. If we identify
with something else, immediately they have to leave us.

* * *

ONLY ONE THOUGHT

Only one thought flashes across my mind,
  only one thought:
Who has given me such impure power of talkativeness,
  this meaningless babble?
Mother, I know my only companion was silence.
Who has taken that silence away from me, Mother,
And who has taken away the cheerfulness of my heart?

* * *

*Question: Yesterday when I was meditating, I got a
message from the silence which said, "Love one another." When we get this kind of message in our meditation, should we meditate on it and take it into ourselves?*

Sri Chinmoy: When we get a message in our mind
during meditation, we have to know whether it is in the
lower mind, the physical mind—the restless, aggressive,
destructive and doubtful mind—or in the calm mind,
the vacant mind, the silent mind. When we receive a
message in the silent mind, we should accept it and feel
that it is the foundation stone on which we can build the

Palace of Truth, Love, Divinity and Reality. This message actually originates in the soul or in the heart, and then enters into the mind. When the mind is absolutely still, calm and peaceful, we can hear that message.

Suppose you are meditating and after a few minutes a thought or idea comes into your mind. Let us say that it is about sacrifice, that you will make some sacrifice for a friend or for some good cause. This is not just an idea at that time; it is an ideal. When you accept an idea as your own, the idea does not remain an idea but becomes an ideal.

Whenever a divine thought enters into your mind, try to expand it. When an undivine thought comes into your mind, either reject it or, if you have enough inner strength, transform it. It is like this. Somebody has knocked at your door. If you know that you have enough strength to compel him to behave properly once he enters, then you can open the door and allow him to come in. But if you do not have the power to compel him to behave, then it would be wise to keep your door closed. Let it remain closed for a day or for a month or for a year. When you gain more strength, then accept the challenge and open the door. For if these wrong thoughts are not conquered, they will come back to bother you again and again. First you reject; then you accept and transform; then finally you totally transcend.

We have to be a divine potter with the dirty clay of our thoughts. If the potter is afraid to touch the clay, if he refuses to touch it, then the clay will remain clay and the potter will not be able to offer anything to the world. But the potter is not afraid. He touches the clay and shapes it in his own way into something beautiful and useful. It is our bounden duty to transform undivine thoughts. But when? When we are in a position to do it safely. If I am not a potter, what can I do with a lump of clay? If I touch it, I will only make myself dirty.

In the spiritual life, a beginner should not allow any thought to enter his mind. He would like to allow his friends to enter, but he does not know who his friends are. And even if he does know who his friends are, when he opens the door for them he may find that his enemies are standing right in front of them, and before his friends can cross the threshold, his enemies are deep inside the room. Once the enemies enter, it is very difficult to chase them out. For that we need the strength of solid spiritual discipline.

There will come a time, as in your case, when you can build on your divine ideas. Build your life of love on this thought that came to you. Love is absolutely necessary in the spiritual life. This is the love which permits us to see that all human beings are God. If we truly love God, we love all mankind as well. We cannot separate divine Love from man and God. Man and God are like a tree. If you go to man, the foot of the tree, with your divine Love, from there it is very easy to go up to God, the top of the tree.

* * *

Keep your mind centered on God. Your futile thoughts will be transformed into fertile ideas, your fertile ideas into glowing ideals and your glowing ideals into the all-fulfilling Infinitude.

EACH THOUGHT

A vivacious infant,
    Each thought
In the vital world.

A helpless orphan,
    Each thought
In the physical world.

A doubting youth,
    Each thought
In the mental world.

A growing God,
    Each thought
In the psychic world.

* * *

Peace is the perfection of one's mind and the divinisation of one's thoughts.

* * *

An idle thought indicates that the mind is on strike. Don't delay, put the mind down quickly and forcibly.

* * *

Do not try to approach God with your thinking mind. It may only stimulate your intellectual ideas, activities and beliefs. Try to approach God with your crying heart. It will awaken your soulful, spiritual consciousness.

* * *

When we live in the mind we live in the fabric of form. When we live in the soul we enter into the formless and eventually go beyond both form and formlessness. We become, at that time, the individual soul universalised and the Universal Soul individualised.

The outer world is synonymous with the mind. The inner world is synonymous with the heart. The world of the eternal Beyond is synonymous with the soul. The outer world has past, present and future. The inner world has the glowing and fulfilling future. The world of the Beyond has only the eternal Now. When we live in the outer world, the ignorant 'I' destroys us. When we live in the inner world, the illumined 'I' satisfies us. When we live in the world of the Beyond, the Infinite 'I' fondly embraces and immortalises us.

* * *

My soul is in charge of my glowing deeds. My heart is in charge of my soaring feelings. My mind is in charge of my transforming thoughts. My vital is in charge of my flowing energy. My body is in charge of my striving life.

* * *

58

I DEPEND

When I am in the body,
I depend on hopelessness and helplessness.
When I am in the vital,
I depend on aggression and regression.
When I am in the mind,
I depend on doubt and fear.
When I am in the heart,
I depend on insecurity and uncertainty.
When I am in the soul,
I depend on love and joy.
When I am in God,
I depend on His Forgiveness and Assurance.

* * *

MY LIFE IS TRANSCENDING

From the blue of the sky
My soul began its descending flight.
In the black of my body
My life is sleeping and sleeping.
In the green of my vital
My life is struggling and struggling.
In the red of my mind
My life is searching and searching.
In the white of my heart
My life is becoming and becoming.
In the gold of my soul
My life is transcending and transcending.

* * *

HE THINKS—HE FEELS—HE KNOWS

His vital thinks
To live with God the Disciplinarian
    Is ridiculous.

His mind thinks
To live with God the Simpleton
    Is ridiculous.

His body thinks
To live with God the Inconsiderate
    Is ridiculous.

His heart feels
To live without God the Beloved
    Is ridiculous.

His soul knows
To live without God the Lover
    Is ridiculous.

* * *

My wealth lies in my mind's divine thoughts, in my heart's pure sacrifice and in my soul's conscious oneness with the Supreme.

* * *

MY KRISHNA IS NOT BLACK

My Krishna is not black,
He is pure gold.
He Himself is woven
Into the universal Beauty, Light and Splendour.

He looks dark
Because I have spilled the ink
Of my mind on Him.
Otherwise, my Beloved is All-Light.

He created Light and darkness,
He is within and without the Cosmos vast.

With this knowledge,
I will have a new acquaintance
With the world at large.

* * *

When I transform my mind into readiness, God will transform His Heart into willingness.

* * *

Learn to love your disturbing and disturbed mind with your soul's light.
You will see your mind listening to your heart's necessity.

* * *

I AM HAPPY

I am happy
Because my mind
Has forgotten how to calculate.

I am happy
Because my heart
Has forgotten how to hesitate.

I am happy
Because my life
Always knows how to tolerate.

* * *

HOPE-BOAT AND LIFE-BOAT

My hope-boat is plying
Between uncertainty and frustration.
My thought-boat is plying
Between disaster and destruction.
My will-boat is plying
Between silence and sound.
My life-boat is plying
Between beauty's Shore and duty's Goal.

* * *

THE HEART

MY HEART

O my heart, I am divinely proud of you. You do not have the shameful and shameless disease, worry! Never do you drink the deadly venom, doubt! Nothing can be simpler than your pure longings. Nothing can be more spontaneous than your glowing feelings. Nothing can be more fulfilling than your selfless love. Nothing has a more immediate access to the Supreme than your inmost cry.

O my heart, your heavenly day within an earthly day is for God-realisation. Your immortalising minute within a fleeting minute is for God-embodiment. Your revealing second within a vanishing second is for God-manifestation.

O my heart, the other members of the family are a-fraid of God. You are never! Their lightless, persistent fear is a lifeless, persistent paralysis. In life's journey others make their own choice. God makes the choice for you. They want to save humanity with their egos' darkest night. You wish to serve humanity with your dedication's brightest day. Their victory is the victory over humanity. Your victory is the victory over yourself.

O my heart, O heart of mine, you are my life-boat. You sail the uncharted seas of ignorance and reach the golden shore of the Beyond.

I am not alone, O my heart. I am with your soaring aspiration. You are not alone. In you and for you is my life's unreserved breath.

Yours is the unfaltering will and unfailing faith in the Supreme. Each petal of the radiant lotus deep within you is perpetually bathed in nectar-rays of the transcendental Delight.

O sweet, sweeter, sweetest heart of mine, you are not only God's. God also is yours.

* * *

EMOTION

Emotion is a gift of God. It fills our days with loving thoughts and glowing deeds.

Emotion tells us that the ever-increasing life-energy is constantly flowing through us, renewing and revitalising our inner being. Emotion not only sweetens and intensifies our inner life, but also awakens our outer life so it may experience perfection in every field of manifestation.

In emotion there is an eternal creative urge. The creative urge finally has to enter into the God-ideal which is Immortality embodied and Perfection revealed.

Emotion has an inner perception of the divine unity. The knowledge of the intellect secretly loves emotion. The understanding of the mind silently loves emotion. The wisdom of the heart openly and soulfully loves emotion.

We must endeavour to uncover within ourselves the deepest depth of emotion so that we can become the widest channels for the divine expression of beauty, joy, power and truth.

Owing to our confused thinking, we misuse emotion. But emotion is not the confusion of experience. It is the reality that grows in perfection. It is the dynamic fulness of completion.

Emotion is not the victim of frustration. Emotion is not demonstration. It is the inner spontaneous joy through which we express ourselves in the world we live in.

When inspiration and aspiration are supported by our psychic emotion, we come into conscious contact with the Supreme, and the perfect Reality then prevails in and through our outer existence.

The psychic emotion is the fountain of abundance. And with this fountain we enter into the world of revealing thought, fulfilling action and transforming realisation.

* * *

I WANT ONLY ONE STUDENT: HEART [A SHORT STORY]

There was once a spiritual Master who had hundreds of followers and disciples. The Master often gave discourses at different places — churches, synagogues, temples, schools and universities. Wherever he was invited, and wherever his disciples made arrangements for him, he gave talks. He gave talks for children and for adults. He gave talks for university students and for housewives.

Sometimes he gave talks before scholars and advanced seekers.

This went on for about twenty years. Finally there came a time when the Master decided to discontinue his lectures. He told his disciples, "Enough! I have done this for many years. Now I shall not give any more talks. Only silence. I shall maintain silence."

For about ten years the Master did not give talks. He maintained silence in his ashram. He maintained silence everywhere. He had answered thousands of questions but now he did not even meditate before the public. After ten years his disciples begged him to resume his previous practice of giving talks, answering questions and holding public meditations. They all pleaded with him and finally he consented.

Immediately the disciples made arrangements at many places. They put advertisements in the newspapers and put up posters everywhere to announce that their Master was going to give talks once again and hold high meditations for the public. The Master went to these places with some of his favourite disciples, who were most devoted and dedicated, and hundreds of people gathered together to listen to the Master and have their questions answered. But to everyone's wide surprise, the Master would not talk at all. From the beginning to the end of the meeting, for two hours, he would maintain silence.

Some of the seekers in the audiences were annoyed, and they left the meetings early. Others remained for the whole two hours with the hope that perhaps the Master would speak at the end, but he closed the meditations without saying anything. Some of the people in the audiences felt inner joy. Some stayed only because they were afraid that if they left early, others would think that they were not spiritual and that they could not meditate well. So some left, some stayed with great reluctance, some stayed in order to prove themselves to others and a few stayed with utmost sincerity, devotion and aspiration.

It went on for three or four years this way. There were many who criticised the Master mercilessly and embarrassed the disciples, saying, "Your Master is a liar. How do you people justify putting an advertisement in the paper that your Master is going to give a talk, answer questions and hold meditation? He only holds meditation, and we don't learn anything from it. Who can meditate for two or three hours? He is fooling us, and he is fooling himself."

Some of the close disciples were very disturbed. They felt miserable that their Master was being insulted and criticised and pleaded with him again and again to give just a short talk and answer a few questions at the end of the meditation. The Master finally agreed.

At the next public function, the Master did not actually forget his promise to speak, but he changed his mind. He went on meditating, but instead of for two hours, this time he went on for four hours. Even his close disciples were sad. They could not get angry with the Master, for it is a serious karmic mistake to get angry with the Master. But they were afraid that someone from the audience would actually stand up and insult the Master. In their minds they prepared themselves to protect their Master in case some calamity took place.

When four hours had passed and there was no sign that the Master would either talk or close the meeting, one of the very close disciples stood up and said, "Master, please do not forget your promise."

The Master immediately said, "My promise. Yes, I have made a promise to you people, so now it is my bounden duty to give a talk. Today my talk will be very short. I wish to say that I have given hundreds of talks, thousands of talks. But who heard my talks? Thousands of ears and thousands of eyes. My students were the ears and the eyes of the audience—thousands and thousands of ears and eyes. But I have failed to teach them anything. Now I want to have a different type of student. My new students will be hearts.

"I have offered messages at thousands of places. These messages entered into one ear and passed out through the other, all in the briefest possible moment. People saw me giving talks and answering questions. Just for a fleeting second their eyes glimpsed something in me and then it was totally lost. While I was speaking about sublime Truth, Peace, Light and Bliss, the ears could not receive it because the ears were already full of rumour, doubt, jealousy, insecurity and impurity which had accumulated over many years. The ears were totally polluted and did not receive my message. And the eyes did not receive my Truth, Peace, Light and Bliss because the eyes saw everything in their own way. When the human eyes see something beautiful, they immediately start comparing. They say, 'How is it that he is beautiful, his speech is beautiful, his questions and answers are beautiful? How is that I cannot be the same?' And immediately jealousy enters. The human ear and the human eye both respond through jealousy. If the ear hears something good about somebody else, immediately jealousy enters. If the eye sees somebody else who is beautiful, immediately the person becomes jealous.

"The ears and the eyes have played their role. They have proved to be undivine students, and I could not teach them. Their progress has been most unsatisfactory. Now I want new students, and I have new students. These students are the hearts, where oneness will grow — oneness with truth, oneness with light, oneness with inner beauty, oneness with what God has and what God is. It is the heart-student who has the capacity to identify with the Master's wisdom, light and bliss. The heart is the real listener; the heart is the real observer; the heart is the real student who becomes one with the Master's light, vision and realisation. From now on, the heart will be my only student."

* * *

MANY A TIME HAVE I SEEN YOU

Many a time have I seen You
In the inmost depths of my heart.
I have broken dark slumber
With my indomitable inner strength.
You are all mine; this secret
Dawns time and again in my mind.
Yet I know not why the darkness of ugliness
Resides still in my heart.

* * *

IN THE DEPTH OF MY HEART
THE BLUE BIRD SMILES

In the depth of my heart the blue bird smiles
  and the blue bird plays.
The festival of lustre-form and celestial delight
  is inviting everyone.
The sun, the moon, the mountains and the ocean —
  all have come.
Today we shall listen to the call of Infinity.
We shall run toward Infinity.
Right in front of us is the ladder of Light.
Our hearts have become the flower of Light Divine.
We are the hope of our Lord Supreme.
The world-creator is none other than our love.

* * *

MY WORLD IS FOR YOUR FEET

My world is for Your Feet.
My life is for Your Dream.
O Silence of Infinity,
O Immortality of Heaven,
Come, come, come.
This heart remains awake.

* * *

ONLY ONE HOPE

Break asunder all my hopes.
Only keep one hope,
And that hope is to learn
The language of Your inner Silence
In my utter unconditional surrender.
In your clear and free Sky
I shall be calm and perfect.
The bird of my heart is dancing today
In the festival of supernal Light.

* * *

MY IMPATIENT HEART CALLS YOU

Mother, tell me,
How can I bear more pain?
If you never awake
Within my heart
I know the night of my sufferings
Will not come to an end.
O Mother, come quickly.
My impatient heart calls you.

* * *

O LIGHT OF THE SUPREME

O Beauty non-pareil, O Beloved,
Do burn the fire of beauty and splendour
    within my heart.
By loving You, eternally beautiful I shall be.
May Lord Shiva's destruction-dance
Destroy all shackles of the finite.
May the Light of the Supreme inundate me,
My heart, my heart, my all.
Having loved the Infinite,
The heart of gloom is crying for the bloom
    of Light.
O Life infinite, give me the eternal hunger,
    aspiration-cry.
The tiniest drop will lose its *raison d'etre* in
    the heart
Of the boundless ocean.
In fire and air Your life of the Spirit I behold.
O Beauty, O Beauty's Gold,
O Light of the Supreme!

* * *

*Question: Why do you tell people to stay in the heart
and not in the mind?*

Sri Chinmoy: There are many reasons why I tell
people to stay in the heart and not in the mind. The
heart knows how to identify itself with the Highest, with
the farthest, with the inmost. In the case of the mind,
this is not so. The mind tries to identify itself with an
object, with a person, with something limited. But this

identification is not pure or complete. When the mind tries to identify, the mind looks at the object with an eye of hesitation, if not actual suspicion. But when the heart wants to identify itself with something or someone, it uses the feeling of love and oneness. When the heart wants to see something, it sees it unreservedly. When the mind wants to see something, it tries to delay and separate. The heart simplifies; the mind complicates. The mind unconsciously gets pleasure in things that are complicated and confused, but the heart gets joy in things that are simple.

The human, physical, earth-bound mind is at our disposal right now. But the higher mind, the overmind, the intuitive mind, the supermind, are not at our command. In our day-to-day life we use the earth-bound physical mind, which is constantly contradicting itself. Unfortunately, we seldom use the heart, which is all love, all sympathy, all concern, all purity, all harmony, all oneness.

Why do I tell people to pay more attention to the heart and less to the mind? Because the heart expands. The soul represents our illumination, and it is inside the heart that the soul abides. In the spiritual life our treasure is the soul. It is only with the help of the soul that we can make the fastest progress in the inner life, and we can contact the soul only by meditating on our heart. All paths lead to the Goal, but there is a particular road that will lead us there faster than the other roads. That road is the heart. It is faster, safer and surer than any other road.

We are the possessors of two rooms. One room is known as the heart-room; the other is known as the mind-room. Right now the mind-room is obscure, unlit, impure and unwilling to open to the light. So we have to remain in the heart-room, the room of light, as much as we can. When we feel that our entire being is surcharged with the inner light that is there, then we can enter into the mind-room and illumine it. But if we enter into the mind-room, which is all darkness, without sufficient light, we will be caught there and will become victims of the ignorant, undivine and suspicious forces of the mind. This is why I tell my students first to strengthen their inner being by meditating on the heart.

The soul's light is available in the heart. If we concentrate on the heart, sooner or later the light of the soul is bound to come to the fore. At that time we will know that we are in possession of the inner light, and we will be able to use it at our own sweet will. Then we can enter into the mind-room to illumine it. But very often we make the Himalayan blunder of entering into the mind-room just because we see that it is all confusion and darkness. We have to know whether we have the necessary light at our command to illumine that darkness. If we do not have the necessary light, we have to enter only into the heart-room. There we can meditate and receive the inner light of the soul until we are inwardly strong. So we should not enter into the mind-room at the very beginning of our spiritual journey. To enter into that room safely we need inner confidence, inner light and inner assurance from the Supreme.

Question: How can we integrate the mind and the heart?

Sri Chinmoy: There are two ways. One way is for the heart to enter into the mind. The other way is for the mind to enter into the heart. Let us take the heart as the mother and the mind as the child. Either the child has to go to the mother, who is calm, quiet and full of love, or the mother has to go to the child, who right now is uncertain, doubtful and restless.

When the mother comes to the child, at that time the child — which is the mind — has to feel that the mother — the heart — has come with good intentions: to calm the mind, to free it, to fulfil it in a divine way. If the doubting and restless mind feels that the heart has come to bother it, and that its restlessness is something very good which it wants to keep, then it is lost. If the child is restless, doubtful, suspicious, and if he cherishes all these undivine qualities and feels they are his best qualities, then what can the poor mother do? The heart will have the good intention of transforming the mind's doubt into faith, and its other undivine qualities into divine qualities. But the mind has to be prepared; it has to feel that the heart has come with the idea of changing it for the better.

The other way is to allow the child to go through everything negative and destructive — fear, doubt, suspicion, jealousy, impurity. Eventually the child comes to a point where he feels that it is high time for him to go to someone who can give him something better. Who is this someone? The mother, the heart. The mother is more than eager to illumine her own child. If the mind is aspiring, it will immediately feel that the heart is the mother, the real mother. And the heart will always feel that the mind is a child who needs instruction.

Both ways are effective. If the mind is ready to learn from the heart, the heart is always eager to teach it. The mother is ready to help the child, to serve the child twenty-four hours a day. It is the child who sometimes becomes irritated, disobedient or obstinate, who feels that he knows everything and has nothing to learn from anybody else. But the mind must learn from someone else. Even the mother, the heart, gets knowledge from someone else—from the soul, which is all light. Let us call the soul the grandmother. From the grandmother the mother learns, and from the mother the child learns. The soul teaches the heart and the heart teaches the mind. If we can see the relationship between the heart and the mind as the relationship of a mother to her child, that is the best way to integrate the two.

* * *

IN THE UNIVERSAL HEART
ALL HEARTS ARE ONE

In the universal heart all hearts are one, inseparable,
   I know.
Yet knowing this I hurt the hearts of others
   day and night.
We are all the slaves of fate;
It dances on our foreheads.
In peace sublime is the extinction-sleep of fate.
I know this secret.
O Jewel of my eye, pour into my heart
   Your golden Silence.

* * *

VISIONS OF THE EMERALD-BEYOND

No more am I the foolish customer
Of a dry, sterile, intellectual breeze.
I shall buy only
The weaving visions of the emerald-Beyond.
My heart-tapestry
Shall capture the Himalayan Smiles
Of my Pilot Supreme.
In the burial of my sunken mind
Is the revival of my climbing heart.
In the burial of my deceased mind
Is the festival of my all-embracing life.

* * *

Question: When you speak of the heart as being the centre of love and the place where the soul resides, do you mean the physical heart, or is 'heart' just a term that you use?

Sri Chinmoy: I am not speaking of the human heart, the physical heart, which is just another organ, or the emotional heart, which is really the vital. I am speaking of the pure heart, the spiritual heart. Some spiritual Masters say that the spiritual heart is in the centre of the chest; some say that it is located a little to the right; some say to the left. There is even one spiritual teacher who says that the heart is a little above the centre of the eyebrows at the place we call the third eye. How can a spiritual Master say this? Because the illumined third eye is light, and the illumined heart is also all light. But according to my own realisation, the spiritual heart is located in the centre of the chest, in the centre of our existence.

The heart is like the commander-in-chief, while the soul is the king. When the soul comes into existence, its first concern is to illumine the heart. When the soul withdraws from the body, automatically the commander-in-chief loses all his power. The heart wants to stay with its king. It does not want to go and join another king or another army. In the outer world our friends may deceive us; but in the case of the soul and the heart, their intimacy is thicker than the thickest. The physical sometimes does not listen to the soul. The mind and the vital may ignore it. But the heart is always faithful to the soul. The heart also knows how to identify itself with others' hearts. The mother does not have to show her love for her child by saying, "I love you, I love you," because the mother's identification with the child makes the child feel that he is loved. The real heart does not need to convince; it has the power of oneness.

Question: Many times I feel many important questions inside myself, but I cannot conceptualise them. How can we be aware enough inside ourselves to know the questions that we have?

Sri Chinmoy: We have to know the source of our questions. If the source of the questions is the intellectual, sophisticated mind, or the physical mind, then these questions have no ultimate value. Even if they are answered most adequately, the answers will be of no use in your inner life. When it is a matter of your heart, there is only one question that can come from the heart, from the inmost recesses of your heart, and that is: "Who am I?" This is the only question truly worth asking and worth answering. It is a question which has to be answered every day, every second in our existence. If you have millions of questions about God and about yourself, you will be able to get most adequate answers to all of them by getting the proper answer to this one question: "Who am I?" All the other questions revolve around this question. When you know the answer to this question, your life's problems are solved. You enter into liberation, salvation, Self-realisation. You become totally and consciously one with God the Omnipotent, God the Omniscient and God the All-Perfect.

Do not bother to search for questions deep inside yourself. Most questions are like ants and bugs. They do not help us in any way to approach our Goal. On the contrary, they stand in our way. Illumining questions, questions that come from the very depth of our heart concerning our inner progress and inner achievement, our self-realisation or God-realisation, are very few in number. Besides asking, "Who am I?" you may want to know the answer to the question, "What am I here for?" You may also have various specific questions about your own spiritual progress, which are bound to come to you spontaneously. But the only really important question is, "Who am I?"

* * *

Man can be happy and safe only when the heart feels faster than the mind thinks.

* * *

Human nature will change only when our heart needs God, and not when our mind wants God and our vital demands God.

* * *

I SHALL NOW CALL MYSELF

I shall now call myself;
I shall now call.
In the forest of my heart, seeing myself,
I shall love myself and love myself.
I shall be my own quest,
My absolute wealth.
The journey of Light supreme will commence
In the heart of freedom.

* * *

O Aspirant! Your heart's cry is a real treasure. Do not allow your obscure, unlit, discouraging and damaging vital to make light of it. Your heart's cry flies like an eagle to reach the highest goal of your purest soul.

* * *

THE SOUL

WHAT DOES YOUR SOUL NEED?

The soul comes into birth for experience. And its experience will' be complete when it brings down all the perfection of the Divine into matter.

Each soul needs involution and evolution. When the soul descends, it is the soul's involution. When the soul ascends, it is the soul's evolution. The soul enters into the lowest abyss of inconscience. Then it evolves again into *Satchidananda* — Existence-Consciousness-Bliss — the triple Consciousness.

The soul enters into inconscience. For millions of years it remains there, fast asleep. All of a sudden one day its eye is opened by a spark of consciousness from the ever-transcending Beyond, and then the hour strikes for self-inquiry. "Who am I?" it asks. The answer is *Tat twam asi,* That thou art. The soul is thrilled. Then again, it falls asleep. Again it enters into self-oblivion. More questions arise after some time: "Whose am I?" I am of That. "Where have I come from?" From That. "To Whom am I returning?" To That. "For Whom am I here on earth?" For That.

Then the soul is satisfied. The soul now is fully prepared for its journey upward — high, higher, highest.
Now the evolution of the soul starts properly. From the
mineral life the soul enters into the plant life. Then it
goes from the plant to the animal life, from the animal
to the human life, and from the human to the divine
life. While in the human, the soul brings down Peace,
Light and Bliss from above. First it offers these divine
qualities to the heart, then to the mind, then to the
vital, then to the gross physical. When illumination
takes place, we see it in the heart, in the mind, in the
vital and in the physical body.

What does your soul need? Your soul needs absolute
fulfilment. It wants to achieve this absolute fulfilment
not in Heaven, but here on earth. If you think it impossible, then you may continue to sleep for a few centuries.
There is no harm in that. But if you feel that the divine
life is possible, then the soul whispers in your ear,
"Arise, awake!" And if you feel it is both possible and
practicable, then the soul smilingly tells you, "Walk,
march, run." Finally, if you feel that the absolute fulfilment of the divine life is not only possible and
practicable but also inevitable, then only will Immortality beckon you. Yours is the Goal, yours is the Kingdom
of Truth and Delight.

On the strength of your present knowledge you tell me
that there is no soul. Had there been a soul, how is it
that during your whole lifetime you have never had a
glimpse of it? I humbly tell you that your experience is
no proof against the existence of the soul. Can we see
the microbe with our naked eye? No, never. Until we
have a microscope, the existence of a microbe is pure
imagination. But the microscope compels us to revise
our proud opinion. In no time it shatters our firm con-

viction and illumines our unlit ignorance. Similarly, until we have an illumined consciousness or the power of spiritual vision, the existence of the soul may seem to be a giant mental hallucination.

You may wonder if the soul is a portion of your heart. No, it is not. A portion of your mind? Ridiculous. A portion of your sense organs? Absurd. An unseen portion of your physical body? Impossible. What is it then? What is your soul, after all?

It is the self-effulgent messenger of God within you. It knows no birth, no decay, no death. It is eternal. It is immortal.

Your soul is unique. God wants to manifest and fulfil Himself within you in an unprecedented way. God has a particular divine Mission to fulfil only through your soul. And to fulfil this particular Mission of His, He will utilise your soul and no other soul as His chosen instrument.

Do you want your life to be of service to God so that you can fulfil His Mission? If so, then here and now give the soul back its throne. You have driven the soul away and placed the ego on your life's throne. Do cordially welcome the soul and unite yourself with it. At that time fear leaves you, ignorance leaves you and, finally, death leaves you. Eternity welcomes you, Infinity welcomes you and, finally, Immortality welcomes you.

* * *

WHEN I AM IN THE SOUL

When I am in the physical, the world attracts me and I tempt the world.

When I am in the vital, I grasp the world and the world hates me.

When I am in the mind, I neglect the world and the world ignores me.

When I am in the heart, I love the world and the world embraces me.

When I am in the soul, I serve God in the world and the world cheerfully fulfils me.

* * *

Question: Do you have any concept of salvation for the soul?

Sri Chinmoy: In the Western world we use the term 'salvation', but in the Eastern world we use the words 'liberation', 'illumination' and 'realisation'. The soul itself has already achieved the highest possible illumination. What it requires now is to reveal its divinity—Light, Peace, Bliss and Power—here on earth. First it reveals itself. But revelation is not enough; the soul feels that manifestation is also necessary. You have something precious. You can reveal it to me, but if you do not actually manifest it, if you do not offer it to me, then I cannot get it. The soul wants to manifest its divinity here on earth, and this manifestation is the liberation and fulfilment of our entire being.

* * *

THE SOUL-BIRD

O world-ignorance,
  Although
You have shackled my feet,
  I am free.
  Although
You have chained my hands,
  I am free.
  Although
You have enslaved my body,
  I am free.
I am free because I am not the body.
I am free because I am the soul-bird
  That flies in Infinity-Sky,
Because I am the soul-child that dreams
On the Lap of the immortal King Supreme.

* * *

Every time the soul enters into the field of creation
and manifestation, it makes a most solemn promise to
God, the Pilot Supreme, to try its utmost to reveal God
here on earth. But, unfortunately, when the soul enters
into the world, the sea of ignorance tries to envelop the
soul. Then the body, vital, mind and heart consciously
or unconsciously get pleasure in identifying themselves
with the ignorance-sea. But the soul is all-forgiving. It
does not cast aside the body, vital, mind and heart. It
has boundless patience.

If the body, vital, mind and heart identify themselves
with the soul, and if they want to see the Truth with the

soul's eye—if that is their promise, their only promise, their inner promise—then the date of God-realisation, God-revelation and God-manifestation on earth is not very far off.

* * *

WHEN I LIVE

When I live in the physical world
    I find it easier to sleep than to work.

When I live in the vital world
    I find it easier to break than to build.

When I live in the mental world
    I find it easier to doubt and suspect
        Than to love and embrace.

When I live in the psychic world
    I find it easier to work than to sleep,
    I find it easier to build than to break,
    I find it easier to love and embrace
        Than to doubt and suspect.

    Unlike in other worlds,
In my psychic world
    I want what I need,
    I get what I want.

* * *

SIX CONFIDANTS

The body takes comfort
  As its confidant.
The vital takes arrogance
  As its confidant.
The mind takes pride
  As its confidant.
The heart takes happiness
  As its confidant.
The soul takes calmness
  As its confidant.
God takes Oneness
  As His confidant.

* * *

If you live in the body, you will be too weak to prevent anything. If you live in the vital, you will be too authoritarian to allow anything. If you live in the mind, you will be too indifferent to love anything. If you live in the heart, you will be too indulgent to control anything. Live in the soul; God will say, do and become everything for you.

* * *

The mind conceals its ideas in the body of the finite.

The heart reveals its ideals in the vision of the Infinite.

The soul fulfils its goal in the Consciousness of the Absolute.

* * *

IMMORTALITY

I feel in all my limbs His boundless Grace;
Within my heart the truth of life shines white.
The secret heights of God my soul now climbs;
No dole, no sombre pang, no death in my sight.

No mortal days and nights can shake my calm;
A Light above sustains my secret soul.
All doubts with grief are banished from my deeps,
My eyes of light perceive my cherished Goal.

Though in the world, I am above its woe;
I dwell in an ocean of supreme release.
My mind, a core of the One's unmeasured thoughts,
The star-vast welkin hugs my Spirit's peace.

My eternal days are found in speeding time,
I play upon His Flute of rhapsody.
Impossible deeds no more impossible seem,
In birth-chains now shines Immortality.

* * *

Question: Does the soul get new experiences in its development, or does it merely uncover what it has always known?

Sri Chinmoy: In essence, the soul, being one with God, is uncovering what it has always known. But, at the same time, it is growing and enriching itself by taking into itself the divine essence of its earthly experiences. Meanwhile, the physical consciousness is becoming more and more conscious of the soul's unlimited divine capacity.

Question: How does the soul communicate with us? What language does it use?

Sri Chinmoy: The soul uses the soul's language, which is light. It is through light that the soul expresses itself. When the soul's light expresses itself to the physical mind, the physical mind gets the message in a way it can understand. It is not actually words that the soul is using. The soul is offering and scattering its light, and the mind is receiving it in the way that it finds most convincing. Unless the mind is convinced, it is not satisfied. So when we hear the soul talking in human language, it is actually the mind that is receiving the soul's light in a way convincing to itself.

Question: Does the soul experience loneliness?

Sri Chinmoy: The soul experiences loneliness only when the body, vital, mind and heart, which are supposed to cooperate with the soul in fulfilling its divine mission on earth, do not cooperate. But it does not waste its time like a human being who feels that just by mixing with others his sense of loneliness will disappear. The soul, in its loneliness, aspires more intensely to bring down Peace, Light and Power from above into the physical, the vital and the mind so that the total being can cooperate and fulfil the Divine. With Peace, Light and Power a higher consciousness descends, and the person becomes conscious of his inner life. With this higher consciousness, the person will naturally respond to the soul's need.

Question: What happens to our soul while we are sleeping? What does sleep do to our soul?

Sri Chinmoy: While we are sleeping the soul may reminisce about its past achievements and try to envision its future possibilities for God-manifestation. In deep inner sleep, the soul gets a kind of confidence that life's outer turmoils are not affecting the inner parts of the seeker's being.

Question: Are all souls good?

Sri Chinmoy: The soul is always good; it cannot be bad. But the more developed souls have more light and wisdom. Young souls have much less to manifest on earth. The soul is like the sun. For some it is covered with teeming clouds and its light cannot be manifested. The lower vital will try to delay the progress of the soul's manifestation. But the dynamic vital, the aspiring vital, will give an additional push to the soul. At the start of the spiritual journey, the potentiality of all souls is the same. But at this point, because of their inner urge, some souls are manifesting their capacity more powerfully. They are running faster in the spiritual race. In India parents often pray to God to give them a child with a powerful soul that will come out of ignorance very quickly and manifest the Divine on earth.

Question: Guru, once you pointed out to us a man whose soul you said had left his body. How could he still have been alive on the physical plane if his soul had left his body?

Sri Chinmoy: The soul leaves the body many, many times while a person is still alive. Your soul has left your body many times during your sleep and has come to me. The soul may leave the body for only a few seconds, but those few seconds of earthly time may seem like many months or even years. The maximum amount of time the ordinary soul can stay outside the body is between eleven and thirteen hours. If the soul leaves the body and does not return after eleven, twelve, thirteen hours, then usually it cannot come back into the body-cage. By that time the cord that connects it to the body will snap. But for half an hour or an hour the soul can easily leave the body and the body can function automatically.

The body is like a machine; the mechanic can leave while the machine is running. After a few hours he can come back and the machine will still be running. Sometimes during sleep our soul may go to various worlds or to a distant part of this world, but after half an hour or forty-five minutes it comes back to the body. This can happen not only during your sleep but also while you are awake. Many times during my deep meditation my soul flies like a bird to my spiritual Centres. My disciples see me as clearly as you see me right now. It is a matter of a few minutes or a few seconds.

While outside the body, the soul may have an experience in one second which would take an hour to narrate. Here on earth you see with your ordinary eyes, and it takes time to observe an experience. But if you see with the soul's light, then you will be able to see every-thing in a fleeting second. When you want to express the experience of that fleeting second with your mind, you can spend at least an hour giving all the details. So when we have a conversation with another soul, even though this conversation may have lasted for only a few fleeting seconds, in those fleeting seconds we get a collection of thought waves which are absolutely real. In one minute the soul can do the work of ten or eleven hours.

If the soul permanently leaves the body, then natural-ly the body will not be able to stay on earth. If the bird flies away from the cage, the cage is useless. It is only when the bird is in the cage that we care for the cage.

Question: Does the soul make demands on a person so that he has to change his ways?

Sri Chinmoy: The soul does not make demands as such. It is not like a mother making demands of her child at every moment, saying, "I am telling you such and such for your own good." What the soul does is send a divine inspiration. This inspiration can at times be so vivid and spontaneous that the person may feel it to be almost an inner imposition made by his inner self on his outer personality. But the soul does not demand. On the contrary, it sympathises with human failings and imper-fections and tries to identify itself with these failings. And then, with its inner Light, it tries to help the person to change his ways.

Question: Can the soul select what the individual is to experience in the manifested world?

Sri Chinmoy: Normally it is the soul that determines the experiences that the individual will have in this lifetime. As a matter of fact, if the individual consciously puts himself into the spontaneous flow of experiences that the soul wants to give him, he will eventually grow into abiding peace, joy and fulfilment. Unfortunately, the individual, being a victim of ignorance, is often not aware of the experiences the soul selects, or, in spite of knowing, does not care for the selection made by the soul.

Question: Approximately where in the physical body does one feel a sense of the soul?

Sri Chinmoy: It is in the spiritual heart. The true spiritual heart, about four finger-breadths in width, is located approximately twelve finger-breadths directly above the navel and six finger-breadths directly below the centre of the throat. It is here that one feels what you have called 'a sense of the soul'.

Question: Do souls differ in their characteristics?

Sri Chinmoy: There is actually no basic difference among souls except in the degree of their manifestation. All souls possess the same possibilities, whether they are housed in the lowest or the highest form of life.

We have to remember, however, that the Supreme

manifests Himself in infinite ways through the different souls. They express His varying aspects of Divinity. For example, one soul may manifest light, another power, a third beauty and so on.

It is by manifesting their hidden potentialities through the process of reincarnation that some souls have become great spiritual Masters. And all souls shall eventually follow them.

* * *

MY NAME, MY AGE, MY HOME

At last I know my name.
My name is God's eternal Game.
At last I know my name.

At last I know my age.
My age is Infinity's page.
At last I know my age.

At last I know my home.
My home is where my flame-worlds roam.
At last I know my home.

* * *

REVELATION

No more my heart shall sob or grieve.
My days and nights dissolve in God's own Light.
Above the toil of life my soul
Is a Bird of Fire, winging the Infinite.

I have known the One and His secret Play
And passed beyond the sea of Ignorance-Dream.
In tune with Him, I sport and sing;
I own the golden Eye of the Supreme.

Drunk deep of Immortality,
I am the root and boughs of a teeming vast.
My Form I have known and realised.
The Supreme and I are one — all we outlast.

* * *

I SHALL DEPEND

I do not depend
And will never depend
On the supposed and borrowed courage
Of others.
I shall depend only on my
Certainty-soul
And
Compassion-Immortality-God.

* * *

Question: How do you explain the soul to a child?

Sri Chinmoy: I am very happy to answer this question because it is only a child who can spontaneously ask a question on the soul. The soul is a conscious portion of God. It came directly from God, it remains in contact with God and it will go back to God. The soul is the light which is called consciousness. A child will not understand the word consciousness, so you can tell him that the soul is something that carries our thoughts, our ideas, our messages to God. The soul is the messenger that goes to God and gives Him our message: it understands our language and at the same time it understands God's language.

Whenever a child tells the truth, whenever he does something good, whenever he does anything that pleases you, you can tell him that it is his soul that is asking him to do this. You can also tell a child that the actual possessor or owner of his body is the soul. As he plays with a toy, so also the soul plays with him. A child knows that he can do anything with his toy and remain unaffected. If he wants to play with it, he can play with it. If he wants to break it, he can break it, and if he is tired of playing with his toy, he can throw it aside. Similarly, in the soul's case, if the soul wants to stay in the body and play with the body, it can do so. If the soul is tired of playing, if the soul wants to go back to its Father, God, it can do so.

Question: Are our desires under the control of the soul?

Sri Chinmoy: Right now our desires are not under the control of the soul. Right now only our aspiration is under the control of the soul. When we are aspiring and the soul says to do something, we do it. But when we are victims to teeming desires and the soul says to do something, we do not listen. The soul, however, will ultimately gain its supremacy.

When a new department head comes into an office, the office workers mock him. They won't listen to him or do the things he asks of them. But gradually, gradually, he understands the situation in the office and he begins to exercise his authority. Then the clerks are afraid they will be fired, so they give him due respect. In the spiritual life also, the soul tolerates everything in the beginning. The physical, the vital and the mind are all unruly members of the family and they mock, they disobey, they do everything wrong.

The physical being is like a naughty child who does not want to take a bath in the pool. He thinks that the water in the pool is very cold, and he does not want to enter. But there is another child beside him, that is to say, the heart, who enters the pool on his own, and gets properly bathed and is happy. The mother, who is in this case the soul, observes the situation and sees that the naughty one is not going to jump into the pool. Finally, after a while she just pushes him into the water and compels him to bathe.

The soul waits for its own time. The world is full of ignorance, but inside the soul is God's infinite Light and adamantine Will. There does come a time when the divine Will is exercised through the soul, although in the beginning the soul remains a witness, like the *Purusha*. The soul just observes what parts of the person are good and what parts are bad. When the good parts want to listen to the soul, the soul welcomes them. It says, "Now, let us run to the Goal." The parts of the being that are still sleeping in ignorance and creating problems will be referred by the soul to the Supreme. Finally, one day the Supreme will use His omnipotent Power and say that the time has come to show them divine Light through divine Authority. At this time, God's choice Hour, when the soul wants to liberate someone from the meshes of ignorance, the darkness of millennia will be expelled.

Question: Is the soul always assured that it will find its true mission during each new lifetime on earth?

Sri Chinmoy: Before taking human incarnation, the soul gets the inner message about its divine purpose on earth. It is fully conscious of its mission and it comes here with the direct approval or sanction of the Supreme. But during the lifetime, the workings of the physical mind sometimes cover up the divine inspiration of the soul and the true purpose of the soul. Then the mission of the soul cannot come forward. However, if we start aspiring with the mind, the heart and the soul, then we can learn the purpose of our existence here on earth.

There is a constant battle going on between the divine and undivine in each human being. The ignorance of the world tries to devour human aspiration. At the present stage of evolution, most human beings live in the undivine vital, where all is desire, anxiety and excitement. That is why they are unconscious of the soul's needs.

* * *

REVEALING SOUL AND
FULFILLING GOAL

If You but knew,
Father, what I have done for You:
Planted and raised a climbing tree
For You to dance on its top, smiling free.

If You but knew,
Father, what I have done for You:
Become the world's lowest slave,
Your Breath to serve in man, the grave.

If you but knew,
Child, what I ever think of you:
You are My Life's revealing Soul,
You are My Vision's fulfilling Goal.

* * *

Question: Do the experiences that the soul gets while it is on earth constitute a kind of expansion?

Sri Chinmoy: The experiences naturally lead to its expansion. When we speak of the soul's expansion, we mean the manifestation of the Divinity inside the soul. Then when we have the experience of the soul, we expand our consciousness and gradually it becomes all-pervading. At the same time we manifest the Divinity that is within us.

* * *

Man, in essence, is not ugly. But hard is it for a man to appear beautiful, for he has lost contact with his soul, the child of All-Beauty.

What is it, after all, that gives to a child his charm and beauty? Is it not the soul's glow? When that touch gets fainter and is finally lost, he becomes a dull and cautious adult.

* * *

Question: Can a person know if he has made contact with his soul and is working from the soul's region?

Sri Chinmoy: It is through meditation and aspiration that he will know. Let us compare his being with an apartment that has three rooms, and let us say that he has free access to these three rooms. He enters into one room and sees it is all dark. In it there is only rubbish and junk; everything is untidy, undivine, obscure and impure. Immediately he has to feel that this is the room of the mind. The unaspiring mind, the doubting mind, the sophisticated mind, the suspecting mind stays in that dirty, undivine room.

Then he enters into another room. There he feels a kind of soothing sensation, and the feeling of hope looms large. Everything is hopeful, everything is fruitful, everything is giving him joy. If he looks at a particular corner, he gets joy. If he looks at an object, he gets joy. Everything is encouraging him, pleasing him, inspiring him. He has to feel that this room is his heart. Here in the heart he is getting inspiration, aspiration, encouragement and a sense of accomplishment.

Then he enters into the third room. There he sees everything is perfect, everything is luminous, everything is fulfilling. There he feels that he has accomplished everything; he feels boundless joy. This room is the soul.

When you first look at the soul-room, you feel that it is yours. Then after some time you feel that you yourself actually are this room — not that it is your possession, but that you have in fact become the room itself. Since everything stays inside the room and does not come out, manifestation in the outer being is still needed, but in itself this room, the soul, is totally perfect.

Question: Does a beautiful soul always choose a beautiful outer being?

Sri Chinmoy: All souls are beautiful in origin. But if a certain soul is a special soul, then naturally in its outer manifestation also we will observe sweetness, beauty, serenity, purity and all other divine qualities. What we are within, we are without. But some people have very fine souls, wonderful souls; yet in their outer manners they may be very crude, unlit and uncivilised. Why is this? It is because the mind and the vital have not been properly touched with the soul's light. These individuals do not care for the integral manifestation of the soul's light, so their lives are lacking in harmony to some extent. In their outer manifestation they may be absolutely unfortunate and miserable because of this.

There is another reason for disharmony between the outer life and the inner life. If we sow the seed of the mango tree, then naturally we will get mangoes. But at times there are other trees around this tree which ruin its beauty. Similarly, if the members of the family do not care for the spiritual life, if they are absolutely unlit, unaspiring, then they can simply crush the finer qualities of a child. How is it that this wonderful child has come into such an undivine family? That is his fate. But generally if one has a beautiful soul, then the outer expression of the soul will also be beautiful.

* * *

THE PILGRIMS OF THE LORD SUPREME

We are the Pilgrims of the Lord Supreme
On the path of Infinity.
At this time we have broken asunder
Obstruction's door.
We have broken asunder the night
Of tenebrous darkness, inconscience,
And the eternal, indomitable fear of death.
The Boat of the supernal Light's dawn is
    beckoning us,
And the World-Pilot of the hallowed bond
Of Love Divine is beckoning us.
The Liberator's Hands are drawing us
To the Ocean of the Great Unknown.
Having conquered the life-breath
Of the land of Immortality,
And carrying aloft the Banner of the Lord Supreme,
We shall return—we, the drops and flames
Of Transformation-Light.

* * *

DEATH
AND
REINCARNATION

DEATH AND REINCARNATION

IS DEATH THE END?

Death is not the end. Death can never be the end.

Death is the road. Life is the traveller. The soul is the guide.

When the traveller is tired and exhausted the guide instructs the traveller to take either a short or a long rest, and then the traveller's journey begins again.

In the ordinary life, when an unaspiring man wallows in the mire of ignorance, it is the real victory of death. In the spiritual life, when an aspirant does not cry for a higher light, bliss and power, it is the birth of his death.

What can we learn from the inner life, the life which desires the extinction of death? The inner life tells us that life is soulfully precious, that time is fruitfully precious. Life without the aspiration of time is meaningless. Time without the aspiration of life is useless.

Our mind thinks of death. Our heart thinks of life. Our soul thinks of immortality. Mind and death can be transcended. Heart and life can be expanded. Soul and immortality can be fulfilled.

What is death after all? Death is a sleeping child. And what is life? Life is a child that is playing, singing and dancing at every moment before the Father. Death is the sleeping child inside the heart of the Inner Pilot. Life is inspiration. Life is aspiration. Life is realisation. Life is not the reasoning mind. Life is not the intellectual mind. Life is not a game of frustration. No, life is the message of divinity on earth. Life is God's conscious channel to fulfil divinity in humanity on earth.

There will come a time when rest will not be necessary at all. Only Life will reign supreme — the Life of the Beyond. This Life is not and cannot be the sole monopoly of an individual. Each human being has to be flooded with this Life of the ever-transcending Beyond, for it is here in this Life Divine that God will manifest Himself unreservedly — here, here on earth.

* * *

DEATH, TELL ME SOMETHING, PLEASE

Death, tell me
Something about yourself, please.

"I shall tell you
The most important thing
About myself:
I love God because He is supremely great.
I love man because he is hopelessly helpless."

* * *

Question: Why is death necessary? Why can't the soul keep on progressing and evolving in the same body?

Sri Chinmoy: Right now death is required; death is necessary for us. We cannot do anything for a long time at a stretch. We play for forty-five minutes or an hour and then become tired and have to take rest. It is the same with our aspiration. Suppose we live for sixty or seventy years. Out of sixty or seventy years we may meditate for twenty days or thirty days and, even then, for only a few hours. An ordinary human being cannot aspire in his meditation for four hours, two hours, or even one hour at a stretch. How can he have the aspiration or reality or consciousness that will take him to the eternal Truth or undying Consciousness all at once?

Right now death helps us in a sense; it allows us to take some rest. Then when we come back, we come back with new hope, new light, new aspiration. But if we had a conscious aspiration, a mounting flame burning within us all the time, then we would see that physical death could easily be conquered. A day will dawn when there will be no necessity for death. But right now we do not have that capacity; we are weak. Spiritual Masters, liberated souls, however, do have mastery over death, but they leave the body when the Divine wants them to.

An ordinary human man who has shouldered the burden of a whole family for twenty, thirty or forty years will say, "I am tired. Now I need rest." For him death really has meaning; the soul goes into the soul's region and enjoys a short rest. But for a divine warrior, a seeker of the Ultimate Truth, death has no meaning. He wants to make his progress continuous, without halt. So he will try to live in constant aspiration, eternal aspiration. And with that eternal aspiration he will try to conquer death so he can be an eternal outer manifestation of the Divine which is within him.

Question: In one of your meditations from your diary you mentioned that death was an obstruction. I always thought you considered death to be a transition that just enables us to be reborn and make continuous progress.

Sri Chinmoy: Yes, I have said that death is a transition. I have said that life and death are like two rooms; life is my living room and death is my bedroom. When I say that death is an obstruction, here I am speaking of death from a different point of view. What is an obstruction? An obstruction is something that prevents us from going farther. It is a limit which we cannot go beyond.

This life is a golden opportunity given to us by the Supreme. But opportunity is one thing and achievement is another. Our spiritual evolution, our inner progress is very steady, very slow and, at the same time, most significant. Naturally there are people who for hundreds or thousands of incarnations will follow a normal, natural cycle of birth and death. Then one day, in God's Eternity, they will realise God. But there are some sincere, genuine aspirants who make a soulful promise that in this incarnation, here and now, they will realise God. They say this in spite of knowing that this is not their first life or their last life. They do not want to wait for some future incarnation. They feel that it is useless to live without God-realisation, and they want to have it as soon as possible. In such cases, if death comes and they are still unrealised, then death is an obstruction. If somebody who is destined to die at the age of fifty is aspiring soulfully, if he can push his death back, with the approval of the Supreme, for another twenty or thirty years, then during this period what will he be doing? He will be continuing his sincere aspiration, his deepest meditation, his highest contemplation. He will be like a racer running towards his Goal with no obstruction. During these extra twenty or thirty years he may reach the farthest end, where his Goal lies.

But if death interferes, then he does not realise God in this life. In the following incarnation very few souls can immediately take up the thread of their past aspiration. As soon as one enters into the world, the undivine cosmic forces come and attack, and the ignorance, limitations and imperfections of the world try to cover the soul. In the formative years of childhood, one does not remember anything. A child is innocent, ignorant and helpless. Then, after a few years, the mind starts functioning. When one is between eight and twelve years old, the mind complicates everything. So for the first eleven, twelve or thirteen years of the next incarnation almost all souls, despite being very great and spiritual, forget their past achievements and deepest inner cry.

There are spiritual Masters or great seekers who get a few high experiences in their childhood or who start thinking or singing about God at a very early age, but usually there is no strong connecting link between the soul's achievements on earth in its past incarnation and these childhood years in the present incarnation. There *is* a link, a very subtle link, but this link does not function significantly for the first twelve or thirteen years.

Some souls do not regain the aspiration of their past incarnation until the age of fifty or sixty. From the spiritual point of view, these fifty or sixty years in their following incarnation are absolutely wasted time. So in this incarnation if one loses fifty years, and if in the past incarnation one has lost twenty or thirty years, then it is eighty years wasted. In this case I say that death is a real obstruction. We have to remove that obstruction with our aspiration, our unbroken aspiration. Aspiration should be like a bullet. It should pass through the wall of death.

But even though it may take some time, eventually the inner being will consciously come to the fore and the person in his new incarnation will start praying and meditating on God most powerfully and sincerely. At that time he will see that nothing from his past has really been lost. Everything has been saved up in the Mother Earth-consciousness, which is the common bank for everyone. The soul will know how much it has achieved on earth; and all this is kept safely inside the earth-consciousness-bank. You deposit money here in the bank. Then you can go to England, and after six years or more you can come back and take out your money. The soul does the same thing after having left the earth for ten or twenty years. All the soul's achievements are kept intact in the consciousness of Mother Earth. Mother Earth gives them back again when the soul returns to work for God on earth.

Nothing is lost except time. But it is better to realise God as soon as possible so that we do not lose our conscious aspiration again in this transitory period. If we can continue on earth for fifty to one hundred years with tremendous, sincere aspiration, then we can accomplish much. If we get real help from a spiritual Master, it is possible to realise God in one incarnation, or in two or three. If there is no real Master or if there is no sincere aspiration, it takes hundreds and hundreds of incarnations.

Question: Can you say something about Eternity and the eternal Life?

Sri Chinmoy: Being a spiritual man, I can say on the strength of my own inner realisation that the soul does not die. We know that we are eternal. We have come from God, we live in God, we are growing into God and we are going to fulfil God. Life and death are like two rooms; going from life to death is like going from one room to the other. Where I am now is my living room. Here I am talking to you, meditating with you, looking at you. Here I have to show my physical body; I have to work and be active. Then there is another room, my bedroom. There I take rest; I sleep. There I do not have to show my existence to anybody; I am only for myself.

Our earthly life comes from the infinite Life, the Life divine. In this earthly life we may stay on earth for a short span of time, say fifty or sixty years. But inside this earth-bound life is the boundless Life. After a while we enter the corridor of death for five or ten or twenty years. When we enter this corridor, the soul leaves the body for a short or long rest and goes back to the soul's region. Here, if the person was spiritual, the soul will regain the eternal Life, the Life divine, which existed before birth, which exists between birth and death, which exists in death and, at the same time, goes beyond death.

While we are living on earth, we can place ourselves in the realm of eternal Life through our aspiration and meditation. But just by entering into the endless Life, we do not possess that Life; we have to grow into it consciously and constantly. When we enter into the life of meditation, meditation must eventually become part and parcel of our every moment. When we are able to meditate twenty-four hours a day, then we are constantly breathing in the endless Life. In our inner consciousness we have become one with the soul.

When we live in the soul, there is no such thing as death. There is just a constant evolution of our consciousness, our aspiring life. But when we live in the body, there is death all the time. As soon as fear comes into our mind, immediately we die. As soon as some negative forces come, we die. How many times each day we die! Fear, doubt and anxiety are constantly killing our inner existence.

* * *

DEATH AND THE SOUL

I have two rooms: a living room and a bedroom. In my living room I work and talk to people. Here people have to see me and I have to mix with them. I call this room life. In the other room, where I sleep, I need not work or talk to anybody, for there I go to rest, either for a long or a short period of time. Life, in the ordinary sense of the term, need not be displayed there. So I call that room death. Needless to say, that room, too, is mine.

You are afraid of death because you feel that death is not yours, whereas life is. You think that life is home, it is familiar, whereas death is a foreign land, totally unfamiliar. But this is not true. Both life and death are in you.

In our inner or spiritual life we call those souls 'dead' who are not aspiring or making any progress. What is required of the one who wants to aspire and make progress? Consciousness. One has to be conscious, fully conscious, of the mind, the vital and the physical and turn inward in order to feel, see and grow into the ever-energising and ever-transforming delight of the soul.

Death is inevitable because our present body is imperfect. It refuses to grow divinely and unendingly. It does not open to the Life eternal. But we shall not always suffer from this limitation. The body will become more conscious; the body itself will aspire to bring down more and more Light, Bliss, Peace and Power into its inner and outer existence, and eventually it will grow into perfection. At that time, death will not be inevitable. In fact, death itself will die.

At present the body dies, and the soul takes rest. But the soul does not forget to carry with it the essence of the experiences that it acquired while it was in the land of the living. While taking its rest, it assimilates the essence of its past. When the assimilation is over, it starts to prepare itself for a new journey. Then it begins to choose its new birth, new environment, new circumstances, new personality and new mission. Afterwards, the soul goes to the Supreme for an interview and, with the divine approval of the Supreme, descends into the physical world.

Birth and death are inseparable. Birth precedes

death; death succeeds birth. What we need to connect both birth and death is Life. Strangely enough, this Life existed before our birth, it exists between our birth and death, and will exist after death, stretching its far-flung arms into Eternity, Infinity and Immortality.

An advanced seeker sees and feels that at every moment he is having a new birth and a new death as his soul is moving from one momentary experience to another. When the body, the vital and the mind live in the soul and experience, nay, become the ever-lasting experience of the Supreme, then alone will God's eternal Life permeate our human existence.

* * *

DEATH, HOW OFTEN DO YOU SPEAK TO SATAN?

Death, how often do you speak to Satan?
"I never speak to Satan.
I hate him!
I hate his brutality;
I hate his ignorance-existence-reality.
He is just impossible!"

Why, Death, why?
"You know why.
I love both Heaven and earth.
I love Heaven's flower of beauty.
I love earth's fruit of duty."

* * *

Question: Will the soul be able to have some kinds of experiences in the worlds it goes to after it leaves the body?

Sri Chinmoy: As soon as the soul leaves this physical body, the physical body enters into the physical sheath, the vital enters into the vital sheath and the mind enters into the mental plane proper. The soul will go through the subtle physical, the vital, the mental, the psychic and then finally to the soul's own region. As it passes through each of these planes, the soul takes up with it the essence of all the experiences it had on the earth.

The soul gets various kinds of subtle experiences in these other sheaths, but these experiences are not going to be manifested. If the soul gets some experience here on earth, the experience is bound to be manifested either today or tomorrow. The soul can aspire in any world. In the higher worlds it will have only aspiration, and this aspiration will eventually take the form of experience. Aspiration itself is an experience. But on earth the experiences that the soul gets here through all the parts of the being are constantly leading it towards the fuller manifestation of Divinity.

Question: Is hell really a place in the vital worlds, or is it just a state of consciousness?

Sri Chinmoy: On the physical-mental level, hell is a place. It is for the vital's experience. If you lead a bad life, you have to go there. There it is real torture, unimaginable torture. Especially for those who commit suicide, the torture is infinitely worse than being fried alive in oil. The suffering that suicides go through in the subtle physical and the subtle vital is unthinkable, unbearable. They will not get another incarnation for a long time. Then after suffering in the vital world for many years, when they finally do get an incarnation, they will be defective: blind, paralysed, mentally or physically defective, and all kinds of things. And this is not just for one incarnation, either. If they are not forgiven by a spiritual Master or by God's Grace, this will go on for quite a few incarnations. Not only that, but right from the beginning they create a disturbance for the entire family that they are born into. For instance, if a former suicide takes incarnation and is insane, he will cause serious problems for his whole family. Also, these souls often increase their own bad karma because they go on in the same way and they do not change. But if there is Grace from God, or if a spiritual Master intervenes, the soul is helped.

So when we live in the gross physical consciousness, in the body consciousness, hell is really a place. But on the highest spiritual level, we have to know that hell, as well as Heaven, is a plane of consciousness. Both Heaven and hell begin in the mind. The moment we think something good, the moment we pray and meditate and try to offer the inner light that we have gained from our meditation and prayers, we begin to live in Heaven. The moment we think evil of someone, criticise someone and cherish wrong thoughts about someone, then we enter into hell. Heaven we create; hell we create. With our divine thoughts we create Heaven. With our wrong, negative, undivine thoughts we create hell within us. Heaven and hell are both states of consciousness deep inside us. When we go deep within, we see that the entire universe is inside us. Inside this physical body is the subtle body, and inside the subtle body, in the heart, we find the existence of the soul. Then, from there, if we go deep within, we see the entire universe.

* * *

DEATH, WHAT DO YOU AND GOD SPEAK ABOUT?

Death, how often do you speak to God?
"I speak to God constantly."

Can you tell me
What both of you talk about?

"We talk about our achievements
            And
Our disappointments.
I tell God about my achievements
            On earth
And my disappointments in Heaven.
God tells me about His achievements
            In Heaven
And His disappointments on earth."

I see.
Thank you, Death.

* * *

Question: What is the purpose of reincarnation?

Sri Chinmoy: In one lifetime on earth we cannot do everything. If we remain in the world of desire, we will never be able to fulfil ourselves. As a child we have millions of desires, and even when we reach the age of seventy we see that a particular desire has not been fulfilled and we feel miserable. The more desires we fulfil, the more desires we get. We want one house, then two houses; one car, then two cars, and so forth. There is no limit to it. When our desires are fulfilled, we find that we are still dissatisfied. Then we become the victims of other desires or larger desires.

Now our dearest is God. Do you think that God will allow us to remain unfulfilled? No! God's very purpose is to fulfil each individual, and Himself through us. He will have us come back again and again to fulfil our desires. If someone is eager to become a millionaire in this incarnation, and at the end of his journey he sees that he has not become a millionaire, then if his desire is really intense, he will have to keep coming back until he really becomes a millionaire. But by becoming a millionaire, he will see that he still remains a beggar in one sense, for he will have no peace of mind. But if he enters into the world of aspiration, he may have no money, but he *will* have peace of mind, and this is the real wealth.

If we go through desire, we see that there is an endless procession of desires. But if we go through aspiration, we see the whole and eventually we become the whole. We know that if we can realise God, inside God we will find everything, for everything exists inside God. So eventually we leave the world of desire and enter into the world of aspiration. There we diminish our desires and think more of Peace, Bliss, divine Love. In order to get a little Peace, a drop of nectar, it may take years and years. But a spiritual person is ready to wait indefinitely for God's Hour to fulfil his aspiration. And his aspiration to achieve this Peace, Light and Bliss will not go in vain.

Now if our aim is to enter into the Highest, the Infinite, the Eternal, the Immortal, then naturally one short span of life is not enough. But again, God will not allow us to remain unfulfilled. In our next incarnation we will continue our journey. We are eternal travellers. We have to continue, continue until we reach our Goal. Perfection is the aim of each aspirant. We are trying to perfect ourselves in an imperfect world. And this perfect perfection we can never achieve in only one lifetime.

It is through aspiration and evolution that the soul develops the full possibility of realising the Highest and fulfilling the Divine. First the physical, the human in us, has to aspire to become one with the Divine in us—the soul. Right now the body does not listen to the dictates of the soul; that is to say, the physical mind revolts. The workings of the physical mind cover up the soul's divine purpose, and the soul cannot come to the fore. At the present stage of evolution, most people are unconscious and do not know what the soul wants or needs. They have desires, anxiety over success, intensity and excitement. All these stem from the vital or ego, whereas anything done with the soul's consciousness is always full of joy. At times we may hear the dictates of the soul, or the message of our conscience, but still we do not do or say the right thing. No, the physical mind is weak; we are weak. If we start aspiring, however, with the mind, and then go beyond the mind to the soul, we can easily hear and also obey the dictates of the soul.

A day will come when the soul is in a position to exercise its divine qualities and make the body, mind and heart feel that they need their self-discovery. The physical and the vital will consciously want to listen to the soul and be instructed and guided by the soul. Then, here in the physical, we will have an immortalised nature, an immortal life, for our soul will have become totally and inseparably one with the Divine on earth. At that time we will have to offer our inner wealth to the world at large and manifest our soul's potentialities. It very often happens that realisation can take place in one incarnation, but for manifestation the soul has to come down again and again to earth. Unless and until we reveal and manifest the highest Divinity within us, our game is not over. We have not finished our role in the cosmic Drama, so we have to come back into the world again and again. But in the march of evolution, in one of its incarnations, the soul will fully realise and fully manifest the Divine in the physical and through the physical.

Question: How long do we have to continue to reincarnate?

Sri Chinmoy: If one aspires, one expedites one's realisation. Otherwise, an ordinary human being takes hundreds and hundreds of incarnations before actual realisation takes place. Aspirants who consciously enter into the path of spirituality and try to discipline themselves on the strength of their inner cry will naturally gain their realisation sooner than those who are still sleeping and are not yet conscious of the inner life.

Now, after one realises God, if it is God's Will, that person need not take any more incarnations. If the person is tired, then he may say, "No, I don't want to be of any help to humanity; I only want to realise God. After realisation I would like to stay in some other plane of consciousness." But some realised souls will want to go back to the earth-consciousness and serve aspiring humanity. It all depends on the individual soul and on God's Will.

Question: Could you please explain how the law of karma affects us in this life and our next life?

Sri Chinmoy: We are carrying the past inside us. It is a continuous flow. "As you sow, so you reap." If we do something wrong, we have to know that either today or tomorrow, either in the physical world or in the inner world, we will get the result. If I constantly steal, one day either I will be caught and put into jail or I will suffer in some other way. And if I do something good, if I pray, if I meditate, if I do divine things, I will get the result of this also.

Sometimes we see that someone who has done something wrong is enjoying the world. But perhaps he did something extraordinary, something wonderful in his immediate past incarnation, and now he is having the result of his good action, while the results of his bad deeds have not yet started to bear fruit. In the evening of his life, or in a future life, he will definitely be punished.

In the case of an ordinary, unaspiring person, karmic dispensation is unavoidable, inevitable. The law of karma is always binding; like a snake it will coil around him. He has to pay the toll, the tax; the law of karma is merciless. But again, there is something called Divine Grace. I was ignorant and I did a few things wrong. But if I shed bitter tears and cry for forgiveness, then naturally God's Compassion will dawn on me. When a person enters into the spiritual life, his karma can easily be nullified if it is the Will of God operating through a spiritual Master. Slowly God's infinite Grace can nullify the results of his bad karma and expedite the results of his good karma. If a seeker not only wants the spiritual life but also sincerely practises the spiritual life every day, then he can stand above the law of karma, for God is bound to shower His boundless Grace on the devoted head and heart of the aspirant. Of course, I cannot go on doing some undivine thing and feel that God will always forgive me. No. But if God sees a soulful cry looming large from within, if He sees that I am sincere and aspiring and want to be free from the meshes of ignorance, He will not only forgive me but He will also give me the necessary strength not to make the same mistake again.

When we come back into our next incarnation, naturally we have to start our journey according to the result of our past karma. If we have done many things wrong, we cannot expect to realise the highest Truth in our next incarnation. But if God's Grace is there, we can easily nullify the wrong things we have already done during this life.

* * *

THE QUICK SURRENDER,
THE BRAVE FIGHT

Old men slowly, helplessly
    And peacefully
Enter into the Hall of Death.

Death proudly, deliberately
    And triumphantly
Enters into the Life-chambers
    Of young men.

O Death, I like the quick surrender
  Of the old men,
    And
I love, admire and adore
  The brave fight
    Of the young men.

* * *

THE PLAY OF
INNER FORCES

LIFE-PROBLEMS

IGNORANCE

We all know what ignorance is and what light is. Ignorance or darkness comes and stands in front of us in the form of temptation. But light does not do this. Light comes and stands in front of us in the form of absolute oneness. Light says, "You and I are one," while darkness says, "No, you and I are two."

Darkness tempts us by saying, "What I have is very sweet, very nice and most fascinating. I have come to offer it to you." Then we ask to try it and we see it, feel it and taste it. Then we are caught and we are doomed.

When light stands in front of us it says, "We are one. You and I are one. What I have inside me, you also have." Light says that it has peace, bliss, delight and power and tells us that if we look inside ourselves, then we will also find the same peace, bliss, delight and power.

But our mind, which lives in the limited consciousness, would rather try to possess something outside of itself. It feels, "What is the use of having something I already possess?" So when darkness offers it something outside of itself in the form of temptation, it tries to grab it. It makes no difference whether it is good or bad. Just because it doesn't have it, the mind wants it. That is why we are always fond of ignorance.

Why do we cherish ignorance? First of all, because we feel it is something which someone else has; for this reason we want it. When we see someone is very rich, we immediately want to become rich too. When someone is happy, immediately we want to be happy. We are always looking around at what others are doing and then trying to imitate them. We feel that if we don't have the thing that others have, then we are fools. Everybody has ignorance. We also have ignorance, but we think that if we do not have a large enough quantity of ignorance, then we are inferior.

A child has a balloon. He feels that his balloon is the best thing on earth. He does not want to think that a balloon is very short-lived and will soon burst. He only cares to know that it is his possession and he does not want to part with it. Ignorance is like a balloon. We feel that if this little toy is taken away from us, then we will be totally lost and have nothing. But when we consciously enter into the spiritual life, we feel that ignorance is constantly tempting us and never fulfilling us. We feel that the more we play with the balloon, the more we are being frustrated and destroyed. We have to know what we want: temptation or fulfilment. If fulfilment is our choice, then temptation has to be discarded.

In our ordinary day-to-day life, ignorance is like a camel: while a camel is eating thorns its mouth bleeds, but it continues to eat thorns because it has formed the habit of doing so. When the soul enters into the body, for one, two, three, four, five or six years it remains dominant. Because the mind is not yet powerful, the soul has the capacity to remain in the fore. But gradually the child starts learning many wrong things from his parents, neighbours, friends and the world in general. When the child is growing up, he sees many shortcomings in his parents but he does not know that these are shortcomings. He thinks that these are things that he needs in order to live on earth. So he starts cherishing in his mind, vital or physical these ideas that come from the outer world through the physical senses. When he starts using his physical senses without being inspired from the heart, darkness enters into his eyes and blinds them and falsehood enters into his ears and poisons them. All the undivine qualities of the world around him enter into him, and he cherishes them consciously or unconsciously.

How can we overcome ignorance? In this world we know only two things: I want or I don't want. We either accept or reject. In God's cosmic Game there are only two things: ignorance and wisdom. Every thought is composed of either ignorance or wisdom, of darkness or light. There is nothing in between. Either darkness is filling the vessel or light is filling the vessel. This is why we have to encourage light to enter into the vessel.

As there is no limit to darkness, so also there is no limit to light. It is up to us to choose. We can live in darkness and ignorance or we can live in light. Today it is difficult for a human being to live in light. It is easier for him to live in darkness because he has become accustomed to it. But he will find it extremely difficult to live in ignorance and darkness after he has begun aspiring sincerely to live in light.

* * *

Question: Is pain necessary?

Sri Chinmoy: There is a general notion that if we go through suffering, tribulations and physical pain, then our system will be purified. This idea is not founded upon reality. There are many people who are suffering because of their past karma or because undivine forces are attacking them, but we can't say that they are nearing their destination. No! They have to aspire sincerely in order to reach their destination. We shall not welcome pain; we shall try to conquer pain if it appears, since very often pain, whether physical, mental or emotional, only interferes with our aspiration.

Physical pain, vital pain and mental pain have to be either conquered or transformed into joy through our constant inner cry for something that will give us real and permanent satisfaction. In the spiritual life the best thing is to take unavoidable pain as an experience which has to be transformed into an experience of joy. Joy is the only eternal reality, the only permanent and everlasting reality. It is absolutely wrong to say that each time we suffer we go one step closer to our goal.

It is not necessary to go through suffering before we enter into the Kingdom of Delight. Many people have realised God through love. The Father has love for the child and the child has love for the Father. This love takes us to our goal. Our philosophy emphasises the positive way of approaching Truth. We have limited light. Let us increase it. Then let us progress from more light to abundant light to infinite Light.

The highest discovery is this: We came from Delight, we grow in Delight and at the end of our journey's close, we retire into Delight. Delight is now in the inner world, while the outer world is all suffering. We see people quarrelling and fighting. Fear, doubt, anger, jealousy and other undivine elements torture us. But when we go deep within, on the strength of our highest meditation, we discover that Delight was our origin, our Source. We see that in Delight we play the cosmic Game and at the end of the cosmic Game we again retire into Delight.

Question: Why do we have to pass through sad experiences such as suffering and sorrow?

Sri Chinmoy: Why do we experience suffering? In this world we are always consciously or unconsciously making mistakes. When we consciously make mistakes, we are quite aware of it. But unfortunately, we do not realise how many things we are doing wrong unconsciously. These unconscious mistakes manifest themselves in the physical world, and the results come to us as suffering. In the case of ordinary, unaspiring human beings, after tremendous suffering, sincerity dawns and the soul leads them to knowledge and wisdom. If people who repeatedly make mistakes have sincere aspiration and want to know why they are suffering, then the soul's light comes to the fore and tells them. If we are spiritual people, consciously we will try not to do anything wrong, but unconsciously we do many things wrong. We can prevent unconscious mistakes only through our aspiration, prayer and meditation. If we aspire, then God's Grace and Compassion protect us.

There is something else that we have to know about what we call suffering. Often we think of God, pray to God and meditate on God, and then we see that all sorts of problems arise in our life. Some disciples have said to me, "I was very happy until I entered the spiritual path. Now I am having more problems than before." But if we are really sincere, we see that we did have the same difficulties before we accepted spirituality, but we were not aware of them before. Spirituality is the path of awareness and consciousness. Previously, many things were happening to us, but we were like a solid wall and were unaware of these things. But now, as seekers, we are affected whenever a good or bad thought enters into our mind. If it is a divine thought we are happy. If it is a wrong thought we are frustrated and disappointed. This is the result of our spiritual awareness. If we are sincere with ourselves, we come to realise that we have always had the same difficulties, the same sufferings, but previously we were not conscious of them.

Again, we have to know that when we enter the spiritual life, the hostile forces attack us. Before, when we lived in ignorance and were a slave to ignorance, ignorance let us sleep. As long as it had us under its control, as long as we were wallowing inside it, it did not disturb us. But when we try to escape from ignorance, at that time ignorance tries to hold us down. So sometimes the seeker will find that he is having some difficulties at the beginning of his spiritual journey that he did not have before, but as he progresses, these difficulties fall away.

God does not want suffering for human beings. He is the Father of Love. When we go to our Father, we don't have to cut our arms or our throat. We will go with all

132

our love because He is waiting for us with His Love. If we say that we have to suffer in order to go to our Father, that is stupidity. God, our Father, does not want our suffering.

But when suffering does come, we have to feel that even in this suffering there is a divine intention. If we really aspire, suffering itself will give us a real experience which will make us feel that we are nearer to our goal. But we should never find fault with God because of our suffering. It is we who have invited suffering through our conscious or unconscious mistakes. When suffering comes to us, we have to pray to God to free us from this suffering. We have to know that suffering is not our goal; the goal is Delight. When we have penetrated into the suffering, when we have gone beyond the suffering, we see that it becomes Delight. And then we can remain in the Delight which is inside the suffering.

* * *

Problems do not indicate man's incapacity. Problems do not indicate man's inadequacy. Problems do not indicate man's insufficiency. Problems indicate man's conscious need for self-transcendence in the inner world, and his conscious need for self-perfection in the outer world.

You have a problem. He has a problem. She has a problem. Your problem is that the world does not touch your feet. His problem is that the world does not love him. Her problem is that she feels that she does not adequately help God in the world. To solve your problem you have to conquer your pride. To solve his problem he has to conquer his greed. To solve her problem she has to conquer her self-styled and self-aggrandised, desiring ego.

Each problem is a force. But when we see the problem, we feel deep within us a greater force. And when we face the problem, we prove to the problem that we not only *have* the greatest force, but actually we *are* the greatest force on earth.

A problem increases when the heart hesitates and the mind calculates. A problem decreases when the heart braves the problem and the mind supports the heart. A problem diminishes when the mind uses its search-light and the heart uses its illumination-light.

If fear is our problem, then we have to feel that we are the chosen soldiers of God the Almighty. If doubt is our problem, then we have to feel that we have deep within us the Sea of God's Light. If jealousy is our problem, we have to feel that we are the oneness of God's Light and Truth. If insecurity is our problem, then we have to feel that God is nothing and can be nothing other than constant and ceaseless assurance that He will claim us as His very own.

If the body is the problem, our constant alertness and attention can solve this problem. If the vital is the problem, our soaring imagination can solve this problem. If the mind is the problem, our illumining inspiration can solve this problem. If the heart is the problem, our perfecting aspiration can solve this problem. If life is the problem, our fulfilling self-discovery can solve this problem.

The individual problem arises when the finite human being wants to possess infinite humanity. The universal problem arises when the Infinite wants to mould, guide, shape, transform and divinely and supremely fulfil the finite, but the finite does not want to listen to the dictates of the Infinite.

A problem is not the harbinger of defeat or failure. A problem can be transformed into the beckoning Hands of the Supreme that can take us to our destined Goal, the Goal of the ever-transcending, ever-fulfilling Beyond.

* * *

Question: In your talk you said that if we see the problem and if we face the problem, then we have greater force than the problem. Do you mean, then, that a problem is not a problem if we know how to look at it?

Sri Chinmoy: If we know how to look at a problem, half the strength of the problem goes away. But usually we try to avoid the problem: we try to run away from it. To have a problem is not a crime, so why should we be afraid to face it? Our difficulty is that when something unfortunate happens in our life, we immediately feel that we are at fault, that we have done something wrong. We must know that there are also wrong forces, undivine forces, hostile forces around us. We believe in the law of karma—that if we do something wrong, we suffer later. But even if we do not do anything wrong, the ignorance of the world may come and torture us. Think of the Christ. He was a great spiritual Master. He did not have any bad karma. He did not do anything wrong. But the ignorance of the world crucified him. Of course, we cannot compare ourselves with the Christ, but at our own level we have to feel that we are not necessarily at fault.

By blaming ourselves and then trying to hide, we do not solve the problem. We have to face the problem and see whether we really are to blame. If somebody else is creating the problem, then we have to stand like a solid wall and not allow the problem to enter into us. If it is my house, my wall, I will not allow anybody to break through. But if I am the problem itself, then this problem is infinitely more difficult to solve. In order to solve the problem of myself, I have to practise the spiritual life and develop inner strength, aspiration and inner detachment. Slowly, gradually, I will become inwardly strong, and then I will be able to solve the problems caused by myself, by my own inner weaknesses.

* * *

As soon as you have conquered a difficulty, you will find that it repeats itself on a higher and subtler level. It is the same essential weakness in yourself which you are made to face in a more refined form.

* * *

A problem exists only in our own consciousness. The same external situation becomes a problem for me but not for you. Why? Because it disturbs some element of my inner harmony, while yours is left untouched.

* * *

There is no other way to spiritual success than to sit at the feet of Patience, trusting to her lords, Time and Progress.

* * *

Adversity makes you dynamic. Adversity forces your eyes wide open. Adversity teaches you the meaning of patience. Adversity endows you with faith in yourself.

* * *

Depression is an ill will self-imposed.

* * *

How to conquer despair? Never cry for outer consolation. Ever cry for inner compassion. Inner compassion is the flood of light. It is also the flood of perfection's realisation.

* * *

What is misery? Emotional misery is the result of desire in the mind. There is also physical misery. This misery is caused by the nerves when they are tensed. When one does not have faith in oneself, it is the beginning of one's misery. When one loses faith in one's Master, he feels within the damaging breath of misery.

* * *

Human experience is frustration after frustration. Divine experience is illumination after illumination.

* * *

Question: Is there any incurable spiritual disease?

Sri Chinmoy: There is one almost incurable disease in the spiritual life and that disease is self-indulgence. This self-indulgence is really a kind of impurity and it lasts for a long, long time. When insincerity disappears, when fear goes away and when doubt vanishes, you will see that self-indulgence still remains either in the physical world or in the mental world of thoughts and ideas.

In comparison to other obstacles, self-indulgence *is* incurable. And it is certainly incurable if the seeker is not strong enough to fight against it. But this is true only in the case of the ordinary seeker. When a seeker is on the verge of self-realisation, he can be freed from self-indulgence. Otherwise, self-indulgence lasts for a very long time. By the Grace of the Supreme one day you do have to be cured of self-indulgence; but for that you need tremendous and constant aspiration.

It is very easy for us to say, "By the Grace of God everything is possible." This utterance we have heard from our forefathers, from our parents, from every spiritual Master. It is true, but this Grace does not come for all and sundry. This Grace comes only for those who really aspire. When you say that by the Grace of God everything is possible and that nothing is incurable, you have to be very careful to see that you are not merely playing with words.

Self-indulgence is an incurable disease precisely because the standard of human aspiration is so very low. At the present stage, human aspiration is unpardonably low, unforgivably low. God, dealing with infinite Compassion, will forgive us no matter what we do, but we will not forgive ourselves! When our sincerity comes to the fore, when our divine justice comes to the fore, we will not forgive ourselves. How can we receive the truth when we know that we are so imperfect and indulgent in our physical and vital nature? Every seeker must feel that self-indulgence is really an incurable disease unless he is ready to run the fastest and is prepared to sacrifice what he has and what he is at every moment. If he is ready to give up everything for God, then nothing remains incurable.

I am not trying to discourage you; I wish to encourage you with all my heart. But in all frankness I have to say that self-indulgence is something most difficult to conquer. It is the most difficult part of the journey for the spiritual aspirant. But undoubtedly one day it will be conquered, simply because God will not allow anybody to remain self-indulgent. God wants perfection from each individual on earth. It is just a matter of time.

* * *

Prosperity and adversity are the two eyes that we all have. Adversity leads us inward to correct and perfect our march of life. Prosperity leads us outward to illuminate and immortalise our human birth.

* * *

In prosperity, our inner strength remains static. In adversity, our inner strength becomes dynamic.

None can deny the fact that every step of progress which the world has made has come from both the smiles of prosperity and the tears of adversity.

Adversity, like poverty, is no sin. One merit of adversity none can deny: it helps us to be stronger within. The stronger we are within, the brighter we are without.

"No suffering, no salvation," so says the teacher adversity to his student, man.

"No soul's delight, no salvation," so says the teacher prosperity to his student, man.

One who is afraid of studying in the school of adversity can never hope for a perfect education in life.

Misfortune threatens prosperity; hope ignores adversity.

How often is our aspiration forced into play by dire adversity! But in glorious prosperity rarely does it peep out.

No fall, no rise. Just as a wrestler often bears away the prize only after he has suffered numerous falls, even so, hell is to be experienced before Heaven is won.

What is failure, if not an important portion, unrecognised, in the configuration of our whole fruitful success?

Failure can have a soothing medicine to relieve it from its pangs and that medicine is consolation. Failure can have an energising medicine to relieve it from its pangs, and that medicine is will power.

The world is strewn with difficulties. In a sense, it is full of thorns. But if you put on shoes you can walk on the thorns. What are these shoes made of? They are made of God's Grace.

* * *

Depression is the most effective smile of a wrong force. Once we allow it to enter, depression tries to crush the strength and joy of our life-force.

* * *

Illness often has very little to do with the divine Will. It is rather the acceptance of imperfection's invasion.

* * *

The pain of the body is often bearable. Not so is the pain of the heart.

* * *

Sorrow is an arrow to pierce into strength. Joy is food to feed strength sumptuously.

* * *

Sorrow lords it over the world. But the very presence of time makes it lose its sting.

* * *

Time is the best physician for suffering. Then comes patience. And then comes tolerance.

* * *

Disappointment is as powerful a negative force as expectation is a positive one.

* * *

Worry unconsciously welcomes trouble. Trouble unavoidably welcomes helplessness. Helplessness tearfully welcomes despair.

* * *

Question: What should one's attitude be to bad things that one did before? What is your view regarding guilt?

Sri Chinmoy: You should feel that the past is buried in oblivion. If you constantly cherish guilt when you have done something wrong, you are being sincere, but this act of mere sincerity does not help. Yes, you have done something wrong, but by thinking of your mistake and having a guilty consciousness, you do not get light or wisdom. If you have done something that is not right, from now on you will be determined to do the right thing, the divine thing. This minute you have used for a wrong purpose. Then use the following minute for a divine purpose. If you do this without thinking of the previous minute when you did something wrong, then what happens? Your positive strength, this will power you have used to do the right thing, will have all its power. But if you think of the past minute with a sense of guilt while you are doing the right thing now, then half your power is again lost in darkness and only half can be utilised for the right action.

If you cherish or brood over your misdeeds, then you are strengthening your guilt unconsciously. You should feel, "If I have done something wrong, I am ready to face it. I have done something wrong, but I have the capacity to do the right thing." By focusing all attention on the right thing, you are adding to your positive strength.

The sense of guilt, the constant feeling of self-reproach is, unfortunately, all-pervading in the Western world. If my Source is God, the Absolute Infinite Light, then someday I must go back to my Source. During my stay on earth, I unfortunately got some unhealthy, unaspiring and destructive experiences. Now I want to erase these unfortunate experiences from my life. For that I have to concentrate only on the right things, the divine things, the things which will fulfil me, and not on the things that have stood in my way.

* * *

Question: When I have problems, I can't seem to really solve them. Even my friends and parents don't always know what is best.

Sri Chinmoy: There is somebody who knows what is best for you, and that is the Supreme. The Supreme is not a mental hallucination. You will be able to see Him, you will be able to speak to Him, you will be able to dine with Him. He is not only your Father, but also your eternal Comrade. You have to give Him responsibility for yourself. If you feel that your family or friends are not guiding you properly, then the first thing is to offer them at the Feet of the Supreme as well. Each time you are attacked by a problem, instead of trying to solve it yourself with your limited capacity or wisdom, please offer it to the Supreme.

His Eyes have better vision than ours. His Ears hear more quickly than our human ears. We talk to human beings who have no time to hear us; they have so many things to do in the outer world. But we very often forget that there is somebody else who is eager to listen. The Supreme is always eager to hear from us, but we do not speak to Him. Sometimes we speak to our own mind, to our own dissatisfied vital, but rarely do we try to speak to our inner being. If we discover the secret of speaking to our inner being, we will solve all our problems and discover the true meaning of our human existence. This human existence is a golden opportunity that the Supreme has granted us. We say that we don't have an opportunity but it is a sheer lie. The Supreme has given us the opportunity, but we do not avail ourselves of that opportunity.

* * *

HAPPINESS

Happiness feeds our heart, inspires our mind, energises our vital and illumines our body.

When the heart is happy, it embraces the whole world. When the mind is happy, it accepts the world as its very own. When the vital is happy, it offers its very existence to the world. And when the body is happy, it serves the world the way the world wants to be served.

Our happiness-moon smiles sweetly, charmingly and soulfully when our hope-kite flies in the skies of Divinity's heights. Our happiness-sun shines brightly when our Dream-Boat touches the Reality Shore.

Possession gives birth to human happiness. Renunciation gives birth to divine happiness. Acceptance of God's Will in God's own way gives birth to supremely divine happiness.

In the domain of lifeless hope, happiness is theoretical and fruitless. In the sea of selfless love, happiness is practical and fruitful. In the domain of teeming fear, happiness bitterly cries. In the sea of brooding doubt, happiness instantly dies.

An aspiring man spreads happiness wherever he goes. An unaspiring man strangles happiness wherever he roams.

The life of happiness is aspiration.
The soul of happiness is realisation.
The goal of happiness is perfection.

Each man has a soul. Each man has a goal. His soul silently tells him that his perennial Source is all happiness. His goal lovingly tells him that in his constant God-manifestation is his own happiness.

Happiness is in God. Happiness is of God. Happiness is for God. A life of dedication knows that happiness is in God. A life of transformation knows that happiness is of God. A life of liberation knows that happiness is for God.

God's invention is happiness. Man's discovery is happiness. God's possession is happiness. Man's achievement is happiness. Man has every right to achieve God's possession, for that is precisely what God wants man to do. Man has every right to discover God's invention, for that is precisely what God wants man to grow into. What is God's supreme possession? Peace. What is God's supreme invention? Love.

A peace-loving man is a quarter God. A peace-achieved man is a half God. A peace-revealing and peace-spreading man is a full God.

A peace-loving man is the serving God. A peace-achieved man is the glowing God. A peace-revealing and peace-spreading man is the fulfilling God in earthbound time.

God's supreme invention is Love. He who consciously loves God manifests the highest divinity. He who soulfully loves God manifests the inmost divinity. He who unconditionally loves God lives in the ever-radiating, ever-manifesting and ever-transcending divinity of the Beyond.

A human God-lover achieves God's constant happiness. A divine God-lover embodies God the Happiness. A human God-lover still has a sense of separativity, so he achieves God's happiness according to his capacity and according to his receptivity. But a divine God-lover, on the strength of his inseparable and constant oneness with God, embodies God, the infinite Happiness.

* * *

BE HAPPY

Be happy.
   You will grow into God's greatest blessing, His highest pride.

Be happy.
   Yesterday's world wants you to enjoy its surrendering breath.
   Today's world wants you to enjoy its surrendered breath.
   Tomorrow's world wants you to enjoy its fulfilling breath.

Be happy.
   Be happy in the morning with what you have.
   Be happy in the evening with what you are.

Be happy.
   Don't complain. Who complains? The blind beggar in you.
   When you complain, you dance in the mire of ignorance-condition.
   When you don't complain, all conditions of the world are at your feet, and God gives you a new name: aspiration.
   Aspiration is the supreme wealth in the world of light and delight.

Be happy.
   Do you want never to be poor? Then be happy. Do you want ever to be great? Then be happy.

Be happy.
> You will get what you like most. You will be what you like best.

Be happy.
> When you are happy, you and God command each other.
> God commands you lovingly. You command God hastily.
> When you are unhappy, the hostile forces command you ruthlessly, doubt commands you openly, bondage commands you triumphantly and fear commands you unconditionally.

Be happy.
> God sees in you His aspiring creation, His transforming realisation, His illumining revelation and His fulfilling manifestation.

Be happy.
> God sees in you another God. God sees you as another God. God sees you and Himself as one.

* * *

FEAR

I FEAR

I fear to speak, I fear to speak.
My tongue is killed, my heart is weak.

I fear to think, I fear to think.
My mind is wild and apt to sink.

I fear to see, I fear to see.
I eat the fruits of ignorance-tree.

I fear to love, I fear to love.
A train of doubts around, above.

I fear to be, I fear to be,
Long dead my life of faith in me.

* * *

FEAR

Whom do I fear?
The Lord, the One?
Not true. I am
My Father's son.

What do I fear?
My ignorance vast —
The sleepless spear,
The eyeless dust.

Why do I fear?
Because my eyes
See not the Smile
Of the golden skies.

QUESTION: You say that if fear is our problem we should feel that we are God's chosen children. Do you mean that we are chosen by God to experience fear?

SRI CHINMOY: Fear is a negative force, a destructive force, and we are the soldiers of God who will fight against it. Fear comes from darkness, from ignorance. If we enter into a room which is pitch dark, we will be frightened. But as soon as we turn on the light, the darkness is illumined and our fear vanishes. We see that there is nothing to fear in the darkness and that there is nothing to fear in the light either.

* * *

How to conquer fear? Sit at the feet of your illumining consciousness-light. This light has the adamantine will power to protect us, liberate us and perfect us.

* * *

HOW TO CONQUER FEAR

Our body is limited: that is why the body has fear. Our vital is unconscious: that is why the vital has fear. Our mind is obscure: that is why the mind has fear. Our heart is unaspiring: that is why the heart has fear.

To free our body from fear, what we need is the glorious experience of our soul. To free our vital from fear, what we need is the dynamic and conscious expansion of our soul. To free our mind from fear, what we need is the transforming illumination of our soul. Finally, to free our heart from fear, what we need is the fulfilling perfection of our soul.

Man's fear does not allow him to see the face of reality, the ultimate Reality. Man's fear does not allow him to reach the Golden Shores of the Beyond. Man's fear does not allow him to fulfil God for God's sake.

But God, the Author of all good, has boundless Compassion, Concern and Love for mankind.

God's Compassion saves man.
God's Concern liberates man.
God's Love fulfils man.

When we unconsciously think of fear or cherish fear, fear smilingly shakes hands with us. When we consciously think of fear or cherish fear, fear triumphantly embraces us. But when we think of our inner courage, God cries with His divine Cry, for He feels that here He has a chosen instrument.

Earth is afraid of Heaven's transcendental Light, and Heaven is afraid of earth's abysmal ignorance. God says to earth, "My child, do not act like a fool. Heaven's transcendental Light is not going to blind you. Heaven's Light is not going to expose you. On the contrary, Heaven's Light is going to illumine you. Heaven's Light is going to transform you."

God says to Heaven, "Do not be a fool. Earth's abysmal ignorance cannot bind you. It cannot destroy you. On the contrary, earth's ignorance will be offered to you. It is you who will transform the face of earth."

God says, "I need both of you: Heaven and earth.

"Heaven, the message of realisation you will have to give to earth. Earth, the message of manifestation, My divine manifestation, you will have to offer to Heaven."

Fear comes from our deep-rooted ignorance. We do not see the light with our inner vision. We see the light with our outer, human, limited, earth-bound understanding.

Let me tell you a short story. An old man walking along the street one evening stepped on a rope. There was no light, and he thought the rope was actually a snake. Filled with fear, he let out a scream, and ran away as fast as he could. While running he fell down and broke his leg.

Some people nearby heard shouting and screaming, so they came with sticks. The old man was shouting all the time that there was a snake there. In the dark the others, too, thought it was a snake. So they started striking the rope, and accidentally began hitting one another.

The shouting and beating continued until another party came with a light and discovered that it was just a piece of rope and not a snake.

So when the light entered, the true reality was discovered. Similarly, in our human life, when light enters into our physical consciousness, every kind of fear is bound to disappear. But we are wanting in light. That is why fear consciously and deliberately looms large in our life at every moment.

But if we are sincere enough to go deep within, and to feel that inner courage belongs to us, then inner courage can dawn at every moment. It is more than willing to come to the fore. Bringing this inner courage to the fore is the conscious awakening of our inner being. Everyone has this inner being but, unfortunately, very few of us want to feed it. We feed our body in order to strengthen ourselves. We study books to feed our mind. We do many things to energise our outer being, but we do practically nothing to feed our inner being.

It is in our inner existence that we can grow into an adamantine will. When we use our adamantine will, which we can easily have at our behest, we can conquer the very breath of fear. Here on earth our inner adamantine and indomitable will can and will reign supreme. Only one thing we need: a conscious awareness of the divine Light which is ours. It is our birthright to realise and embody this inner Light.

There can be no fear, there cannot be even an iota of fear, when we live in the effulgence of our soul. To live constantly in the divine effulgence of our soul only one thing is needed: a conscious inner cry. This inner cry is called aspiration, the mounting flame deep within us. When this flame rises up towards the highest, it illumines everything around it. Darkness is transformed into light, fear into strength, doubt into certainty, ignorance into wisdom and death into Immortality.

* * *

Question: How can we overcome fear?

Sri Chinmoy: Fear can be in the physical, vital, mental and even the heart. First of all, one has to know where the fear looms large. If there is fear in the gross physical, then that person should concentrate on the navel *chakra*. If one can concentrate on the navel centre and be one with the life force, the life energy in the physical, then one can conquer fear there.

If one wants to conquer fear in the vital, then one should concentrate on one's own inner being. But this is difficult for beginners, so I tell them that they should try to expand the dynamic vital in themselves. We have two types of vital. One is aggressive, and the other is dynamic. The dynamic vital wants to create something sooner than at once in a divine way, an illumined way. So if we can concentrate on that vital, or focus our attention on that vital, then we expand our consciousness in the vital. Then there can be no fear.

To conquer fear in the mind, one has to empty the

mind daily. The mind is full of doubt, obscurity, ignorance, suspicion and so forth. Early in the morning you can try for ten minutes or so not to have any thoughts — good, bad, divine or undivine. If a thought comes, try to kill it. Then, after some time, allow only the divine thoughts which are your friends. In the beginning you do not know who your friend is and who your enemy is, so you have to be very careful. Later on, you can allow only your friends to enter. Your friends are divine thoughts, progressive thoughts, illumined thoughts. These thoughts will undoubtedly conquer fear in the mind on your behalf. Feel that your mind is like a vessel. First you empty it, and then you wait for Peace, Light and Bliss to descend. But if you do not first empty the vessel, then Peace, Light and Bliss will not be able to enter.

Why is there fear in the physical, the vital and the mind? Precisely because we do not want to expand our consciousness. I am separate from you. You are separate from me. That is why I am afraid of you and you are afraid of me. But when we realise the Highest, immediately we feel the length and breadth of the universe as our very own. In expansion only can we expel fear. If we expand our consciousness, then we become one with others. We feel that we belong to them and they belong to us. How can we be afraid of anybody when we represent divinity in humanity and others represent the same divinity in humanity? So there can be no fear.

The aspiring heart has no fear, but the unaspiring heart does have fear. The aspiring heart has a flame — a burning flame that mounts towards the highest. Where there is light, there cannot be fear. But to conquer fear in the unaspiring heart you have to take help directly from the soul. When you meditate on the heart centre, every time you breathe in, try to feel that you are digging inside. This is not violent digging, but a divinely intensified feeling you have inside your heart that you are going deep, deep, deep within. Each time you breathe in, feel that you are going deep within. If you do this regularly, after a few days or a few months you are bound to feel a twinge or hear a very tiny sound. When you hear the sound, try to see if the sound is caused by something or if it is spontaneous. We need two hands to clap, but in the heart sound is not produced by two things struck together; it is automatic, spontaneous. When you can feel that kind of sound inside, like a celestial gong, then you are bound to conquer fear in your unaspiring heart.

* * *

The difference between fear and doubt is this: fear cherishes itself, doubt nourishes itself.

* * *

NO LITTLE ENEMY

There is no little enemy.
   A wee fear
      Tortures our whole existence.
   A tiny doubt
      Devours our entire being.
   A puny jealousy
      Destroys our universal oneness.

* * *

Question: How can I overcome the fear of failure?

Sri Chinmoy: You have to know what failure is and what failure can do. Fear is bound to go when you know that failure is not something shameful, damaging, destructive or painful. Feel that failure is something natural. When a child starts to walk, he often stumbles and falls down. But he does not feel that stumbling is a failure. He thinks that it is a natural process to stand up for a moment and then fall again.

If you think of failure in that light, not as something that is against or totally distant from reality but as something that is forming, shaping, moulding and becoming reality, then there cannot be any fear. We take failure as something contrary to our expectation and our God-realisation. But failure is not contrary to our realisation. Failure is something that is urging us towards our realisation. What we call failure, in God's Eye, is only an experience.

Always take failure as an experience. Do not take it as a finished product or as the culmination of an experience, but rather as the process of an experience. If you think that failure is the end of your experience, then you are mistaken. In a long race one may start very slowly, but then gradually he increases his speed and eventually he reaches his goal. But if he thinks that since his start was slow, he will not be able to reach the destination, then he is making a deplorable mistake. If there is no failure, naturally you will run the fastest. But if there is failure, take it as an experience that is just beginning. The end will be success. And then who can say that you have failed?

Who is the judge? If you are the judge, then no matter what you do and what you achieve, you will always feel that you have failed. But if somebody else is the judge, then he will know whether your so-called failure is real. He will call your experience a failure only when you do not want to overcome what you feel is wrong within you. When you give up the spiritual life, that is failure. Otherwise, there is no such thing in my terminology as failure.

* * *

COURAGE

Courage is the most devoted servant of one's own faith in oneself and God.

Timidity says, "God is forever unknowable." Courage says, "God is at present unknown, but only for a while."

Cowardice is an extra load to carry in the march of our day-to-day life.

Courage is an ever-willing extra porter to carry our wealth, inner and outer, according to our soul's volition.

Courage is perfection only when it springs from our oneness with the Vision of God.

There is no other way to please our inner self than to be a perfect emblem of courage.

Enthusiasm in its purest expression is courage.

Without courage, life is a path without progress.

Against one's inner courage, death itself contends in vain.

Courage is God's successful inspiration in man's body, mind, heart and soul.

* * *

To rise triumphantly out of every trial, what we need is inner courage. What is inner courage? Inner courage is the constant acceptance and fulfilment of God's Will.

* * *

Inner courage mends our outer existence. Outer fear ends our inner existence.

* * *

Courage is absolutely necessary in the spiritual life. The very acceptance of the spiritual life demands enormous courage. It is only a divinely courageous soul, only a divinely inspired soul, that can swiftly reach the highest Goal.

This courage is not the courage of a haughty, rough person who will strike others to assert his superiority; it is totally different. This courage is our constant awareness of what we are entering into, of what we are going to become, of what we are going to reveal. We have to jump courageously into the ocean of spirituality, but we have to know that we are not jumping into the sea of uncertainty. Uncertainty and spirituality never go together. When we speak of courage, we have to know that courage means certainty.

It is not by hook or by crook that we are going to have God-realisation; it is through constant self-offering. Self-offering is the most powerful weapon, for it is in self-offering that true courage lies. When we know, feel and realise that God is ours and we are God's, we get spontaneous courage streaming forth.

* * *

Difficulties indicate the strength of unwanted forces. Endurance indicates the inevitable victory of the soul's ever-fulfilling, ever-glowing Light.

* * *

Self-confidence means God's inner guidance.

* * *

SPEAK AND DON'T SPEAK

In your aspiration-life
Speak to faith.
Faith will strengthen your success.

In your aspiration-life
Speak to courage.
Courage will widen your horizon.

In your aspiration-life
Don't speak to doubt.
Doubt will slacken your vigilance.

In your aspiration-life
Don't speak to fear.
Fear will weaken your progress.

* * *

DOUBT

WHY IS IT EASIER TO DISBELIEVE THAN TO BELIEVE?

Why is it easier to disbelieve than to believe? It is easier to disbelieve than to believe because disbelief is an act of descent, whereas belief is an act of ascent. Descending is easier than ascending.

It is easier to disbelieve than to believe because disbelief is an act of breaking, and belief is an act of building. Building is more difficult than breaking.

It is easier to disbelieve than to believe because disbelief is an act of our self-centered mind, whereas belief is an act of our self-giving heart.

Disbelief begins its journey in the doubting mind and ends in the destructive vital. Belief begins its journey in the illumining soul and continues to march in the vast kingdom of the aspiring heart.

A man of disbelief, with his eyes firmly closed, tells us what others are, what the world is and what he himself can do for the entire world if he wants to. A man of belief, with his heart's door wide open, tells us what God has done for him, what God is doing for him and what God will do for him.

Disbelief has a perfection of its own. Disbelief finds its perfection in the cyclone of separation. Belief has a perfection of its own. Belief finds its perfection in the music of universal oneness.

Disbelief tells the world, "Be careful, be careful. If not, I shall devour you." Belief tells the world, "Come in, come in, please. I have been eagerly waiting for you."

Disbelief hates the world. Why? It feels that the world is never of it and can never be for it. A man of disbelief always feels that this world does not belong to him and that he can never lord it over the world. This is precisely why a man of disbelief dares to hate the world.

A man of belief loves the world. Why? He believes that this world of ours is verily the aspiring Body of God, the glowing Dream of God and the fulfilling Reality of God.

In the spiritual life if one cherishes disbelief, one is simply lengthening the distance to the ultimate Goal. But if a seeker has abundant belief in his spiritual life, in his own quest for the ultimate Truth, then undoubtedly he is shortening the distance. Finally, if his inner being is surcharged with boundless faith, then he feels that the Goal itself, the Goal of the Beyond, is running towards him, and not that he is trying to reach the Goal.

There comes a time when a man of disbelief, being totally frustrated, wants to kill the world around him out of exasperation. But to his wide surprise he sees that the wild ignorance of the world has already stabbed him. With his proud knowledge he wanted to kill the world; but before he could kill the world, the world and his own wild ignorance have killed him.

A man of belief wants to love the world. To his wide surprise he sees that his entire existence is in the very heart of the world. The world has already placed a throne in the inmost recesses of its heart for the man of belief to sit upon.

In our spiritual life disbelief is nothing short of a crime. When we disbelieve, we pour slow poison into our system; we kill our possibility and potentiality, and wallow consciously and deliberately in the pleasures of ignorance.

Why do we disbelieve? We disbelieve because we are afraid of oneness, afraid of the vast. We feel that when we enter into the vast, we lose our identity, we lose our individuality, we lose our very existence. But we forget the undeniable truth that when we enter into the vastness, it is nothing short of the enlargement of our divised consciousness.

For an ordinary person, an unaspiring human being, it is extremely difficult not to disbelieve. An aspiring person, an aspiring seeker, knows that there is something within that is pushing him forward to the Light, to the Reality, for his is the life of conscious awareness. An unaspiring person feels that something from without is pulling him backwards, pulling him to something unknown, to something that will bind him.

When we consciously disbelieve someone, we do not realise the fact that the inner magnet within us pulls the undivine qualities of that particular person into us. What happens when a person has achieved something but we do not believe it? The person and his achievement remain the same whether we believe it or not. But the person also has imperfections, limited capacity, impurity; and our disbelief is a magnet that pulls only his imperfections. If we have belief and if we offer our belief, then we have to feel that we have a magnet that draws the good qualities, the divine qualities, the illumining qualities of the other person.

When we disbelieve God, when we disbelieve the Reality, God remains the same. But what happens is that ignorance, the teeming vast, gets the opportunity to envelop us more powerfully and more completely. And when we believe in God, God's Compassion gets the utmost opportunity to work in and through us most powerfully.

The deeper we enter into the spiritual life, the more we become aware of the capacity of disbelief and belief. Disbelief is nothing short of destruction. Belief is nothing short of a new creation. Each time we believe in something, we see the face of a new creation within and without us. And when we go one step ahead, when our inner faith looms large, then we see in us a perfected man and a liberated soul.

* * *

In the inner life we see the role of fear and doubt, courage and certainty.

Fear. What is it? When we follow the spiritual life, we come to realise sooner than at once that fear is a real enemy. What does it do? It buys our coffin long before we are destined to die.

Doubt. What does it do? It starts digging our grave while we are still alive, while we are still performing our earthly duties.

Courage. Courage is the outer expression or manifestation of our inner indomitable will. At every moment we can stand in front of the reality, see the reality and grow into reality if our existence is inundated with inner will and outer courage.

Certainty. Certainty tells us that God is ours. God is not the sole monopoly of any individual. Even realised souls cannot dare to claim that God belongs to them alone. No, far from it. Each individual has the right to proclaim that God is his, and that he belongs to God. Certainty makes him feel that God and he are eternally one, and that God-realisation is his birthright.

The living universe and the evolving universe, the dying universe and the perishing universe. When we aspire, when we consciously, soulfully and spontaneously try to go beyond the boundaries of the finite, we live in the living and evolving universe. When we consciously or unconsciously cherish doubt, jealousy, fear, imperfection, bondage, limitation and death, we live in the dying and perishing universe.

* * *

Doubt will leave us only when we feel that we are destined to do something for God. We get tremendous power from the word 'destined'. This word brings boundless courage to the fore. Even if somebody is weak by nature, if someone can convince him that he is destined to work for God, then immediately, from the inner world, heroism comes forward. He will fight against any obstruction with a strength and inner determination that will surprise him. Obstructions may come to him in the form of impurity, obscurity, jealousy, fear and doubt, but the word 'destined' will smash the pride of all the negative forces. Anything that is undivine will have to surrender to this word. So if we have the kind of inner and outer conviction that tells us we are destined to serve God, then the goal can unmistakably be reached.

* * *

Doubt is the worst possible impurity in the human mind.

* * *

Doubt is a down-dragging force in the low and un-aspiring stage of a seeker's evolution.

* * *

DOES BELIEF COME SPONTANEOUSLY OR BY EFFORT?

Belief comes spontaneously. Belief comes by effort. In the spiritual life a sincere, advanced and surrendered seeker can and will have spontaneous belief. Belief by personal effort, without the divine Grace and God's unconditional Protection, cannot be as effective as spontaneous belief.

Spontaneous belief is a gift from God that allows the human in us to see, feel and grow into the very image of God. Belief by personal effort is a human earthly discovery, although to some extent it also is necessary.

Believing is seeing. Seeing is believing. When believing is seeing, a seeker becomes a perfect instrument for the Supreme to use in His own Way. When seeing is believing, a seeker makes a solemn promise both to God and to himself that he will realise and fulfil God on earth. But there is no certainty, no guarantee. He may fulfil his divine promise and he may not, for at any moment during his long journey he may be assailed by teeming doubts, fears, jealousies, anxieties and ignorance-night.

Belief by effort is the acceptance, the mere acceptance, of Truth and Light. This belief is usually mental and intellectual. But spontaneous belief is the conscious and constant oneness with Truth and Light. It is not that belief by personal effort is of no use; personal effort has its own value, but it is not as strong and sure as spontaneous belief.

Not only ordinary human beings but also many spiritual giants have suffered from doubts and other undivine qualities in their human nature before devotedly and wholeheartedly launching onto the spiritual path. So we must not be doomed to disappointment when we are assailed by doubts in our spiritual life. Belief that comes from within is at the head of the divine spiritual army, and this army destroys our doubts or, rather, let us say it illumines our doubts, perfects our imperfections and transforms our bondage and limitation into divine plenitude.

We have two principal organs: the eye and the ear. Our eyes quite often, if not always, believe themselves. Our ears very often believe others. These are our human eyes and our human ears. But the divine eye, the third eye, will believe only in the vision of Divinity, and the divine ears will believe only in the truth of Reality. When we listen to the inner command, when we have the capacity to grow into constant obedience to our Inner Pilot, we feel within and without the presence of spontaneous belief. Belief is the reality of our inner obedience. This is divine belief, spontaneous belief. Belief by effort is a restricted, disciplined human understanding.

Belief is power. A real seeker of the infinite Truth knows this. An insincere and unaspiring seeker is aware of the truth that belief is power, but he cannot go beyond understanding or awareness; whereas a sincere, genuine, devoted and surrendered seeker knows that belief is dynamic power, and he has this power as his very own.

We see a tree. The tree bears flowers, and soon afterwards we see fruits. The flower is the harbinger of the fruit. In the spiritual life, belief is the flower. Belief is a divine angel which enters into us as the harbinger of the Lord Supreme.

We can cultivate belief. If we do not have belief we *can* develop belief. How? We can do it by mixing with sincere spiritual people who care more for God than for pleasure. There are also people who care only for God in human beings, and if we mix with those people we can cultivate belief. When we have belief we can walk with God in His Garden of Light and Delight.

But in the spiritual life spontaneous belief need not be and cannot be the last word. There is something infinitely higher and deeper than belief, and that is faith. When we have belief, we can make tremendous progress for a day or for a month or for a year. But then, if we unconsciously or consciously become a victim to undivine forces, our belief loses its strength. Then we cannot make fast progress in the spiritual life in spite of having belief.

The strength of belief, even spontaneous belief, is not enough to take us to the ultimate Goal. Belief is like a child's instrument that you can play upon for a limited number of hours or years. But when you have faith, you come to realise that you are an eternal player and, at the same time, you are an eternal instrument. And when you go farther and deeper, you come to realise that the player is somebody else, the Lord Supreme, and you are His instrument. He is the eternal Player, and you are eternally His chosen instrument.

Spontaneous belief will make you feel what you eternally are: God's chosen child. But if you do not have faith, you will not have the abiding satisfaction and the feeling that you and He are eternally one, that you represent the One and that your very presence on earth is the manifestation of the One Absolute Supreme. It is only when your outer being and your inner being are surcharged with faith that you can manifest God here on earth. Faith in oneself and faith in God must run together.

If you say that you have no faith in yourself but you have all faith in God, then I wish to say that you cannot go very far. You have to have faith, constant faith and abundant faith, not only in God, but also in yourself since you are God's son or God's daughter. When you truly feel that you are God's child, you will find that it is beneath your dignity to make friends with ignorance. Reality, Eternity, Immortality and Infinity are not vague terms; these are your birthright. When you have that kind of faith, God will shower His choicest Blessings upon your devoted head and surrendered heart.

But faith in oneself must not exceed its own boundary. I said before that you have to have faith, constant faith in abundant measure. But you have to remember the source of your faith as well; you have to remember where it comes from. At some time you may think: "Oh, I am working so hard for my realisation of the absolute Truth, for my perfection. It is all my effort, my effort. One percent of the work will be done by the Grace of the Supreme, and ninety-nine percent will be my personal effort." But when that most auspicious day dawns and you realise the Absolute, you will see that just the opposite is true: your faith enabled you to contribute one percent in personal effort toward your realisation, and God supplied the other ninety-nine percent as His divine Grace, unconditional Grace. And when you are about to manifest your realisation, a higher and more profound truth will dawn on you. You will realise that the one percent of faith you had, which was absolutely necessary, was also God's gift to you.

You were chosen from among countless people to run toward the Light. Others are still fast asleep. It was sheer Grace, God's unconditional Grace, that inspired you to come out of ignorance and look toward the Light. Since it was He who inspired and invited you to join consciously in His cosmic Game, you have to feel that the one percent of faith you had in the beginning also came directly from God, the Absolute Supreme.

Some people do not have belief; they want to follow the negative path. No matter how far they go, their minds tell them that there is no God. But I wish to tell you, on the strength of my own oneness with God and with humanity, that they will not have even temporary satisfaction on this earth, not to speak of abiding satisfaction. A day will dawn when they will feel that their lack of belief, their denial of God, is not giving them what they want. They will be compelled to look for a fulfilling belief.

We who have started walking along the spiritual path are the forerunners. All will eventually run toward the same transcendental Goal. The majority of mankind will not always lag behind. All children of God, no matter how unconscious and unaspiring, will one day run toward the common Goal. This Goal is the supreme discovery of one's Divinity and the constant and perfect manifestation of one's everlasting Reality.

* * *

We doubt God at our own sweet will. We doubt God precisely because we think He is invisible. We doubt Him because we think He is inaudible. We doubt God because we think He is incomprehensible.

But to see Him, what have we done? To hear Him, what have we done? To understand Him, what have we done?

To see Him, have we prayed soulfully every day? The answer is no. To hear Him, have we loved mankind devotedly? No! To understand Him, have we served the divinity in humanity? No! We have not prayed to God. We have not loved mankind. We have not served the divinity in humanity. Yet we want to see God face to face. It is impossible.

God can be seen on the strength of our inner cry, which we call aspiration, the mounting flame within us. Every moment this flame is rising towards the highest. If we know how to cry within, then this flame will climb high, higher, highest; and while it is climbing, it will illumine the world around it.

* * *

Doubt can be conquered. It has to be conquered. How? The only answer is constant and soulful concentration on the mind, meditation on the heart and contemplation on the entire being.

* * *

Each human being can be at once a fighter and a forgiver. When self-doubt tortures him, he must play the role of a fighter. And when his own ignorance humiliates him, he must play the role of a forgiver.

* * *

How to conquer doubt? Observe the vow of inner silence; do inner meditation and selfless service. Your doubt will have no strength to shout-at you. It has to die, and it will—for good.

* * *

PUNISHMENT

Doubt is self-punishment,
Faith is self-enfoldment.

Fear is self-punishment,
Courage is self-refreshment.

Division is self-punishment,
Unity is self-enlightenment.

Hate is self-punishment,
Love is self-fulfilment.

* * *

CARRIERS

Doubt, don't come to me!
   If you come
   I shall carry you to Faith.
   Faith and I shall kill you.

Fear, don't come to me!
   If you come
   I shall carry you to Will.
   Will and I shall kill you.

Faith, do come to me!
   Carry me to the real starting point.

Will, do come to me!
   Carry me to the ultimate Goal.

* * *

ALL ARE UNSELFISH

Doubt shares its capacity
  With the mind.
Therefore, unselfish is doubt.

Arrogance shares its capacity
  With the vital.
Therefore, unselfish is arrogance.

Lethargy shares its capacity
  With the body.
Therefore, unselfish is lethargy.

Insecurity shares its capacity
  With the heart.
Therefore, unselfish is insecurity.

Uncertainty shares its capacity
  With the soul.
Therefore, unselfish is uncertainty.

Man shares his ignorance-capacity
  With God.
Therefore, unselfish is man.

* * *

Question: If you told me you could swim across the ocean, I would say, "Let me see you do it." I wouldn't accept the fact that you could until I saw you do it, and then after I saw you do it, I'd say, "Well, now you can teach me."

Sri Chinmoy: All right. But if you asked me to prove my capacity to swim, you would have to let me do it in my own way. If you asked me to prove my capacity with my hands tied behind my back and my feet tied together, I don't think I would be able to prove anything to you. Or if you refused to let me get into the water, or if you closed your eyes and refused to watch my performance, I don't think I could prove anything to you.

There *is* a way for a spiritual Master to prove the truth of his philosophy or of his realisation, but you must allow him to do it in his own way. I would ask you to give up your doubts, your impurities, your attachments, your desires for a few months, and meditate with me sincerely, devotedly and soulfully. If you allowed me to prove myself in this way, you would very soon see and feel the truth. But if you said, "No, I don't want you to prove yourself in that way; right now I want you to show me God, Truth and Light right before my very eyes," then what could I do? I would be helpless at that time. If I brought God, Truth and Light before you, which I could do, at that time your inner eyes would be tightly shut and you would not see anything; so you would still doubt my capacity and my truth.

In the outer world you need eyes to see if somebody is doing something. Similarly, in the inner world you need the third eye to see if somebody is doing something inwardly. One has to use one's inner vision to see the authenticity of the spiritual Master. The outer eyes, which serve the mind, are of no use for seeing inner things. If you want to prove the authenticity of a spiritual Master, meditate and go deep within, make your mind quiet and try to enter into the universal Consciousness. Only then will you see whether the spiritual man is telling the truth or not. Only then do you become a competent judge.

But you cannot expect to become a qualified judge overnight. If you want to learn to be an electrician, you place yourself in the hands of a qualified electrician for a year or two and follow his instructions carefully. At the end of that time, if he has not taught you well, you can say, "You were not qualified," or "You did not know what you were doing." God-realisation is an infinitely more difficult subject. If a spiritual man says, "I can lead you to God," you have to follow his instructions to the letter for at least a year or two even to get preliminary experiences that will show you that you are on the right track. If you doubt him from the very beginning, you are not giving either yourself or him a chance. If your Master says, "I have seen the Light, and I will take you to the Light," you have to give him an opportunity to take you to the Light. You have to be patient, and you have to give him complete obedience. I use the word 'surrender', but complete obedience is necessary to make even a beginning. For that, you have to reject the doubting mind totally. With tremendous self-discipline you have to force yourself to stop doubting, even if you must tell yourself that it is only for a temporary period. Say, "I will stop doubting for two years, and give this man a chance to show me the Light." But if you doubt his teachings while trying to learn from him, you are simply destroying your opportunities.

If you want to see something in the outer world, you have to go to the place where it is being shown. In the inner world it is also like that. When a spiritual person says that he is doing this or that, you have to go to *his* level, to *his* plane, in order to see it. Everything has to be seen or felt or judged in its own world. I am no judge of science because I have never entered into that world; I am not competent to judge it on its own level. Physical truth has to be seen in the physical world, and spiritual truth has to be seen in the spiritual world..

Westerners have a special problem with this developed mind. It is really a disadvantage in the spiritual life to have a highly developed intellectual mind. But if you transform it and transmute it, it can become a very useful instrument. I wish to tell you a traditional Indian story on this subject.

A seeker who had studied thousands and thousands of spiritual books went to a Master and said, "Master, I have studied all that the books can teach, and now I wish to learn from you."

The Master said, "You are not fit to be my student."

The seeker asked, "How is it that I am not fit to be your student? Here you have all kinds of ignorant people as your students, while I have studied many books and all the scriptures."

The Master replied, "Because what you have learned, you now have to unlearn, whereas they have not to unlearn anything. You have a giant burden on your shoulders. Unless you unburden yourself, you will not learn anything from me. But these innocent students of mine are not burdened with book information; they are fresh."

Then the Master asked the seeker to bring him an almanac and open it to a particular page. "Here it is written that at this particular hour it will rain heavily. Now squeeze the paper. Is it raining here? Squeeze the whole book. Is it raining? You have squeezed the book as hard as you can, but no rain. Book knowledge is theoretical knowledge. Experience alone is practical knowledge. Just unlearn all that you have learned for so many years, and then you will be fit to be my student."

Indian Masters are sometimes very, very strict, or perhaps we should say very rude, to their students when they come with intellectual questions. Sometimes they snub their students mercilessly. They want to show their students that unnecessary intellectualisation will only hinder their spiritual development.

* * *

NO LITTLE FRIEND

There is no little friend.
    An iota of faith
    Energises my entire being.

A small fraction of love
    Elevates my whole existence
        To Heaven.

An insignificant portion of surrender
    Makes me one,
        Inseparably one,
            With Infinity.

* * *

PURITY

SIMPLICITY, SINCERITY AND PURITY

Simplicity, sincerity and purity. These are the three things that we need in our inner life. Simplicity, sincerity and purity.

Simplicity we need at every moment. If the mind is not simple, if the mind is complicated and complex, then there can be no peace in the mind. A child is simple. He is all joy. In our day-to-day existence, unfortunately we do not pay any attention to simplicity. If we go deep within, if we have a simple mind, a simple existence, we shall feel how lucky, how happy and how fortunate we are.

Sincerity is the life of our heart. If we have sincerity, then we have to know that we are already marching towards our destined Goal. Sincerity is our safeguard. A sincere seeker is running towards his destined Goal, either consciously or unconsciously, at every moment. If we want to make constant progress here on earth, then what we need is a sincere heart.

Purity. This purity does not mean that we have to

take a bath ten times a day. No! It is the inner purity that we need and not just the outer cleanliness. When we are pure, we can receive the divine Peace, Light, Bliss and Power in abundant measure. When we can maintain our purity, then Peace, Joy, Light, Bliss and Power can dawn on earth. The role of purity is of paramount importance in our spiritual life.

* * *

PURITY AND POWER

Have purity first; then only will you never be devoid of power.

Look at the miracle of a drop of venom and a drop of purity. The former poisons the blood in your veins. The latter purifies the human soul in your body.

Power is not necessarily purity, but purity is sheer power.

There is no one who can fly as high as a divine dispenser of power. There is no man who can ruin his heart as quickly as a misuser of power.

To have experiences without the strength of purification is like living in the most dangerous part of the forest. This does not mean that experience must always wait for complete purification. What is actually needed is a good understanding and a true relation between growing experience and growing purification.

Knowledge is a secret power. When you have won knowledge, power is bound to follow it.

Purity is the ceaseless shower of God's omnipotent Grace on aspiring human souls.

Purity is the immediate gift from the universal Treasure-house to God's hopeful children.

* * *

THE ROLE OF PURITY
IN THE SPIRITUAL LIFE

Purity! Purity! Purity! We love you. We want you. We need you. Stay in our thoughts! Stay in our actions! Stay in the breath of our life!

How to be pure? We can be pure by self-control. We can control our senses. It is unbelievably difficult, but it is not impossible.

"I shall control my senses. I shall conquer my passions." This approach cannot bring us what we actually want. The hungry lion that lives in our senses and the hungry tiger that lives in our passions will not leave us because of the mere repetition of the thought, "I shall control my senses and conquer my passions." This approach is of no avail.

Nor is it advisable always to think of our impurity and brood over it. If we meditate on the positive—that is to say, on light—then light will descend into us. But if we think constantly of night and are afraid of night, then we are unconsciously entering into the domain of night. Whenever we think of night, of darkness within us, we enter into night's domain. But if we always think of light, which is, after all, our true joy and saviour, then we are running towards our destined Goal.

What we must do is fix our mind on God. To our utter amazement, the lion and tiger of impurity, now tamed, will leave us of their own accord when they see that we have become too poor to feed them. But as a matter of fact, we have not become poor in the least. On the contrary, we have become infinitely stronger and richer, for God's Will energises our body, mind and heart. To fix our body, mind and heart on the Divine is the right approach. The closer we are to the Light, the farther we are from the darkness.

Purity does not come all at once. It takes time. We must dive deep within and lose ourselves, with implicit faith, in contemplation of God. Then we need not go to purity; purity will come to us. And purity does not come alone. It brings with it everlasting joy. This divine joy is the sole purpose of our life. God reveals Himself fully and manifests Himself unreservedly only when we have this inner joy.

The world gives us desires. God gives us prayers. The world gives us bondage. God gives us freedom: freedom from limitations, freedom from ignorance.

We are the players. We can play either football or cricket; we have a free choice. Similarly, it is we who can choose either purity or impurity to play with. The player is the master of the game, and not vice versa.

Let nothing perturb us. Let our body's impurity remind us of our heart's spontaneous purity. Let our outer finite thoughts remind us of our inner infinite will. Let our mind's teeming imperfections remind us of our soul's limitless perfection.

The present-day world is full of impurity. It seems that purity is a currency from another world. It is hard to obtain this purity, but once we get it, peace is ours, success is ours. Then we can face the world bravely. Our

Inner Pilot is constantly vigilant. The undercurrents of our inner and spiritual life will always flow on unobstructed and unafraid once purity is ours.

* * *

Question: What is the highest kind of purity I can aspire to?

Sri Chinmoy: Purity in the physical. You should always try to invoke light in the unaspiring body. The lower physical and the emotional vital below the navel have to be purified totally. Human beings have purity to some extent in the heart. In the mind the quantity is very small. In the vital purity is totally mixed with impurity. There dynamism and aggression play together, but aggression is impurity and dynamism is purity. Below the vital is the physical. There, because of inertia and sloth, darkness reigns supreme. And where there is darkness, you can rest assured that impurity is the lord.

You have to aspire for purity in the gross physical. It is the physical in you that needs radical transformation, and for that what you need is physical purity. Purity in the physical can be established only by bringing down light from above into the physical and lower vital consciousness, especially below the navel centre. How can you do it? Through constant elevating prayer and constant inner cry for light. Light and darkness cannot stay together; it is impossible. Similarly, purity and impurity cannot stay together. When you pray for purity, you have to feel that what you actually need is light. And you must not just repeat the word 'purity' like a parrot. You should meditate on the transcendental Light. When light descends into your emotional vital and physical body, then automatically, spontaneously, the light will purify the conscious and the unconscious or lower worlds within you. First it will purify and then it will illumine your consciousness, which is now unconsciously expressing the physical truth: the world of temptation, frustration and destruction.

Question: Is it possible for a person to become unintentionally involved in the vibrations of someone who is impure?

Sri Chinmoy: Yes, it is quite possible. In spite of being absolutely pure oneself, one can become a victim of others' impurity. What actually happens is that the person who has purity does not have enough inner strength to prevent others' impurity from entering into his system. That is why spiritual teachers very often tell aspirants not to mix with the outside world, with people who are not pure. The aspirants may be absolutely pure themselves, but if they are not also very strong, then they are helpless. Their purity can be torn to pieces like a rose. The rose is beautiful to look at, for it is the embodiment of purity. But if someone wants to, he can easily tear the rose to pieces.

In our day-to-day life we very often come across people and places that are very impure. While walking along the street a spiritual person may sense tremendous impurity at a particular spot where an ordinary person may not notice anything at all. To an ordinary person all places are practically the same. But a spiritual person knows that purity and impurity vary tremendously from place to place and from person to person. So what you are saying is absolutely true. One can easily be attacked by the impurity of others. The only way to prevent this is by energising ourselves with the soul's power. The soul's power is always alert and can easily come to our aid.

* * *

THE POWER OF PURITY

Purity is the light of our soul expressing its divinity through the body, the vital and the mind. When we are pure we gain everything. If we can retain our purity, we will never lose anything worth keeping. Today we may have great thoughts or great inner power, but tomorrow we are bound to lose them if we are not pure. Purity is the Breath of the Supreme. When purity leaves us, the Breath of the Supreme also leaves, and we are left with only our human breath.

Purity means following the dictates of our Inner Pilot without allowing undivine forces to enter into us. Wherever there is a lack of purity, there is obscurity, which is the harbinger of death. What we call obscurity today, is death for us tomorrow. If there is no purity there is no certainty. If there is no purity, there is no spontaneity. If there is no purity, there is no constant flow of divinity inside us.

Purity is like a divine magnet. It pulls all divine qualities into us. When we have purity, the world is filled with pride in us. If Mother Earth houses a single pure soul, her joy knows no bounds. She says, "Here, at last, is a soul I can rely upon."

Once purity is established, especially in the vital, much is accomplished in one's inner life and outer life. In human purity abides God's highest Divinity. Man's purity is God's Breath. Purity is tremendous power. We can accomplish anything with purity. But if we lose our purity, although we may have power, wealth or influence, we can easily fall, we will crumble.

All spiritual aspirants, without exception, have seen and felt the necessity of purity. Today they climb the inner Mount Everest on the strength of their highest purity, but tomorrow they fall down into the lowest abyss. Purity lost, everything is lost; God Himself is lost. Purity won, the world is won; the entire universe is won.

* * *

THE FIRST AND THE LAST

The first woman
  Tempted
The first man
  To eat.

The last woman
  Shall inspire
The last man
  To be divine,
  To be perfect,
  To be supreme.

* * *

MAN, BE CAREFUL OF WOMAN

Sri Ramakrishna said:
Man, be careful of woman.

Mother Kali said:
Son, your advice needs some explanation.

Mother, what I meant was this:
Man, be careful of the human in woman.

Son, still it is not quite clear to me.

Mother, let me simplify it for you.
What I meant was this:
Man, do not use your human eyes to see
        and corrupt
The divine in woman.

Son, now I understand your philosophy.
    It is simply fascinating,
    It is divinely illumining,
    It is supremely fulfilling.

* * *

Sincerity is our life's
        protector.
Purity is our life's
        perfecter.

* * *

ONE MAN AND ONE WOMAN
CAN SAVE THE WORLD

One man can save the world.
Who is that man?
  That man is the man of Compassion.

One woman can save the world.
Who is that woman?
  That woman is the woman of Perfection.

Where does the man
Of Compassion live?
He lives in the abode
  Of God's transcendental Pride.

Where does the woman
Of Perfection live?
She lives in the abode
  Of God's eternal Gratitude.

                    * * *

Aspiration is the first step toward God.
Surrender is the last step toward God.
In between there are only three steps:
      The mind's sincerity,
      The heart's purity
            and
      The life's humility.

                    * * *

WHY IS SHE CHOSEN,
WHY IS HE CHOSEN?

Why is she chosen?
She is chosen
   Because
She cries and cries
In her heart.

Why is he chosen?
He is chosen
   Because
He dares and dares
In his mind.

Why is she chosen?
She is chosen
   Because
She knows what surrender is.

Why is he chosen?
He is chosen
   Because
He knows what service is.

* * *

True, my heart of purity alone can see the Face of God. Equally true, my heart of impurity is not ignored by God. On the contrary, my heart's impurity is well taken care of by God's constant Compassion.

* * *

SOME INNER QUALITIES

OBEDIENCE, INNER AND OUTER

Inner obedience, inner obedience:
  What is it,
If not a divine opportunity?

Outer obedience, outer obedience:
  What is it,
If not a glowing beauty?

My inner obedience
Carries me to my Lord Supreme
Sooner than at once.

My outer obedience
Brings me to my Lord Supreme
Slowly, steadily and unerringly.

* * *

PATIENCE

What is patience? It is a divine virtue. Unfortunately not only are we badly wanting in this divine virtue, but also we neglect it most foolishly.

What is patience? It is an inner assurance of God's unreserved Love and unconditional Guidance. Patience is God's Power hidden in us to weather the teeming storms of life.

If failure has the strength to turn your life into bitterness itself, then patience has the strength to turn your life into the sweetest joy. Do not surrender to fate after a single failure. Failure, at most, precedes success. But success, once achieved, gives you the name of confidence.

Have patience in the body; you will be able to accept the whole world. Have patience in the vital; you will be able to hold the whole world. Have patience in the mind; you will be able to neither forget nor lose the world. Have patience in the heart; you will feel that the world is not only with you and in you, but also for you as well.

Time is a flying bird. Do you want to capture the bird and encage it? Then you need patience. Your fondest dreams will be transformed into fruitful realities if you just know the secret of growing the patience-tree in your heart.

Patience is your sincere surrender to God's Will. This surrender is by no means the effacement of the finite self which you now are, but the total transformation of your finite existence into the Infinite Self.

In silence patience speaks to you: "Try to live the inner life. You will not only see and reach your goal, but also become the Goal."

Patience can never be imposed on you from outside. It is your own inner wealth, wisdom, peace and victory.

* * *

Question: How can we develop patience?

Sri Chinmoy: In order to develop patience, we have to feel that we have begun a spiritual journey, an inner journey, which has a goal, and that this goal wants us and needs us as much as we want and need it. This goal is ready to accept us, to give us what it has, but it will do this in its own way at God's choice Hour. We must know that God will give us His Wealth in time.

Patience will never tell us that it is a hopeless task. Patience will only tell us either that we are not ready or that the time is not ripe. We may have the feeling that we are ready, but we have to know that our integral being, our whole being, is not ready. Our soul may be ready, our heart may be ready, our mind may be ready, but our vital and physical may not be ready to reach the goal, which is Light and Truth. When our whole being is ready, the goal itself will dawn within our aspiring consciousness. When the hour strikes, the goal will draw us towards itself like a magnet.

When we are in the spiritual life, we have to feel that patience is not something passive. On the contrary, it is something dynamic. In patience we develop our inner strength, our inner will power. It is true that if we have will power we can easily acquire patience. But it is equally true that when we have patience, our inner will power develops itself in a special way.

Question: In my meditation and in my spiritual life, I feel that I am fighting against time because of my eagerness to reach my goal. Is this the wrong attitude?

Sri Chinmoy: If you feel that you are fighting against time, then I wish to say that you are making a deplorable mistake. This incarnation of yours is not the first and it is not the last. You have meditated, let us say, in your previous incarnations; and in this incarnation you have also meditated for a number of years. If you feel that each moment is leading you towards your destination, then this progress itself is a kind of partial goal. We cannot separate divine progress, real progress, from our goal. Rather than fighting against time, we should try our utmost to derive spiritual benefit, spiritual progress, from each second. Each time we make progress we have to feel that we have touched something of the Goal itself, a tiny portion. In this way, we feel that we are always advancing.

If we want to see or achieve the entire Goal, then we have to surrender to eternal Time, God's Time. What does this mean? Right now we feel that it is our responsibility to realise God at this very moment, in the twinkling of an eye. This is our own sense of need. But if we feel that God needs our realisation infinitely more than we ourselves need it, then we see that our realisation becomes His responsibility. God takes this responsibility on His shoulders most sincerely. After all, it is He who wants to manifest in and through us. And if we remain unrealised, then how can He fulfil Himself in and through us? So it is God's bounden duty to make us realise Him. But we have to know that He has His own choice time. We cannot pull this time. We cannot get it by hook or by crook. Realisation is His Gift; He has to offer it to us at His choice Hour. On our part we have only to be earnest, sincere, dedicated, devoted and surrendered to His Will. That is what He expects from us — sincere aspiration and surrender.

* * *

HUMILITY

My humility does not mean that I want the world to ignore me. That is not humility. My humility says that I should neither veil my ignorance nor make a parade of my knowledge. To be violently dissatisfied with oneself and curse one's fate is not the sign of humility. The true signs of humility are one's constant aspiration and one's inner cry for more Peace, Light and Bliss.

The seed of humility is exceptionally fertile. It may not germinate plants of power and force, but it does yield flowers of sweetness, grace, modesty and light.

Love for the Divine is in its essence a spontaneous spiritual humility.

Humility has no need to sit on the King's throne. But the King cannot help but bring the throne to humility. And who is the King? God's Compassion.

A prayer, in its simplest and most effective definition, is humility climbing the sky of all-fulfilling Delight.

Only the true sense of humility can raise us from our knees as high as we aspire.

We must realise that there is only one way of acquiring infinite future possibilities. That way lies in the great power: humility.

* * *

MY HUMILITY

God is my Superior, my only Superior. I am humble to Him. This is my supreme duty. God's children are my equals. I am humble to them. This is my greatest necessity. Pride is my inferior. I am humble to pride. This is my surest safety.

My humility is not self-denial. My humility in silence affirms what I truly have in my world without and what I surely am in my world within.

My humility is not abstinence from self-love. I do love myself. I love myself because in me the highest Divinity proudly breathes.

Self-conceit tells me that I can easily destroy the world. It tells me that the world is at my feet. But my humility tells me that I have neither the capacity nor the desire to destroy the world. My humility tells me that the world and I have the real capacity and the sincere desire to cry for perfect Perfection. My humility further tells me that the world is not at my feet; far from it. I carry the world devotedly towards its self-realisation. The world carries me lovingly and openly towards my self-manifestation.

When I am all humility, I neither underestimate nor overestimate my life. What I do is judge my life exactly, the way my Lord Supreme judges my life.

Humility is not a self-imposed, willed virtue. It is an inner state of consciousness that feels pure joy in its expression.

* * *

ADMIRATION

Admiration is not the **sign of inferiority. Rather** it is often a sign of the reciprocal **recognition of two souls.**

Familiarity and admiration **can rarely be** long-enduring friends, unless the uniqueness of the one finds an echo in the other.

It is easy for our admiration to win over another's love. But often it is too difficult for our love to win over another's admiration.

Can we separate our admiration from our sincerity? Decidedly not. For admiration demands a truthful selflessness.

Self-love must know that its annihilation will begin when admiration enters.

Admiration begins to show the psychic touch when it reaches out toward those eternal qualities possessed by seers, saints and sages.

* * *

AMBITION

Ambition is the fond embrace of possession and expression.

Life is an ever-progressing reality. This is the firm conviction of ambition.

Ambition is an attempt at self-expression and self-extension. When it is based on the ego's enlargement, we call it self-aggrandisement. When it is based on the soul's illumination, it ceases to be ambition and becomes a divine mission.

If you cast aside your ambition while still in the un-aspiring life, lo, you become a lethargy-prince.

If you embrace ambition in your aspiring life, lo, you become a condemned convict. You can never come out of the finite.

In your outer life ambition is the highest height. In your inner life ambition is the darkest night.

In your outer life the closer you come towards the land of fulfilling ambition, the mightier is your hopeful security. In your inner life the farther away you go from the shore of ambition, the greater is the strength of God's Protection for you.

Before you become an aspirant, ambition is your highest aim. After you become an aspirant, ambition is not only a low aim, but a serious fall.

To be sure, ambition is not aspiration. Ambition wants to command the world. Aspiration cries to serve the Creator in His creation.

Ambition is a human passion, never to be satisfied. Aspiration is a divine glorification, ever to be satisfied.

Ambition is the end of human realisation. Aspiration is the beginning of divine realisation.

Ambition is the chosen child of man. Aspiration is the chosen child of God.

* * *

How to conquer pride? Early in the morning think a few times of the ones who are infinitely superior to you in love and power. In the evening try to feel that you are sleeping in the Lap of the Supreme's supreme Love.

* * *

How to conquer arrogance? Try to feel that your arrogance will be paid back in its own coin. Nay, what you used was a hand-bomb and what you will have to encounter is an atom-bomb.

* * *

MY HUMAN PRIDE AND MY PRIDE DIVINE

My human pride feels that I can do everything. My divine pride, the pride that has surrendered itself to the Will of God, knows that I can do everything only when I am inspired, guided and moulded by the Supreme.

My human pride wants the world to understand me — my love, my help, my sacrifice. My divine pride, which is the feeling of oneness with all in God, does not wish the world to understand my selfless activities. It feels that if God understands me and knows my motives, then there can be no greater reward.

My human pride drinks the hot water of life — sufferings, struggles and doubts — without a spoon. The result is that my tongue gets badly burnt. My divine pride drinks the same hot water, nay, infinitely more in quantity, but it uses a spoon to drink with. So I suffer not. And this spoon is the spoon of Liberation, freed from the shackles of ignorance.

My human pride is afraid of saying and ashamed of doing many things. My divine pride is not afraid of saying or doing anything, for it knows that God is at once the Doer and the Action. It asks, "Whom am I to be afraid of? What am I to be ashamed of?"

My human pride crushes humanity with man-acquired power. My divine pride liberates humanity with God-given Power.

When I say that God is mine and I can use Him at my sweet will, I harbour my human pride. But when I say that I am God's, and my very existence is at His behest and at His Feet, I cherish divine pride.

To my human pride, the material world says, "We shall either succeed or we shall fail and perish." To my divine pride, the spiritual world says, "Together shall we endeavour, together shall we succeed."

* * *

TWO KILLERS

Lord, when You kill me
  With Your Love supreme,
I kill You with my undying ingratitude.

Lord, when You kill me
  With Your Power supreme,
I kill You with my hopeless helplessness.

Lord, when You kill me
  With Your Indifference supreme,
I kill You with my bleeding insecurity.

* * *

Our wild impatience destroys our spiritual growth. Unlike other trees, our patience-tree bears three kinds of fruit: inspiration, aspiration and realisation.

* * *

When you are bitter and irritable, just throw your bitterness and irritation into their source: ignorance; and then throw yourself into your Source: Light.

* * *

How to conquer anger? Feel the necessity of perfecting yourself. When anger wants to enter into you, say, "I am so sorry. I eat only one food. The name of my food is Peace. I won't be able to digest you. If ever I eat you, I will be destroyed within and without. I don't want to be destroyed. I have to do much for the divinity in me and the humanity around me. O anger, you are knocking at the wrong door."

* * *

How to conquer worry? Ignore it deliberately. To be sure, worry also has its own pride. It will ignore you totally. It will feel that it is beneath its dignity to come to you and offer all its problems and responsibilities.

* * *

WORRY

Worry! Worry!
Why do you worry?
Just pray in the morning,
   Concentrate at noon,
   Meditate in the evening,
   Contemplate at night.
   That's all!
Look, your worries are buried
   In oblivion-hush.

Worry! Worry!
Why do you worry?
Turn around;
Look, God is looking at you.
Enter into your mind;
Look, God is devotedly thinking of you.
Enter into your heart;
Look, God is all for you.
Enter into your soul;
Look, God has already done
Everything for you.

* * *

CURIOSITY

A curious man does not want the truth. He does not need the truth. He just wants to hear from others what the truth looks like. On very rare occasions, he may want to see the truth from a distance. But he is afraid of personally approaching the truth. He feels that the moment he approaches the truth, the volcanic power of the truth will destroy him, his earthly existence, which is nothing other than ignorance.

Curiosity commits two unpardonable sins. It kills our spontaneous love for light, the illumining light that transforms our life and enables us to realise the highest Truth. It also extinguishes our inner flame, which is a normal and natural fire. This inner flame we call aspiration. The higher this flame of aspiration rises, the sooner we reach the Shore of the Golden Beyond.

Curiosity is afraid of two things: the highest reality and divinity. When reality—that is to say, the transcendental Reality—looks at curiosity, curiosity immediately runs away, looking for an escape, a hiding place, for curiosity feels that in no time it will be exposed. When divinity looks at curiosity, curiosity, out of tremendous fear, curses divinity. It feels that a perfect stranger is entering into its very breath.

Curiosity has, however, two intimate friends: doubt and jealousy. Doubt feeds curiosity just at the moment when the divine Peace, Love, Bliss and Power of the spiritual Master want to help mankind unconditionally. Doubt feeds curiosity at that very moment. Jealousy makes curiosity feel that it is far inferior to the genuine seekers of the infinite Light. So jealousy does not permit curiosity to make friends with the spiritual seekers or to take spiritual help from them. Jealousy says, "If the spiritual seeker or Master is so great, then what of it? Let me remain in the meshes of ignorance. No harm." Here jealousy leads curiosity to remain where it already is.

Curiosity is not spirituality. But we cannot become

sincere overnight. If I am not sincere, I cannot become sincere in the twinkling of an eye. It is impossible. But if, out of curiosity, I want to see what is happening in the sincere spiritual seekers who feel that God is the only necessity, then I may try to act sincere myself, because I see something divine and fulfilling in them.

So if one goes to a sincere spiritual seeker or a spiritual Master out of curiosity, one may still see something which he has not seen before. I have some students or disciples who came to me with curiosity and very limited aspiration. I must say that I also have most sincere students and disciples. But I do not throw cold water on those who are right now not fortunate enough to have genuine aspiration. I tell them, "Don't worry. If you have come to me just out of curiosity, no harm. Mix with the sincere seekers. See what they are getting from their genuine spiritual life. And if you feel that their spiritual life has changed their nature or is giving them a new light and peace, giving them a new meaning to their life, then try to follow their example. Be one with them."

I have come across quite a few totally and exclusively curious human beings who have been transformed into serious, sincere seekers. Truth, either today or tomorrow, has to be realised, so if we do not have utmost sincerity right now, no harm. Sincerity grows, like everything else. Like a muscle, sincerity can be developed. If we do not have strong aspiration right now, no harm. We can develop aspiration, our inner cry.

To the many, many sincere seekers I say: run fast, faster, fastest towards your destined Goal. And to the curious seekers I say: do not stop with the achievement which is your curiosity. Please try to go one step further.

Then you will see today's curiosity transformed into tomorrow's sincerity, and in your sincerity you will see the inner cry, the mounting flame which we call aspiration.

Today's aspiration is tomorrow's realisation. This is the only truth, this is the only realisation that I can offer to you, dearest sisters and brothers, seekers of the infinite Truth. Start here and now.

* * *

When I was an animal, I evolved through selfishness. Now that I am a man, my evolution can be achieved only through self-sacrifice.

* * *

THE INNER VOICE, WILL AND FREEDOM

THE INNER VOICE

Conscience is the inner voice that offers to us this most important message: Love is building the palace of Truth.

* * *

Is there any way left for a man to be free? Certainly there is. The moment he feels his mind to be a thought of God, he can be at large like a bird in the sky; his life, however fleeting, is a breath of his Inner Pilot.

* * *

Question: Very often I may not recognise my inner self. I do not know whether the voice I hear is the inner voice or the outer voice, and this is extremely confusing.

Sri Chinmoy: I fully understand. But if you get a teacher who is a realised soul, you can go to him for help and find out if what you are doing is correct. Or if you do not get a spiritual teacher, please go deep, deep within and see if you get a voice or a thought or an idea. Then go deep into the voice or thought or idea and see if it gives you a feeling of inner joy or peace, where there are no questions or problems or doubts. When you get this kind of peace and inner joy, you can feel that the voice that you have heard is correct, that it is the real inner voice which will help you in your spiritual life.

To be true, pure, strong and brave, what we need is the inner voice. Our inner voice is the truth-power within; our outer voice is the money-power without. Man is not pure enough to see the truth-power operating in his outer world of desire and demand. Man is not fortunate enough to see the money-power operating in his inner world of aspiration and need. The truth-power used for humanity and the money-power used for divinity can and will change the face of the world. Truth-power will awaken and illumine the slumbering and unlit humanity. Money-power will serve and fulfil the yet unfulfilled divinity on earth.

The inner voice is the heart's wealth. When an aspirant uses this wealth, it soulfully smiles. When an unbeliever and disbeliever in God attempts to use this wealth, it is mercilessly suffocated.

The inner voice tells us to help the world only in accordance with God's express Will. If help is rendered otherwise, it is bound to turn into dire calamity later on. He is not only divinely liberal but also supremely blessed whose help to another is God-inspired and God-ordained.

To give, on second thought, a thing requested is to give once. To give a thing for the asking is to give twice. To give a thing unsought is to give thrice. To give a thing when God wants it to be given is to give the thing for good, along with one's own body and soul.

We shall never hear the song of the inner voice if we consciously or unconsciously make friends with anxiety. What is anxiety? Anxiety is the destructive breath of life's poverty.

There can be no greater choice or higher prize than to listen to the inner voice. If we willfully refuse to listen to the inner voice, our false gains will lead us to an inevitable loss. But if we listen soulfully to the inner voice, our true gains will not only protect us from imminent destruction but will also surprisingly hasten our realisation of the transcendental Truth.

An aspirant must realise that the inner voice is not a gift but an achievement. The more soulfully he strives for it, the sooner he unmistakably owns it.

Sincerity tells man he should be truly proud that he has the all-discerning inner voice. Humility tells man he should be supremely proud that the wrong-shunning, right-performing and good-fulfilling inner voice has him.

The inner voice is at once man's untiring guide and true friend. If a man goes deep within, the inner voice will tell him what to do. If he goes deeper, the inner voice will give him the capacity. If he goes still deeper, the inner voice will convince him that he is doing the right thing in the right way.

There is a word that is very sweet, pure and familiar to us. The word is conscience. Conscience is another name for the inner voice.

Conscience can live in two places: in the heart of truth and in the mouth of falsehood. When conscience strikes us once, we must think that it is showing us its unconditional love. When it strikes us twice, we must feel that it is showing us its unreserved concern. When it strikes us thrice, we must realise that it is offering us its boundless compassion to prevent us from diving deep into the sea of ignorance.

Conscience and passion need not contradict each other if man aspires to offer his heart's light to his passion and his heart's surrender to his conscience.

The inner voice is the temple within us. The inner voice is the deity within us. The inner voice is the divine duty within us. The inner voice is the supreme necessity within us.

God has commanded the inner voice to be the friend of aspiring souls and the judge of unaspiring souls.

The inner voice is not only constant constancy, but also perfect Perfection.

Question: Can we answer our own questions through our daily meditation?

Sri Chinmoy: Any question you have can be answered during your meditation or at the end of your meditation. If you go deep within, you are bound to get an answer. But when you get an answer, please try to determine whether it is coming from the soul, the heart or the mind. If it is coming from the heart or the soul, then you will get a sense of relief, a sense of peace. You will see that no contradictory thought is following the answer. But if the answer does not come from the heart or the soul, then the mind will come to the fore and contradict the idea you have received.

* * *

MY INNER PILOT DISCOURAGES ME

In the morning
   My Inner Pilot
Discourages me from bitter complaining.

In the afternoon
   My Inner Pilot
Discourages me from constant competing.

In the evening
   My Inner Pilot
Discourages me from useless brooding.

At night
   My Inner Pilot
Discourages me from fruitless dreaming.

* * *

Conscience and intuition are the inner experiences of the soul that try to protect and perfect our outer life.

* * *

COMPLETE TRANSFORMATION-CHANGE

There is only one serious danger,
And that danger is doubt.
My Inner Pilot warned me of that danger.

There is only one serious temptation,
And that temptation is supremacy.
My Inner Pilot warned me against this temptation.

There is only one dark death,
And that death is fear.
There is only one true life,
And that life is love:
Love of the soul for the body's
Complete transformation-change.

* * *

I DO THE IMPOSSIBLE, HOW?

I have decided what I want.
I shall listen to the voice within.
I believe
It is all-loving ,all-fulfilling.
I know
It is all-loving,all fulfilling
And it is exactly so.
My belief is my power;
My knowledge is my power.
I do the impossible because
My life of constant surrender
To the Will of the Supreme
Has taught me how.

* * *

WILL

WILL AND WILL POWER

Will is myself. Will is my Self. My will is absolutely God's and God's alone.

As my inner will is, in the world of realisation, so is my outer life, in the world of manifestation.

To my mind's doubt, nothing is real. To my heart's will, everything is real. To conquer my doubt is to grow into the breath of my will.

I am not afraid of my emotions and frustrations. My emotions and frustrations live in my God-surrendered will and will always rejoice in God's adamantine Will.

When my inner will energises my outer existence, all my imponderable troubles and excruciating pangs dissolve into thin air.

Doubt wants to blight my mind.
Fear wants to kill my heart.
Ignorance wants to veil my soul.

Aspiration wants to illumine my life.
Surrender wants to fulfil my life.
Will wants to immortalise my life.

* * *

My earthly will has always a beginning and an end.
My heavenly will has no beginning and no end. It has
always been and will always be the same. My will is
Eternity's abode of truth, built on the rock of God's
Vision-in-Reality and God's Reality-in-Vision.

* * *

What can will power do? Will power can remove all
our confusion—confusion in the physical, the vital, the
mind and the heart. How is it that everyone has not
realised God? Why are there very few spiritual Masters
and realised souls on earth? There is just one reason. It
is because of confusion in either the mind, the vital, the
physical or in our inner existence. The moment this veil
of confusion is removed, we see the golden Face of the
Supreme within us.

What else can our will power do? This will power,
which is the soul's light, can enter into reality sooner
than at once. We knock at the door of reality with our
sincerity, our purity, our aspiration, our dedication and
our devotion. We knock at the door of reality, but it
may take a few days or months before this door actually
opens for us. But when divine determination, divine will
power, knocks at the door of reality, immediately the

door opens wide. Why? Is reality afraid of man's determination? No! Reality opens its doors immediately to will power because it sees two things at once. It sees that will power has the capacity to embody reality, whereas other qualities may not have the necessary strength to immediately embody reality when it is thrust upon them. Reality also sees that when it wants to manifest itself on earth, it is human will power transformed into divine will power which takes up the challenge to help. Man's other divine qualities hesitate; when reality wants to manifest through them, they feel that the time is not ripe. They say, "We are preparing ourselves. Please give us a little more time." But when reality comes to will power, reality feels tremendous joy and delight because reality sees that human will power is ready to place it on its shoulders and carry it all around.

If God comes and stands right in front of us, with our purity we will say, "O God, I am most grateful that You have given me purity." With our humility we will say, "O God, I am most grateful that You have given me humility." With our peace we will say, "O God, I am most grateful that You have given me peace." We will offer gratitude, but we will still feel some hesitation about using these qualities. We will feel that perhaps we are not humble enough, perhaps we do not have enough peace. Instead, either outwardly or inwardly we should say, "O God, I have this quality; now You utilise me." But when we have will power we immediately say, "O God, You have given me purity, peace and other divine qualities. Now I am ready to serve You. Please tell me what I can do."

No matter how feeble our will power is in comparison to God's adamantine Will Power, human will power will say, "God , I am ready to fulfil You. Please tell me what I should do. I want to be Your instrument. I want to be Your dynamic hero and warrior. My power may be limited, but this limited quality I am ready to use. Do You want to sit on my shoulder? Then sit. Do You want me to run for You? Then I will run. If You want to bring me something to do, I will do it. On the way I may break my legs, but I will do my best for You." This determination, this will power, is never, never afraid of doing anything or saying anything. It knows that its strength comes forth from the soul, and the soul has God as its very own.

* * *

DETERMINATION AND WILL

If we want to develop determination, then we must think not of the lower, emotional vital, but of the dynamic, energetic vital. We must think of ourselves not as the aggressive vital, which most gladly enjoys depression and frustration, but as the vital that is full of determination. If the vital wants to achieve something by hook or by crook, then it is the undivine vital. But the undivine vital only destroys our possibilities and potentialities. By adopting foul means, by misusing our determination, we cannot get anything. But if the vital wants to work devotedly and with tremendous sincerity, that is to say, if it needs the truth and if it will not take rest until it achieves the truth, then that is the divine vital. The divine vital longs for everything positive. It needs Light. Without Light, it will not be fulfilled. It needs divine Power: the Power that builds, not the power that destroys. It needs divine Love: the love that expands, not the human love that ends in frustration.

Let us say that a child has started to study in primary school. He says, "I am determined to get my Master's degree; before that, I will not give up studying." If his determination is very sincere, then the child will one day reach his goal. Similarly, in the spiritual life if the vital makes the promise that it will bring down from above Peace, Light and Bliss in boundless measure, then eventually it is bound to bring down Peace, Light and Bliss.

But the determination of the vital is not enough; we also need the will of the soul. Determination ultimately comes from the soul. When we use this power on the physical, vital or mental plane—that is to say, on the outer plane—we call it determination. But when we use it on the inner or psychic plane, we call it will power, the light of the soul. 'Will power' is the spiritual term that we use for determination. When the light of the soul enters into the vital, we can have one-pointed determination. This one-pointed determination is divine determination, real will power.

In ordinary human life, when we are determined to do something, we maintain our determination for five minutes and then all our determination is gone. If we try to achieve determination on our own, it will not last. But once we know what the soul's will power is, we see that it lasts for many years, even for a lifetime.

Divine determination automatically comes if we meditate on the heart, on the heart's light. Each seeker can develop the capacity to bring light to the fore. If we meditate somewhere else rather than on the heart, our determination may fluctuate. Suppose we are determined to get up the next morning at five o'clock. Tomorrow we may get up at five o'clock with greatest difficulty. But the day after tomorrow, we simply forget to get out of bed. We have not made a determined promise and so we get up at eight o'clock or ten o'clock. Why? Because we have not charged our battery. If we get divine light from our soul during our meditation and if we sincerely pray to the soul to wake us up at five o'clock, then the soul will be pleased. Even if we go to bed at two o'clock in the morning, we will be able to get up at five o'clock. The soul will get us up. It is the soul that can take the responsibility to do what is necessary on our behalf. The seekers of Truth and Light will always try to have free access to the soul's will. If we make a conscious effort to identify with our soul's will and with the determination of our inner being, only then can our efforts have power.

* * *

GOD'S WILL AND MY WILL

When God's Will is my will, I have not to give up anything, for He is with everything and in everything. When I act contrary to God's Will, I injure my body, torture my life and encage my soul-bird. When I am in perfect slavery to venomous doubts, my will becomes empty of God's Will. When I am absolutely obedient to Truth's inevitability, I grow into God's adamantine Will. When I live the life of faith, God's Will transforms my earthly dreams into heavenly visions. When I live the life of proud self-assertion, God's Will forgets me, earth hates me and Heaven disowns me.

I encircle the Supreme in the arms of my utter helplessness. He encircles me in the arms of His all-sheltering Protection. I squander His Blessings and Compassion. He grows His Hope in me and feeds His Promise to me.

My will is the opening of my aspiring heart to the Supreme. I meditate on Him, not because I want Him to know that I meditate, but because I want to receive Him in an infinite measure. During my meditation, when I swim in the sea of love and devotion, He comes down to me. During my meditation, when the sun of wisdom and peace dawns within me, He lifts me up to Himself.

I silently pray. He secretly hears. My heart's mounting flame rises up and touches the Throne of His Compassion.

The Supreme never demands my belief in Him before He has given me evidence, infinitely more than necessary, upon which I can found my implicit faith. If I want to doubt Him, He has given me abundant opportunity to do so. Verily, here lies the magnanimity of His Compassion-Light for me.

My will and God's Will. When my will is approved by God's Will, my pure heart does not have an abiding inner bliss. But when my heart unreservedly and soulfully obeys God's Will and I accept it as my own will, infinite joy grows within my heart and eternal joy flows through my heart.

* * *

THY WISDOM

Thy Wisdom fills my heart.
Everything, everywhere,
Present, future, past
I am — and all I bear.

My rapture knows no bounds;
My sombre eyeless dole
Beyond the ken of all.
It is I who build my Goal.

My life's ignorance-dream
I drive toward Thy Will.
I alter now the course
Of my bosom's goalless rill.

* * *

A real aspirant is he who has consciously made his life a devoted channel for the inflow and outflow of God's Will.

* * *

To obey God's Will is to escape from one's self-created prison.

* * *

When I desire, impossibility frowns at me. When I aspire, possibility beckons me. When I will, I smash the pride of impossibility and transform possibility into inevitability.

* * *

The difference between thought and will is this: thought hesitantly considers; will instantly ventures.

* * *

There is only one way to get your emotions under control, and that way is to be the conscious expression of your express will power.

* * *

The human mind and the Will of the Supreme are perfect strangers to each other.

* * *

FREEDOM

I ESCAPED

    I escaped
From the Embrace of God.

    I escaped
From the sea of ignorance.

    I escaped
From the perdition of despair.

    I escaped
From the den of destruction.

      I know not why.
      I know not how.

And now I see,
   No escape, no escape.
   I am caught by my own
   Choice of freedom.

             * * *

OUTER FREEDOM AND INNER FREEDOM

The mother of freedom is light. The father of freedom is truth. The wife of freedom is peace. The son of freedom is courage. The daughter of freedom is faith.

Freedom rings where light shines. Freedom rings when truth sings. Freedom rings if peace expands. Freedom rings because courage demands. Freedom rings; hence faith blossoms.

Human freedom is an experience of the body, in the vital and for the mind. Divine freedom is an experience of the soul, in the heart and for the mind, the vital and the body. There is practically no difference between animal freedom and human slavery. In the domain of the destructive vital, our animal freedom roars. In the abyss of our sleeping, inconscient body, our human slavery snores.

God's Freedom lies in His constant service to mankind, in His unconditional Self-giving. Man's freedom lies in his God-achievement, life-perfection and life-fulfilment.

The freedom of the doubting mind is undoubtedly a reality. But this reality is fleeting, flimsy. The freedom of the loving and aspiring heart is an everlasting reality and an ultimate sublimity.

Freedom of earthly thought is good, but quite often it opens itself to false freedom. Freedom that comes from following the heavenly Will invokes God's Presence in us. It invokes His divine Promise in and through us and His supreme Self-assertion and Self-manifestation in and through us.

What is false freedom? False freedom is our constant and deliberate acceptance of ignorance and our conscious existence in ignorance. What is real freedom?

Real freedom is our conscious awareness of our inner divinity and our constant inseparable oneness with our Inner Pilot.

What can false freedom do? False freedom can do much. It can totally destroy us. It can destroy our inner possibilities and potentialities. It can destroy our inner wealth. What can real freedom do? Real freedom also can do much. Real freedom can make us grow into the very image of our Supreme Pilot.

Forgetfulness takes away our freedom, but God's Forgiveness brings it back. Teeming desires take away our freedom, but God's Compassion brings it back. Self-importance, self-assertion take away our freedom, but God's Light brings it back.

It is our self-awareness that retains our freedom, and God's divine Pride in us that perfects our freedom. In the perfection of our earthly freedom we grow, we sow the Heaven-seed within us. And in the fulfilment of our inner freedom we see Heaven and earth as complementary souls, for earth offers its wealth and capacity, which is receptivity, and Heaven offers its wealth and capacity, which is Divinity and Immortality.

True freedom does not lie in speaking ill of the world, or in speaking ill of an individual or individuals. Again, true freedom does not lie in merely appreciating and admiring the world or humanity at large. True freedom lies only in our inseparable oneness with the world's inner cry and its outer smile. The world's inner cry is God the Realisation. The world's outer smile is God the Manifestation.

Freedom is expressive. This is what the body tells me.
Freedom is explosive. This is what the vital tells me.
Freedom is expensive. This is what the mind tells me.

Freedom is illumining. This is what the heart tells me.
Freedom is fulfilling. This is what the soul tells me.

We have two types of freedom: outer freedom and inner freedom. Outer freedom constantly wants to prove its capacity. It wants to prove its sovereignty. Inner freedom wants to prove that it belongs to God and God alone.

Outer freedom has a new goal every day. It wants to discover this goal only in pleasure. But inner freedom has only one eternal Goal, and that Goal is to achieve the conscious awareness of God and the conscious manifestation of God in and through itself.

Outer freedom is satisfied only when it is in a position to say, "I have no superiors. I am my only master." Inner freedom is satisfied only when it can soulfully say, "I don't want to be superior to anyone, but I want God to be my superior, my only superior."

The inner freedom is to see what we should. The inner freedom is to be what we must. What we should see is the golden face of Truth. What we must be is the flowing Life of God's Vision and the glowing Breath of God's Reality.

We fight for the outer freedom. We cry for the inner freedom. With the outer freedom we see and rule the four corners of the globe. With the inner freedom we see the Soul and become the Goal of the entire universe.

My outer freedom is my self-imposed and self-aggrandised obligation. My inner freedom is the birthright of my eternal aspiration and my endless realisation.

The paramount question is whether or not my inner freedom and my outer freedom can run abreast. Certainly they can. Certainly they must. My inner freedom knows what it has and what it is: realisation.

My outer freedom must know what it wants and what it needs: transformation.

When the freedom of my life without is soulfully and unreservedly transformed, it immediately becomes the mightiest might and the highest pride of the freedom of my life within.

My outer freedom is my life-boat. My inner freedom is my life-sea. My God is my Supreme Pilot. Today I am my journey's searching and crying soul. Tomorrow I shall be my journey's illumining and fulfilling goal.

My soul of freedom is my God's compassionate and constant necessity. My goal of freedom is my God's smiling and dancing transcendental assurance everlastingly fulfilled.

* * *

GO AND ASK

Father, what is sin?
"Daughter, I really do not know.
Go and ask a Christian mind."

Father, what is salvation?
"Daughter, I really do not know.
Go and ask a Christian soul."

Father, what is bondage?
"Daughter, I really do not know.
Go and ask a Hindu mind."

Father, what is liberation?
"Daughter, I really do not know.
Go and ask a Hindu soul."

* * *

GOD IS STILL MY BOSS

Darkness, you want me
   To help you.
      Therefore
You have come to me.
      Alas,
You have more freedom
   Than I have;
I have no freedom at all.
God is still my boss.

Ignorance, you want me
   To serve you.
      Therefore
You have come to me.
      Alas,
I tell you my only secret:
I have no freedom at all.
God is still my boss.

* * *

Question: Is there any spiritual significance to the energy crises, wars and other problems the world is having now?

Sri Chinmoy: The divine forces are trying to bring Light into the world, but right now the world is run by the undivine forces. There is a great difference between the Supreme's approval, the Supreme's sanction and the

Supreme's tolerance. The Supreme has created us and He has given us very limited freedom. Right now we are using that freedom in a very undivine way. We are all acting like mad elephants, and He is just tolerating us. The Supreme does not want us to behave this way; He does not want hostility, conflicts, fighting and quarreling between nations, but He has given us limited freedom, and we are doing these things. But a day will come when the Supreme will not tolerate them.

There is no spiritual significance in the world upheaval in the sense that from this something very spiritual, divine or magnificent will come about. It is we who are creating that kind of suffering. On rare occasions, suffering helps us in purifying our life. But the present problems are being created by undeveloped, obscure, impure people. We are suffering and we shall suffer more because of our own ignorance.

* * *

SPIRITUALITY

THE SPIRITUAL LIFE

What is spirituality? It is the common language of man and God. Here on earth we have hundreds and thousands of languages to allow one person to understand another; but when it is a matter of God and man, there is only one language, and that language is spirituality. If one follows the path of spirituality, one can easily speak to God face to face.

* * *

Question: Could you explain what inner hunger is?

Sri Chinmoy: If you are dissatisfied or frustrated, if you feel that you have not achieved something that you wanted to achieve, this does not necessarily mean that you have inner hunger. But suppose you feel that within you there is something vast, something luminous, something fulfilling, something positive, which you don't have right now. You think that inside you there is peace, but you do not have access to it. If you think that you have something inside you that is divine, and that you need this very thing, that means that aspiration is there. Hunger comes from your spiritual need. If you need something and you know where that thing exists, then you will try to get it. When you have this hunger, the next thing is to satisfy it.

If you enter into the spiritual life because of frustration, dissatisfaction or despair, you may not remain in the spiritual life. Today you are dissatisfied with someone or something, and tomorrow you will say, "No, let me try it again. Perhaps this time I will get satisfaction." You have failed and that is why you are dissatisfied, but tomorrow you may try again in a human way. But after a while, you will see that only dissatisfaction and frustration come from desire. If you do not fulfil your desire, you are disappointed. Or even if you get the thing you wanted, still you will not be satisfied. In desire-life there is no satisfaction.

Then finally you say, "No, I am not going to desire anything in a human way. I came from the Vast and I just want to enter into the infinite Vast." This is aspiration. When you aspire, you try to enter into the vast ocean of Peace, Light and Bliss. But when you desire, you try only to possess the object of your desire. When you aspire, you just jump into the reality and feel that reality as yours.

When God is asked for some material object, only God knows whether He will give it or not, because only God knows whether it is something that the person really needs. If a person gets the thing he is crying for, it may only increase his desire. Again, if he does not get it, he will be frustrated and displeased with God. But God has to decide whether it is best that he get the thing or not.

In your case, since you are a sincere seeker, if you pray to God or meditate on God for Peace, Light or Bliss, even if He does not grant it to you the way you want, you will still be satisfied, for you will still have inner joy and inner peace. You will simply say, "He knows best. Perhaps I am not ready. That is why He is not giving me what I asked for. But He will give it to me the day I am ready." In the life of aspiration it is not actually your achievement that gives you satisfaction. It is your aspiration. The aspiration itself is your satisfaction.

In the spiritual life we do not progress by hook or by crook. Spirituality cannot be achieved by pulling or by pushing; it is something spontaneous. I cannot thrust the spiritual life upon you and I cannot take your spiritual life or inner cry from you. But if you have something spiritual in you, I can inspire you. If you have one spiritual coin, then through my inspiration you can get millions of spiritual dollars. But to start with you have to have a little flame.

There are many who are fast asleep. For them spirituality is out of the question. No matter how sincerely we try, we cannot awaken them. You are on a spiritual path; that means that you are already up and awake. But if you try to pull down spiritual Light, you are making a mistake. Only when this Light comes on its own, when on the strength of your aspiration you bring it, can you receive it. Otherwise, when the Light descends, if you don't have enough receptivity, the vessel will only break.

How can you receive this Light from above? For that you need constant practice. If you practise daily, without fail you will expand your consciousness. An unaspiring person has a consciousness which is earth-bound; it does not expand at all. But when you aspire, your consciousness expands and your receptivity increases. So if you pray or meditate, then you can easily hold the Light and Peace that descends.

Question: I am looking for more joy in my life, but I don't feel confident about jumping into meditation to get it.

Sri Chinmoy: When life is not giving you joy but you feel that you want joy, that means you are hungry. In the spiritual life, when you are hungry, you will eat spiritual food. When you are not hungry, you will not eat. For fifteen or twenty years you did not sincerely and intensely care for the spiritual life. Since you have not meditated intensely for so many years, if you jump all at once into the sea of spirituality you won't be able to swim. You cannot change your nature overnight. It has to be done slowly, steadily, gradually. First move around in the water; then gradually you will learn how to swim. Then there will come a time when you will be able to swim well. But since you have inner hunger, that means you are ready to start swimming.

Question: When you spoke of the need to transcend the past, you said that the world is continually evolving. Could you say more about this?

Sri Chinmoy: Each person has to know and feel how much he has progressed. When he accepts the spiritual life and walks along the path of spirituality, he is bound to see inner progress. In the inner world he achieves Peace, Light and Bliss; but in the outer world his nature is still imperfect. It takes time to manifest these divine qualities in one's outer behaviour. If we look only at the outer activities, we will be disappointed. But if we go deep within, we will see how much Peace, Light and Bliss this person has already achieved. In the course of time, he will be able to manifest what he has inside himself. What we have within, we are bound to manifest either tomorrow or the day after.

Question: What happens if, after practising spirituality for a while, you decide you want to take a rest and then continue your journey at a later time?

Sri Chinmoy: In the ordinary life, after you have covered one mile you can remain where you are for a while and take rest before continuing on your journey. But in the spiritual life it is not like that. In the spiritual life, once you take rest, doubt enters into you, fear enters into you, suspicion enters into you. All kinds of negative forces enter into you and destroy all your possibilities. Your potentiality remains the same; eventually you will realise God. But the possibilities that you once had, the golden possibilities, you have lost. If you stop meditating and leave the spiritual life, the progress that you have made will be destroyed. People will not receive a good vibration from you; nobody will get inspiration from you; you won't be able to give your soul's smile. You will fall back into your old ways and be lost to ignorance.

However, the essence of the progress that you made will remain inside the soul. The essence is never lost, even though in your outer life you cannot use it. The quintessence of the progress that you made will remain inside your heart, and after five or ten years, when you want to meditate again, or in your next incarnation, this quintessence will come to the fore. If you pray to God most sincerely to enter into the spiritual life again, your previous progress will loom large in your life.

So always be on the alert and run as fast as you can toward your Goal. Do not stop until the race is won; otherwise, the pull of ignorance will take you back again to the place from which you started.

Question: Sometimes people say that the dream is always better than the reality and that the search for something is better than the actual achievement of that thing, because when the goal is reached there is no place else to go. Does this also apply to the spiritual life?

Sri Chinmoy: In the spiritual life we have to know that there is no end to our journey, because God is not and cannot be satisfied with any particular standard. Today's dream will transform itself into tomorrow's reality. But again, tomorrow's reality will be meaningless in comparison with the reality we are aiming at the following day. There is no end to our reality, because we have the infinite Divine within us constantly. It is our goal to change the face of reality from bright, to brighter, to brightest and from high, to higher, to highest. Even in the highest, the reality has to go beyond, beyond, beyond, because God does not, cannot and will not ever accept any end to His creation. Creation is His progress, His own movement; and God wants endless progress in infinite ways.

Question: I often find that in the spiritual life I go up and down. I always hope that I will not fall down again, but it happens constantly.

Sri Chinmoy: In the beginning everybody experiences ups and downs in the spiritual life. When a child is learning to walk, in the beginning he stumbles and falls again and again and again. But after a while he learns to walk properly, and finally to run. Eventually he can run as fast as his capacity will allow. But a small child cannot expect to run as fast as his father does, because his father has much more capacity.

You experience ups and downs. When you are up, you have to feel that you are getting a glimpse of your eventual capacity. When you are down, you should simply feel that this is only a temporary incapacity. Just because you see that those who are more advanced than you in the spiritual life are running, you must not be discouraged. Once upon a time they also stumbled.

Right now the sky may be full of clouds, but a day will come when the sun will shine again with its full effulgence. When you experience low moments of fear, of doubt, of lack of aspiration, you should feel that this won't last forever. Like a child who has fallen, you must try to stand up again. Some day you will be able to walk, then run, and finally run the fastest without falling.

Question: Now that I have entered into the spiritual life, I have more problems with desires. Is the Supreme giving me these extra desires to strengthen me?

Sri Chinmoy: When we have entered into the life of aspiration and spirituality, the Supreme will not bring extra desires and impurities into our mind or life. It is He who has given us aspiration, so why should He give us desire, which is directly opposite to aspiration? No. He will not deliberately impede our progress in this way. These desires seem suddenly to appear, but they are not really new to us. They existed before in our life, but we did not notice them so much because our life was totally enveloped in myriad desires.

Before we entered the spiritual life we were all unconscious; the tiger in us was sleeping. But when the tiger sees that we are trying to leave its domain it says, "Where are you going? What right have you to leave me? I will devour you before you leave me." As long as the desire-tiger is confident that we will stay with it all the time, it does not feel the necessity to threaten or frighten us. But when we start trying to come out of our bondage-cage, the ignorance-tiger tries to prevent us. It attacks us most vehemently with doubts and other undivine forces as soon as it feels that we are threatening to leave it.

While we are in the ordinary life there is no intensity. Today we have one desire, tomorrow four and the next day ten or twenty. But we are rarely intense even in trying to achieve and fulfil our own desires. Our desires are mere wishes. We do not have the capacity or the willingness to work to fulfil them. We want to be rich or famous or great or brilliant or beautiful, but far from working to achieve these desires, we will not even pray sincerely for their fulfilment.

When a seeker enters into the spiritual path, if he has not wholeheartedly accepted it, or if he is not far advanced, then during his meditation the same desires may come forward. He will begin to think, "This person is very rich, this person is very beautiful, this person has some good qualities which I do not have." While he is praying for Peace, Light and Bliss, one part of his being may be consciously and deliberately cherishing the desire to become a multimillionaire. At that time, the intensity of the seeker's meditation meets with these earthly desires. Then what happens? The intensity enters into the desires and makes them much stronger than they previously were.

It is through the unillumined mind that desires try to approach us even after we have entered into the life of aspiration. The best thing we can do is never to allow any impurity in the form of desire, doubt, anxiety, jealousy or any unaspiring thoughts to enter our minds during meditation. If a desire comes to us while we are not meditating, it is not good to cherish it; but it is infinitely worse to cherish it during meditation. If we cherish desire or any impure thought during meditation, then we are simply strengthening the power of the negative forces and making our own spiritual journey more difficult.

When desires come into our life of aspiration, we must not be afraid of them. We must take them as hurdles. It is true that if there are no obstacles or impediments in our way, we will run faster. But if there are impediments, each time we cross one hurdle we get additional strength and encouragement to try to cross another one. If we have no hurdles, we are fortunate. But if we do have some because of our long association with ignorance, we should feel confident that we will be able to transcend them because we have aspiration, the inner impetus to pass all obstacles and reach the Goal.

If we go deep within, we *can* see each difficulty as a boon. Formerly we were alone with our difficulties. Now we have become conscious aspirants, so God's Grace has entered into our lives. God's Grace is constantly helping the seeker. It stands between the difficulty and the seeker. If one sees millions of difficulties when he sincerely enters into the spiritual life, then he can see them also as millions of blessings, because God's Grace is in them, illumining them. The sooner difficulties appear before us the better, because then we can surmount them right away. We should not be ungrateful to God, nor should we curse our fate when difficulties appear. We should be grateful that God has brought out all our impurities to be illumined and transcended as soon as possible. We have to face and conquer our enemies either today or tomorrow. By making ourselves worthy of God's Compassion and Grace, we will easily be able to overcome our difficulties.

Question: How can I win the battle that is going on inside me between the light and the darkness?

Sri Chinmoy: In our inner existence we are constantly fighting with truth and falsehood. Many times it happens that, in spite of knowing the truth, we do not follow the truth, because we feel that it would be extremely difficult, while something which is not true may be more convenient to our current outer needs. At that time, we make the greatest blunder.

If we take falsehood as our very own, what happens? Truth remains silent. But if we are eager to follow the truth, then falsehood comes and strikes us, insults us, discourages us. At the same time, truth is not extremely eager to claim us because it has seen how many times we have touched its feet and promised that we would listen to it, but time and again this has been all idle talk. We say that we will follow the path of truth, but the next moment we go and listen to falsehood because we get more pleasure there. Truth has heard our false promises hundreds and thousands of times.

When we really do try to fulfil the promise that we made to truth, we may feel falsehood pulling at our mind. "Where are you going?" it says. "You promised me that you would always remain with me." But if the day comes when truth sees that we are absolutely sincere, at that time it fights most powerfully against falsehood. And if we become totally one with truth, we will see that all the dark forces inside us and around us have no choice but to surrender.

Again, some people cry for light sincerely, but without satisfactory results, simply because God's destined Hour has not yet arrived. If a farmer feels that on the very day he starts working to cultivate his land he should get a bumper crop, he will get disgusted and abandon the field when he sees no result after a few weeks of sincere effort. Although sincerity is important, time is still a great factor. The field can only produce satisfactory fruit at God's own time. Our timing and God's timing need not be, and very often are not, the same. If we are one hundred percent surrendered, we will feel that if we are not getting satisfactory results, we will wait forever for God's Hour. But if we are not surrendered, we will not accept God's Will. We will become depressed and disheartened and give up the battle, and we will certainly be the losers.

What we need is light. But if light does not come, we must be ready to wait an Eternity for infinite Light to surcharge our inner and outer being. Then falsehood will immediately feel that we are ready to wait for millions of years in order to bathe in the sea of Light, and it will lose its interest in us. If God wants to, He can give us what we want at once, but if He feels that this is not the appropriate time, we have to wait. Then, if we have patience, which itself is the extension of light or of consciousness, we can feel that we are increasing the light that we have and the light that is entering into us.

Question: I'm not as receptive as I would like to be. Why is this?

Sri Chinmoy: Our receptivity is lessened by the hostile forces that attack us. They can attack us just because our consecration to the Supreme is not yet complete. Sometimes the aspirant's mind revolts, sometimes the vital revolts and sometimes the physical or even the subtle physical revolts. If there is any such opening, the hostile forces can attack us.

There is also another reason why we are not receptive. Until we are really sure of what we actually want, the life of desire or the life of aspiration, then the hostile forces will stand between our desire and our aspiration. Aspiration brings us to the goal, to the reality, but desire immediately makes friends with our enemies. Hostile forces are always on the alert; they try to divide us. They want to separate us from our aspiration. Then what do they do? They bring in desire and try to kill aspiration. Very often they succeed. But a spiritually alert person will take aspiration and enter into desire in order to transform it. If desire enters into aspiration, aspiration is ruined. If aspiration enters into desire, the desire is transformed.

In your case, if you become a victim of hostile attacks, these attacks come primarily for two reasons. The first reason is that your physical is mercilessly revolting against the heart's psychic aspiration. You can't get rid of all your undivine and negative qualities permanently because you are unconsciously cherishing negative thoughts. You still feel that these qualities are fulfilling for your outer life, your vital life. Your inner aspiration is running much faster than your physical capacity or urge. The physical is constantly playing the part of a robber. The soul is gaining something for you and the physical is robbing you and squandering it. You get the light from the soul and throw it all around. The physical gets light but does not utilise it for its own illumination.

The second reason for these attacks in your case is uncertainty. Whether you are aware of it or not, you are afraid of the Infinite. On the one hand, you want to dive into the sea of Infinity. On the other hand, you have a feeling of uncertainty. You wonder what you are going to get from the sea of Infinity. You have to know that you are going to get the infinite wealth of the immortal Consciousness which pervades the entire universe. Your soul wants it, but your physical mind is afraid. So long as there is fear, even an iota of fear, in you, the hostile forces have the power to attack you mercilessly. If there is no integral acceptance or aware-ness of one's own real goal, then the hostile forces are bound to torture one. But if you do not have fear and if you are sure of your goal, then the hostile forces can never attack you. If you can accept Infinity as something which is your own but which you have forgotten about, if you can see that you have always been that Infinity, then fear does not come.

* * *

HIS CORRECTION
AND HIS MANIFESTATION

He corrects
His countless shortcomings
  By thinking of God's Perfection.

He manifests
God's Transcendental Perfection
  By becoming the Soul of God's Aspiration.

* * *

YOGA

Question: What is actually meant by Yoga?

Sri Chinmoy: Yoga means union, union with God. Yoga tells us that we have a divine quality called aspiration within us and that God has a divine quality called Compassion. Yoga is the common link between our aspiration and God's Compassion.

Question: Can anybody practise Yoga?

Sri Chinmoy: Yes, anybody can practise Yoga and it can be practised irrespective of age. But we must understand what Yoga really involves. Unfortunately, in the West there are many people who think that Yoga means physical postures and breathing exercises. This is a deplorable mistake. These postures and exercises are preliminary and preparatory states leading toward concentration and meditation, which alone can take us to a deeper, higher and fuller life.

Yoga is not something unnatural, abnormal or unearthly. It is something practical, natural and spontaneous. Right now, we do not know where God is and what God looks like. But by practising Yoga, we can see Him at first hand. As in the material world, we achieve success in our chosen activity by constant practice, so also in the spiritual world, by practising Yoga, we achieve the goal of goals — God-realisation.

Question: Can Yoga help us in our everyday life?

Sri Chinmoy: Certainly. Yoga helps us in our everyday life. As a matter of fact, it is Yoga that can serve as the supreme help in our daily lives. Our human life is full of doubt, fear and frustration. Yoga helps us to replace fear with indomitable courage, doubt with absolute certainty and frustration with golden achievement.

Question: Do Yoga and meditation require the renunciation of all religions?

Sri Chinmoy: Meditation does not interfere with any religion. Religion does not have anything to say against meditation because true religion is the realisation of God. Among my disciples there are Catholics, Protestants and Jews. The real aspirant who has launched into spirituality and Yoga will find no difficulty in remaining in his own religion. I do not tell my disciples to give up their own religion. True Yoga will not demand the renunciation of any religion. If the disciples remain in their own religion and practise the spiritual life, they will be able to run as fast as possible toward the Goal. Their own religion will give them constant confidence in what they are doing.

In the physical manifestation, each religion is like a house. You have to stay in a house; you cannot stay in the street, for the world may not need or welcome you. But a time comes when your consciousness expands and the whole world becomes your house. At that time, you cannot be bound by the limitations of any one particular house. You accept all religions and, at the same time, you go beyond the domain of religion and achieve conscious oneness with God. Each religion is like a river, but when the river enters into the ocean it has played its part. At that time, the river feels that it has become the ocean itself; it has become one with the source. So religion is like a river and God-realisation is the ocean.

If you follow religion, I wish to say that you are on the road to your destination. But if you want to reach the highest ultimate Truth, then you have to concentrate, meditate and contemplate. That does not mean that you will not go to church or synagogue any more. No! But you have to feel that you have got the inner call deep within your heart to run fast, faster, fastest towards your Goal. And that means that you have to practise the inner life, the life of self-discipline and meditation.

Now, when you practise Yoga, if you want to give up your religion, no harm. For your goal is to realise God, who embodies all religions and, at the same time, is far above them. Yoga embraces all religions and goes beyond them. Yoga aims at conscious oneness with God. When you are one with God, you are one with everything. So the seekers of the infinite Light and Truth can, if they want, go beyond religious barriers. If they want to get some glimpses of light, truth, peace and bliss, then they can stay in their religion. But if they want the highest Truth, God-realisation, then they have to consciously transcend religion.

* * *

In Yoga breathes Self-realisation. Self-realisation embodies Self-perfection. Self-perfection is followed by the absolute manifestation of God.

* * *

True Yoga and life go together. If you want to separate them, you will fail. Yoga and life are as inseparable as the Creator and His creation.

* * *

Yoga guides life for the experience of existence. You may call this a theoretical experience. Yoga guides life toward the fulfilment of existence. This you must call a practical experience.

* * *

ASPIRATION

ASPIRATION-FLAME

God had a glowing dream. The name of that dream was aspiration. Man has a climbing cry. The name of this cry is also aspiration. God was originally one. With His Aspiration, God wanted to become many. He wanted to divinely enjoy and supremely fulfil Himself in and through an infinite number of forms.

Man is many. With his aspiration, man the dividing and divided consciousness, man the obscure mind, man the unfulfilled being, wants to become one with the world-consciousness, the world-life and the world-soul. He unmistakably and soulfully feels that this is the secret and sacred way to feel the deepest depth of Reality and the highest height of Truth.

Aspiration is the inner flame. Unlike other flames, this flame does not burn anything. It purifies, illumines and transforms our life. When purification takes place in our lower nature, we hope to see the Face of God. When illumination dawns in our outer nature, we feel that God is near and dear, that He is all-pervading and all-loving. When our nature, both lower and outer, grows into the Transformation-Flame, we shall realise the truth that God Himself is the inmost Pilot, brightest journey and highest Goal.

Some people are under the impression that desire and aspiration are the same thing. Unfortunately, or rather fortunately, that is not true. They are two totally different things. The difference between desire and aspiration is very simple and clear. Desire wants to bind and devour the world. Aspiration wishes to free and feed the world. Desire is the outgoing energy. Aspiration is the inflowing light. Desire says to man, "Possess everything. You will be happy." Poor man, when he wants to possess just one single thing, he sees that he has already been mercilessly caught and possessed by everything in God's creation. Aspiration says to man, "Realise only one thing, and that thing is God. You will be happy." Fortunate and blessed man: on his way upward and inward, long before he sees God, he feels sublime peace in his inner life and radiating joy in his outer life. Then he feels that the realisation of the supreme Beyond can no longer remain a far cry.

Aspiration has, not one, but three genuine friends: yesterday, today and tomorrow. Yesterday offered its inspiration-flight to aspiration. Today offers its dedication-might to aspiration. Tomorrow will offer its realisation-delight to aspiration.

Aspiration is our inner urge to transcend both the experience and the realisation already achieved. This is absolutely necessary because God the Infinite is constantly transcending His own Infinity, God the Eternal is constantly transcending His own Eternity and God the Immortal is constantly transcending His own Immortality.

The childhood of aspiration wants to realise the Supreme in an earthly and individual way. The adolescence of aspiration wants to realise the Supreme in a divine and glorious way. The adulthood of aspiration wants to realise the Supreme in the Supreme's own way.

Aspiration is realisation. Aspiration is revelation. Aspiration is manifestation. Aspiration is realisation if and when the aspirant needs God-realisation and God-realisation alone. Aspiration is revelation if and when the aspirant feels that God-revelation is absolutely for God's sake. Aspiration is manifestation if and when the aspirant feels that God-manifestation is his birthright.

Aspiration can be developed. It is like crossing a street, one step at a time. Each time we aspire, we perform in the very depth of our consciousness a miracle of welcoming the Beyond.

Life has an inner door. Aspiration opens it. Desire closes it. Aspiration opens the door from within. Desire closes it from without.

Life has an inner lamp. This inner lamp is called aspiration. And when we keep our aspiration burning, it will, without fail, transmit to God's entire creation its effulgent glow.

* * *

Question: What do you mean when you say that the unaspiring man's Eternity is uncertain?

Sri Chinmoy: An unaspiring man is not sure of anything. He is at the mercy of all his whims. At this moment something may make him feel that he is absolutely useless and hopeless. At the next moment his ego will come forward and he will feel that he is everything, that he is the Lord of the universe. Nothing is certain for the unaspiring man, even his own life. He lives in constant fear. He may feel that while he is sleeping somebody will come and kill him. An unaspiring man will never feel certain that there is a tomorrow, since he does not feel Eternity's flow. For him, tomorrow does not exist, not to speak of Eternity.

But for an aspiring man, Eternity is certain because he knows and feels that he is in the flow of Eternity. He is the river which is entering into the ocean. For an aspiring man nothing is uncertain. He knows that inside him he has everything. Right now he is like a child. His Father cannot give him millions of dollars because, since he is only a child, he will misuse it. He knows that he can use at this time only a dime or a quarter. But he is certain that when he grows up his Father will give him all His Wealth: infinite Peace, Light and Bliss. He is certain he will get all of this.

* * *

Desire is a wild fire that burns and burns and finally consumes us. Aspiration is a glowing fire that secretly and sacredly uplifts our consciousness and finally liberates us.

Thirst for the Highest is aspiration. Thirst for the lowest is annihilation.

Desire is expectation. No expectation, no frustration. Desire killed, true happiness built. Aspiration is surrender, and surrender is man's conscious oneness with God's Will.

* * *

Desire means anxiety. This anxiety finds satisfaction only when it is able to fulfil itself through solid attachment. Aspiration means calmness. This calmness finds satisfaction only when it is able to express itself through all-seeing and all-loving detachment.

In desire and nowhere else abides human passion. Human passion has a dire foe called judgement, the judgement of the divine dispensation.

In aspiration and nowhere else dwells man's salvation. Man's salvation has an eternal friend called Grace, God's all-fulfilling Grace.

Desire is temptation. Temptation nourished, true happiness starved. Aspiration is the soul's awakening. The soul's awakening is the birth of supernal delight.

* * *

Question: How can I separate myself from my physical desires?

Sri Chinmoy: First of all, since you have accepted the spiritual life, you have to ask yourself whether desire satisfies and fulfils you or not. In your inner being you will feel that it neither satisfies nor fulfils you. Before you actually desire, you have in mind the object or fruit of your desire, and you think that when you attain that object, you will be happy. Unfortunately, what you eventually get is frustration. When you enter into the physical or lower vital desire with your mind, you are caught. You enter into the very jaws of a devouring tiger. When you concentrate on desire, you can feel inwardly that in the beginning there is no light, in the end there is no light and in the middle there is no light. There is only darkness from the beginning to the end and darkness means the absence of divine satisfaction. If you can feel this result before you actually desire, then you can easily turn your life away from desire.

You have to feel that what you want is aspiration and not desire. The moment one begins to aspire he feels true satisfaction. This true satisfaction comes because aspiration has the capacity to identify itself consciously and soulfully with the farthest corner of the globe, with the deepest and inmost being and with the highest transcendental Self. If you feel the real necessity of aspiration, you will see that physical, vital and mental desires will stop knocking at your heart's door.

At every moment you have to aim at your goal. If you want to concentrate and meditate on the sun as it rises early in the morning, then you have to face the east, and not some other direction. If you are looking toward the west and running toward the east, you will stumble. If you want to be certain of your goal of God-realisation, then you will not look behind you or around you, but only toward the light. You can conquer your physical desires only by running toward the light. Don't think of your physical desires, but think only of your aspiration. If you can run forward with one-pointed determination, limitations and desires will fade away from your life. Aspiration is the only answer. For outer things you cry; for inner things you can also cry. If you can cry sincerely, you can fly spiritually.

> When I think, I sink.
> When I choose, I lose.
> When I cry, I fly.

* * *

We have to have the inner cry, and this inner cry has to be the cry of a child. The child cries for his mother. The mother comes running toward the child, no matter where she is. The child may be in the living room or the kitchen, but the mother comes running to feed the child. Similarly, when we have the inner cry, spontaneous cry for Light and Truth, God out of His Infinite Bounty will show us the Light, and in that Light we will grow.

* * *

ASPIRATION-CRY

Aspiration is a cry within our heart. As a child cries, so also in the heart you will feel a cry. A child is within you, shedding tears. He is weeping because he wants to transcend himself. This mounting cry, this climbing cry inside our heart we call aspiration. When we aspire with our heart's tears, we see that God is coming down to us from above. The heart is crying and yearning like a mounting flame burning upward. This flame of the heart wants to go up beyond the mind, so it is always rising. And God is constantly descending with His Grace, like a river flowing downward. Ours is the flame which always burns upward; God's Grace, like a stream, is coming down from the Source. It is just like two persons meeting; one is on the first floor and the other is on the third floor. So what happens? We go up to the second floor and God comes down to the second floor. There we meet and fulfil each other. When aspiration and Grace meet together, we come to experience the divine fulfilment of union with God.

With aspiration we begin our journey, and with aspiration we continue our journey. Since there is no end to our journey, and since God is infinite, eternal and immortal, our aspiration will constantly flow toward God's Infinity, Eternity and Immortality. Aspiration is the endless road that leads eternally toward the ever-transcending Beyond.

* * *

When an unaspiring man looks upward, he feels that his life is obscure. When he looks forward, he feels that his life is immature. When he looks backward, he feels that his life is premature. And finally, when he looks inward, he sees that his life is a giant failure.

When an aspiring man looks upward, he feels that his life is protection and salvation. When he looks forward, he feels that his life is determination and realisation. When he looks backward, he feels that his life is imperfection and frustration. When he looks inward, he feels that his life is illumination and perfection.

* * *

DESIRE AND ASPIRATION

Some human beings progress very, very slowly in their spiritual life because they have no aspiration. But there are people who not only have no aspiration but also have no desire either for themselves, for humanity or for God. Those people are in the most deplorable situation. God says to them, "Something is better than nothing. It is better for you to have some desires and get some temporary satisfaction from the life of desire than to live in the stone-consciousness, wallowing in the pleasures of idleness and making no progress at all. Then, when you see that you get nothing but frustration from the fulfilment of desire, you will begin to aspire."

There are elderly people who are like this—they have practically no desires but, at the same time, they have no aspiration either. They know that they are approaching death, but that does not inspire them either to cry for fulfilment of their desires or to pray or meditate on God. They do not even have any particular desire to live.

But there are also highly spiritual people who don't have any desires because they have transcended them. They serve God in humanity with the utmost dedication and unconditional love. This form of desirelessness is the only satisfactory one.

If one has desire but no aspiration, that is better than having neither desire nor aspiration. He will have many necessary experiences and eventually he will see that there is no fulfilment in desire. Then he will jump into the sea of aspiration. But if one enters again into the realm of desire after having entered into the world of aspiration, that is a real catastrophe. If one does not aspire, we can say that he is just an ignorant fellow; he does not know that there is something called inner peace, inner bliss, inner light. If someone has not seen the light and he stays in a dark room, God will not blame him because he is not aware that there is a room full of light. But after having had inner experiences, if one wants to go back to the ordinary world, then he will be a victim to frustration and inner destruction. Once one has seen the effulgence of light in the illumined room, if the vital pulls him back again to the dark room, his inner psychic pain will be most excruciating. When he saw the light, the joy that he received had intensity. In the dark room there also is intensity, but this intensity is like a sharp knife, and he just stabs himself.

Once you enter into the spiritual life, never, never go back to the ordinary life. If you go back to the ordinary life, you will be an object of ridicule in the outer world and an object of distrust in the inner world. People will say, "This fellow has failed; that is why he has given up and come back to us." The divine forces in the cosmos will say, "Oh, he does not care for us. He cares more for the life of ignorance," and they will not try to help you any more. Also, you will always make a conscious or unconscious comparison between the divine life you have left and the life you have returned to. This comparison will always be unfavourable to the ordinary life. Your soul, the divine spark within you, will make you feel that you have given up something most precious. Then frustration will loom large in your ordinary life.

* * *

In the life of aspiration, between fear and doubt, choose neither; between faith and surrender, choose both.

* * *

Doubt is a fatal disease, but not the final end.
Lack of aspiration marks the end of our real life.

* * *

Man thinks that the perfection of evolution is his speculation and imagination.
God knows that the perfection of evolution is the glowing Song of His fulfilling Aspiration.

* * *

Man means aspiration's evolution.
God means evolution's aspiration.

* * *

Aspiration is a love-living God.
Desire is a love-dying man.

* * *

SPIRITUAL DISCIPLINE

SPIRITUAL PRACTICE

Any method of spiritual discipline will have two inevitable and inseparable wings: absolute patience and firm resolution.

A progressive self-giving and an absolute confidence in God can easily challenge the strength of impossibility in one's spiritual journey.

March forward just three steps and God is won. Now what are the three steps? The first step is aspiration. The second step is self-giving. The third step is reliance on the Divine in oneself.

In the early stages of spiritual practice, to leave everything to the Divine and to think that personal effort is unnecessary is to dance before you can walk.

Tapasya (intense or austere discipline) says to the aspirant: "I shall make you see God." Surrender says to the aspirant: "I shall make God see you."

Faithfulness is the only key that both *tapasya* and surrender possess to open God's Door.

In the ultimate analysis, no distinction can ever be made between *tapasya* and surrender. Surrender, when complete and effective, is the result of, and nothing other than, the most arduous *tapasya*.

The more complete the aspirant's surrender, the brighter the smile of his psychic being.

Surrender is fondly influenced by the psychic being. Knowledge is boldly influenced by the will.

Surrender is the most suitable net to entrap the Divine. It is at once wisdom and power in action.

Spontaneous obedience is the husk. Conscious surrender is the rice.

Demanding surrender says to God: "Father, I am looking at You. Be pleased to look at me. Let us look at each other." Devoted surrender says to God: "Father, I need not look at You. You just look at me. That will do."

There are three ways to fulfill the soul's need: either the aspirant steps forward to see the Divine; or the Divine steps forward to make the aspirant see Him; or both the aspirant and the Divine step forward simultaneously toward each other.

When the aspirant bitterly starves his questioning mind and feeds his surrender sumptuously, God says: "The time is ripe. I come."

Surrender can never be a one-day achievement. Likewise realisation, when attained, is not a one-day wonder.

Although regularity in spiritual practice may appear mechanical, it is a constant blessing from above and shows the development of some inner strength.

To see God only during your surrender at meditation is to declare that God is absent from you more than He is present.

True meditation has a free access to the inner being. True self-consecration has a free access to the right consciousness and attitude.

When the mind and the vital close their eyes for good, surrender, the inner strength, opens its eyes for good.

The body's discipline is sex-control.

The vital's discipline is dynamic aggression-control.

The mind's discipline is thought-control.

The heart's discipline is emotion-control.

Man's discipline and his soul's divine pride go together.

* * *

Question: How can one have a disciplined life?

Sri Chinmoy: A disciplined life can come from only one thing, and that is aspiration, inner cry. When we cry for outer things, sometimes we get them, sometimes we don't. But if our inner cry is sincere, we see that fulfilment always dawns. A child cries for milk. He is crying in his cradle in the living room. The mother may be in the kitchen, but wherever she is, the mother comes running to feed the child with milk. Now why? The mother feels the cry of the child is genuine and sincere. Similarly, in the spiritual life we have an inner cry. If we have that inner cry, then it does not matter when we cry. It may be at noon, in the morning, or in the evening. At any hour, that inner cry reaches God and God is bound to fulfil that inner cry. If one wants to discipline oneself, if one is dissatisfied with his loose life and if one feels that from a disciplined life he can have real fulfilment, perfection and satisfaction, then God is bound to help that particular sincere seeker. If there is an inner cry, then nothing on earth can be denied. No fruit can be denied an individual who has an inner cry.

We cry as human beings for name and fame, for many things. But we do not cry for one thing which is of paramount importance, and that is God's inner Wealth. What is His inner Wealth? His inner Wealth is divine fulfilment, divine perfection. No human being is perfect. But our aim is to be perfectly perfect. This perfect Perfection can only come from self-discipline. Self-discipline is the precursor of self-discovery. Self-discovery is the harbinger of God-manifestation.

God is all ready. He is more than eager to offer His perfect Perfection. But for that perfect Perfection we have to grow into a mounting cry which we call aspiration, constant aspiration. When this flame of aspiration rises toward the Highest, it illumines everything around it which is dark. The higher it goes, the greater and more fulfilling is our manifestation.

* * *

Each aspirant has to be a divine soldier. He must consciously and constantly use his divine energy to drill himself into a liberated soul.

* * *

Temptation runs rampant until it is caught by self-control. When self-control reigns supreme, frustration sees the face of realisation.

* * *

DETACHMENT AND RENUNCIATION

A spiritual seeker must know that austerity is an abnormality inasmuch as it is a disturbance of the natural balance of forces in the different parts of our consciousness. Austerity does not give self-mastery. In true detachment is the real self-mastery. Just as earth has temptations for an ordinary man, so Heaven has temptations for an advanced seeker.

* * *

ATTACHMENT AND DETACHMENT

From the body we get the message of attachment. From the soul we get the message of detachment. The body is limited; hence, the body wants to bind us and limit us. It wants to bind and limit our outer capacity and our inner potentiality.

The soul, in its potentiality and capacity, is limitless and endless. Therefore, the soul wants to free us from the meshes of ignorance and liberate us from the bondage-night.

What is attachment? Attachment is the dance of our outer pleasure.

What is detachment? Detachment is the song of our inner joy.

Attachment ends in the prison-cell of frustration and destruction.

Detachment fulfils itself in the palace of Divinity and Immortality.

I am a fool if I consciously live in the physical. I am a greater fool if I constantly admire and adore my physical body. I am the greatest fool if I live only to satisfy the needs of my physical existence.

I am a wise person if I know that there is something called the soul. I am a wiser person if I care to see and feel my soul. I am the wisest person if I live in my soul and for my soul constantly and soulfully, unreservedly and unconditionally.

When we are attached to the body, we in no time become impulsive. When we are attached to the vital, we very soon become explosive. When we are attached to the physical mind, we ultimately become destructive.

But when we are in the body, detached, we consciously feel our aspiring consciousness. When we are in the vital, detached, we expand and widen our aspiring consciousness. When we are in the mind, detached, we supremely fulfil our unlimited consciousness here on earth.

Many people, unfortunately, mistakenly feel that attachment and devotedness are one and the same thing. But attachment means that we are in the finite and attached to the finite, and devotedness means that we devote ourselves to the Infinite and are liberated by the Infinite.

Detachment is often misunderstood. Spiritual seekers sometimes think that to be detached from someone means to show him utter indifference, to the point of total neglect. But this is not true detachment. When we are indifferent to someone, we do nothing for him. We have nothing to do with his joy or sorrow, his achievement or failure. But when we are truly detached, we work for him devotedly and selflessly, and offer the results of our actions at the Feet of the Lord Supreme, our Inner Pilot.

It does not matter if the result is success or failure. If we are not at all attached to the results, we get an immediate expansion of consciousness. If we do not care for the fruit of our action, the Supreme rewards us in His own way.

If we work devotedly and selflessly, action does not bind us. There will be no difficulty in working for God's sake if we work without caring about the result. This is true detachment; this is spiritual detachment. When we can renounce the unlit, unaspiring action, we can enter into the divine action, which is our real life; and in this there is always fulfilment.

* * *

DETACHMENT AND RESPONSIBILITY

The more Light we get from within, the swifter comes our progress and achievement. Each achievement sparks an iota of detachment. But total detachment is something we do not get until practically the end of our journey, after a long period of spiritual practice. Nobody can say he *started* his spiritual journey with detachment. One can never get detachment all at once. For years, even for quite a few incarnations, one has to concentrate, meditate and do selfless service; then only one can achieve detachment. Detachment is something extremely difficult to achieve, but it is something which we all have to have.

In a family, each member has a responsibility toward the other members. Physical, moral and all other kinds of obligations we have as long as we live. The mother has to care for the son because the mother brought the son into the world. The son has to care for the mother because the son feels an obligation, to some extent, to fulfil or please the mother. But often the mother does not truly care for the son, or the son for the mother. When affection or true understanding is missing among family members, immediately we can know that it is lack of concern, not detachment. Lack of concern everybody knows; we see it in our day-to-day life. Lack of concern is often mistaken for detachment. But detachment is something far superior to lack of concern. Detachment, not lack of concern, is what a spiritual seeker needs.

Detachment does not mean that we will have no concern for others. Detachment means that we will perform our duties as well as possible, but not care for the results. In detachment we do the right thing in the right way and at the right moment. Everything is done precisely because the Inner Pilot has commanded it. Then, if we go still deeper, we feel that the Inner Pilot is everything. He is the Doer, He is the Action itself and He is the Enjoyer.

Suppose one is an athlete, a runner who has been practising for a long time. Finally he runs in the Olympics and he comes in last. He will say to himself, "I have practised for so many years. How is it that I have stood last?" But now he must be detached. From what? From the fruits of his actions. A runner has to practise with all hope that he will be the winner. He has to get up early in the morning, take various kinds of exercise and do everything else that is necessary to improve his performance. But the result of his actions he has to place at the Feet of God, who is the only Doer.

The supreme philosophy is, "God is the Doer and the Enjoyer," and this is absolutely true. But here on earth, on the physical plane, we definitely have to do what we feel is best. We have to work and do the needful. In every way we have to do our duty as well as we can in order to reach our goal. Sometimes we try to see the result of our work with our mental eye, and our mental eye shows us that the result will be defeat. If we know that the result will not please us, then we find it extremely difficult to work well and with enthusiasm. If success is all that we care for, then naturally we will be discouraged. But at this point we are making a mistake; we do not know the true meaning of detachment. We have to act with hope, enthusiasm and determination, and whatever happens to us is not our business. When the action is over, it does not remain in our hands. When the result is out, we will be totally detached whether we stand first or last. If we stand first, we will be happy. Again, if we stand last, we will also be happy because we have surrendered the result of our action to God.

Real joy comes if we can feel the moment we begin working that the work itself is the result. Then we don't have to wait for twenty minutes or two months or two years for the result. What we want is the satisfaction that will come only after a few months or a few years, when we reap the fruits of our action. But if we are wise enough, we enter into the work and see that the work itself is joy. First of all, we have to know that out of millions of people on earth, it is we who have been chosen to do this particular job. Then, the moment we start working, we have to feel that the very work gives us what we want. If we want to get satisfaction, joy and fulfilment from any kind of work, then we have to feel the moment we enter into it that the work itself, not the future result, is all joy.

How can we be detached in our work? There are two ways. One way is to feel that nothing remains permanently on earth. No matter how great one is in the human world, nothing remains forever — nothing. Name and fame will all be buried. We can claim nothing as our very own, not even ourselves. Today I use the terms 'I, my, mine'. But tomorrow this 'I' goes away to some other world. What is the use of attaching myself to someone or something which I now call mine if I cannot take it with me after sixty or seventy years? It is simply foolish!

The same thing is true about attachment to others. Although I know that I am attaching myself to someone whom I cannot claim as my own, I say that that person is mine. I cannot show him, I cannot prove it to him. How can I show my heart? I cannot show my inner feelings. If it is a good feeling, I try to offer it. If it is a bad feeling, I try to cover it. Often, if we are doing good work, we are eager to show it. If we are doing bad work, we are reluctant to show it. But whether the work is good or bad, whether we have good feelings or bad feelings, the object of our attachment does not last. We finally come to realise that nothing we call our own can last permanently. This is one way to be detached.

Another way to achieve detachment is to know that apart from the finite light there is a higher Light, an infinite Light. This Light gives us true joy. Knowing this, how can we be attached to the people and things that are constantly tempting us? The more we detach ourselves from these temptations of the finite, the more we are attaching ourselves to the Infinite. In this divine attachment is our real satisfaction. If we really care for the spiritual life, then our business is to focus all our attention only on the Supreme. If we are deeply attached to the Supreme, to the inner life, then naturally we remain detached from other people and things, from the world which is not aspiring. What we call our attachment to the Supreme will be seen as Wisdom-Light in the future, because in Him only, and not anywhere else, can we grow. In Him only, and not anywhere else, are we fulfilled.

Some Indian seekers who follow the path of devotion go the length of saying that devotion is nothing but attachment to God. As human desire is attachment to a human being, so spiritual devotion is a form of attachment to God. We cannot be attached to two things or two persons at the same time. When we go deep within, we see that we can be attached only to one person or one thing. Attachment and devotion are like concentration. We cannot properly concentrate on two fingers at once. We see two fingers, but we focus our attention either on one or on the other. Similarly, when we really offer to the Supreme our purest attachment, which is devotion, it can only go to Him. And inside Him the rest of humanity can be found. In the beginning we have an ordinary family with a few members. But there comes a time when we have to expand our family. Humanity itself becomes our family. The more we grow within, the larger becomes our family. And it is always inside the Supreme that humanity stays.

We can identify with another person's sufferings and feelings and still remain detached if we enter into that person with our soul's Light. Our soul's Light always expands. It does not bind and, at the same time, it cannot be bound. With our soul's Light we can identify ourselves with anybody on earth and not be affected. If we enter into the person with our inner soul's Light, which is all freedom and perfection, and if we spread this inner Light in the sufferer, at that time he gets the best help from us. Afterwards, we can fly away like a bird without being touched by the person or being attached to him.

The Boat of the Supreme is carrying us to the Golden Shore. The Boat is *in* the water, but it is not *of* the water. The Boat is right now in the sea of ignorance, but it is not affected. It is carrying us to the Golden Shore, where there is no ignorance, no doubt, no bondage—where all is perfection and plenitude. In our human life also, we have to feel that if we have the soul's Light within us, we can stay inside anybody. He may be the most imperfect person or the worst sufferer. Yet, although we are helping him most sincerely and effectively, we will not be attached to him or pulled down by him. So first we have to discover our inner Light, our soul's Light. Then only will we be truly qualified to help others without being attached to them or to their suffering. Then only can we be of truest and purest help to suffering humanity.

* * *

Question: While striving for detachment, how can we safeguard against indifference?

Sri Chinmoy: There is a great difference between detachment and indifference. When you are indifferent to something or someone, at that time you are almost, *almost* hostile to his progress. There is a kind of inner malicious hope that he will not pass his examination, not do the right thing, not be admired or adored by anyone. You may say you are indifferent to convince your own mind. But you will observe whether he is succeeding, and if he is, it will pinch you. And if he fails, you will get tremendous malicious pleasure. Indifference is like that. It observes in a secret way and gets tremendous joy when it observes failure and suffers tremendous jealousy when it observes success. We say we are indifferent, but if the other person becomes great, our jealousy will kill us, and if he fails, we dance with joy.

But detachment is a spiritual quality. When we are detached, our physical is detached, our mind is detached, our vital is detached and so on. The thing in me that wants to bind you and the thing in you that wants to bind me from inside are warning each other, "I am not the right person to bind you and you are not the right person to bind me. There is someone else, the Divine, the Supreme, who is the only one. It is He who has infinite Light, Peace and Bliss, so run toward Him as I am running toward Him. I shall help you with my inner capacity, which is my prayer, meditation and concentration. But if I grab you and claim you with my vital, physical and mental longing, this is no help at all. Instead let me offer to you my prayer, meditation and concentration, and these things you have to offer to me. In this way we strengthen each other."

In detachment two persons grow together through their souls' Light. Their souls' qualities make a bridge on which they can go to their common goal. The bridge is not the goal, but both use the bridge. They say, "Let us walk together along the path that leads to our common destination." So when we are detached, all the time we make ourselves feel that the human in somebody else or the human in ourselves is not the goal, but that we both have a common goal which we have to reach together with our heart's aspiration and our soul's Light. Detachment we have when we use our inner light and inner reality, rather than our physical reality.

* * *

Foolish is he who thinks that affection should be turned into indifference in order that God might come to him. Alas, he has yet to learn that God is all affection.

Affection and attachment need not always go together. The rejection of all relations can never be a promising sign of progress towards realisation.

Controlled desire is good. Better is non-attachment. Best is it to feel oneself removed from the snare of nature. Suppression is as hostile and undeserving as attachment. It is our non-attachment only that is the master of nature.

Desire and hunger have one common enemy: detachment.

Detachment and not possession should be the bridge between you and the object of your love.

Spiritual detachment intensifies the seeking of our hearts, purifies the vibration of our bodies and transforms the ignorance of our consciousness into knowledge.

Granted, loneliness is a kind of spiritual disease. But human association can never be its lasting medicine. The only permanent cure for it is inner experience.

* * *

RENUNCIATION

From the strict spiritual point of view, the so-called earthly renunciation is not necessary for an aspirant. If renunciation means leaving one's family aside, if renunciation means not caring for society or humanity, then I wish to say that no matter what we renounce today, there will be something else tomorrow to stand in our way. Today the family is the obstacle; tomorrow it will be our friends; the day after tomorrow, it will be our country, and the day after, the world. There is no end to this kind of renunciation.

Certainly we have to renounce in the spiritual life. What are we going to renounce? We are going to renounce fear, doubt, imperfection, ignorance and death. We are not going to renounce individuals; we are going to renounce qualities which stand in the way of our union with the Divine. When we enter into the spiritual life, we get the opportunity to renounce, or rather, to transform these qualities. When we speak of renouncing or transforming something, we immediately think of ignorance. Truly it is the one thing that we have to transform in our spiritual life.

If somebody says he is going to renounce the world in order to realise God, then I wish to say that he is mistaken. Today he will renounce the world and tomorrow he will find that the God he is seeking is nowhere else; He is in the world itself. So what is preventing him from seeing God in the world? It is his attitude. In order to see God in humanity, he has to remove the veil of ignorance that lies between him and the rest of the world. When the veil is rent, when the veil is, in fact, removed, there is nothing to be renounced. One sees God, one feels God, one is in God, here and beyond.

* * *

A perfect renunciation and a complete self-surrender are the obverse and reverse of the same ambrosial coin.

* * *

No renunciation can be commanded. No renunciation can be demanded. Renunciation has to grow from within. Renunciation has to flow from without. Man renounces the futility of his ignorance-night. God announces man, Infinity's Light.

* * *

The real transformation of human nature comes not through an austere, ascetic life or a complete withdrawal from the world, but through a gradual and total illumination of life.

* * *

SERVING THE WORLD

IS THE SPIRITUAL LIFE AN
ESCAPE FROM REALITY?

An unaspiring man thinks that undying pleasure is the only reality. An aspiring man feels that a divine experience is the only reality. A God-realised man knows that God, the supreme Lover, alone *has* the Reality, and that God, the supreme Beloved, alone *is* the Reality. Reality is also God the fulfilling Light and man the fulfilled life.

The abode of transcendental fulfilment has three doors: love, freedom and delight. The love-door is open only to him who serves crying humanity. The freedom-door is open only to him who serves struggling humanity. The delight-door is open only to him who serves awakening humanity.

The spiritual life is never an escape from reality. On the contrary, the spiritual life is the conscious and spontaneous acceptance of reality in its totality. For a spiritual seeker the idea of an escape from reality is absurdity plus impossibility, for spirituality and reality need each other to be supremely fulfilled. Without reality's soul, spirituality is worse than useless. Without spirituality's breath, reality is more than meaningless. Spirituality with reality means man's inner cry for perfect Perfection. Reality with spirituality means God's omnipotent Will for total and absolute manifestation.

The acceptance of life with a divine attitude is not only a lofty idea but the very ideal of life. This ideal of life is realised, revealed and manifested through God's soul-elevating inspiration and man's life-building aspiration. Acceptance of life is the divine pride of true spirituality. To live a spiritual life is our only responsibility.

Escape is a base thought. It acts like a thief, the worst possible thief. Into the heart of tenebrous gloom escape gains easy and free access. He who indulges in the idea of an immediate escape unmistakably commits lingering suicide.

No, we must never make a cowardly escape. We must always be brave. Divine courage is our birthright. We are the hero-warriors of the supreme Reality chosen to fight against the teeming, brooding and threatening ignorance-night.

* * *

Question: What is the spiritual value of the earth?

Sri Chinmoy: Those who accept life, those who accept Mother Earth as something real, feel that they have a bounden duty to perform here. This duty is nothing other than conscious realisation of God. Unconscious awareness of God everybody has. But a seeker becomes consciously aware of God's Presence. He meditates on God and gradually his own consciousness develops to such an extent that he feels God's Presence constantly, everywhere. He feels that it is his bounden duty to reveal God's Presence, which he feels and which he sees with his own heart and his own eyes. Finally, he feels that he has to manifest his realisation of the highest Truth. This manifestation has to take place here on earth and nowhere else. Realisation of the highest Truth has to take place here and manifestation of the Truth, the highest Truth, the ultimate Truth, has to take place here on earth.

A real seeker, a sincere seeker, is a divine hero. He has to fight against teeming darkness and he has to fulfil God's Will here on earth. Otherwise, earth will remain earth and Heaven will remain Heaven. There will always be a yawning gulf between earth and Heaven. This earth of ours must be transformed into Heaven, into a place of Joy, Peace and Delight.

We must not negate the body. The Indian spiritual Masters who did not care for the body at all said, "Meditate, remain in the other world, realise God and then leave the body." But if you love God and if you really want to serve God, then here on earth is the golden opportunity to manifest Him and fulfil Him. If you get your realisation and you say to God, "I don't want to work for You. I'm tired, exhausted, totally exhausted; now I want to take rest," God may allow you to take rest. But the real divine hero will say, "I have worked hard, but now I wish to offer the fruits of my realisation to the world at large." Then God will say, "Work on earth. Do it."

Our path is the path of acceptance. Acceptance of what? Acceptance of this material world. While operating in matter, Spirit has to sing the song of Immortality. The material life and the spiritual life must run together. The material life can be perfected only by listening to the inner dictates of the soul. We have to accept the world as it is, but we must not think that the world has completed its task. No, far from it. We have to work and work for the earth-consciousness. We have to free it from limitations, imperfections, bondage and ignorance.

Question: When you say that earth can easily be transformed into Heaven, do you mean physically as well?

Sri Chinmoy: You have to know what we mean by Heaven. Heaven does not mean a place with big houses, big palaces or estates. No! Heaven is in our mind. When we enjoy divine thoughts, we are in Heaven. When we cherish jealousy, lower vital thoughts or other undivine thoughts, we are in hell. Heaven and hell are states of consciousness.

What does each human being have? Consciousness. It is through consciousness that we see reality. When we pray, when we aspire, our finite consciousness becomes infinite; our so-called unaspiring consciousness becomes aspiring. This is Heaven. If we say that we all will become divine, this is certainly true. We will have a divine life, but that does not necessarily mean a physically immortal life. When we think of Heaven, we feel that it is immortal. The consciousness of Heaven *is* immortal. But very often we feel that the physical will remain immortal as Heaven is something immortal. But this physical body will live for sixty, eighty, one hundred, perhaps even two hundred years and then go.

The very conception of Heaven is something bright, luminous, delightful and, at the same time, immortal. But we have to know what is immortal in us. It is consciousness, the aspiring consciousness in us. When we say that earth will be transformed into Heaven, that means that anything that is within us or in the world which is now imperfect, obscure or unaspiring will be transformed eventually into perfection.

Question: Will you please explain how it is that the soul evolves only on the planet Earth?

Sri Chinmoy: The soul manifests only on this planet because this planet is in evolution. Evolution means constant progress, constant achievement. When one wants to make progress, when one wants to go beyond, then this is the place. In other worlds, beings are satisfied with what they already have achieved. They do not want to go one inch beyond their achievement. But here on earth you are not satisfied, I am not satisfied — nobody is satisfied with what they have achieved. Dissatisfaction does not mean that we are angry with somebody or angry with the world. No! Dissatisfaction means that we have constant aspiration to go beyond and beyond. If we have only an iota of light, then we want to have more light. Always we want to expand.

This planet has that inner urge. On the one hand, it is obscure, it is ignorant, it does not care for divine life. But, on the other hand, it has that tremendous inner urge of which most human beings are not yet aware. When the inner urge is functioning, then there is no end to our possibilities, no end to our achievements. And when we achieve the Infinite, then naturally we surpass the achievements of other worlds.

Question: Is there a link or bridge between the inner world and the outer world?

Sri Chinmoy: Yes, there is a link between the inner world and the outer world. What actually happens is that we are not paying any attention to the inner world. Most of the time we are on the surface. Twenty-four hours a day we are moving, talking, shouting and living in the hustle and bustle of the outer world. We don't get five minutes to meditate or concentrate on our inner, real world.

A true spiritual seeker feels that if we feed the inner world, then only can the outer world have its true meaning. The body is the outer world. Three times a day we feed the body without fail; we have been doing it and we shall keep on doing it until we breathe our last. But again, there is deep inside us a divine child called our soul. We don't get time to feed this child. Unless and until the soul, which is the conscious representative of God in us, is fulfilled, we can never be fulfilled in our outer life.

Now how do we make the connecting link? If we know the divine art of concentration, if we know the divine art of meditation, if we know the divine art of contemplation, easily and consciously we can unite these two worlds. And to our widest surprise we shall see that the outer world, which is now full of complexity, disharmony and so forth, is bound to become harmonious, simple, straightforward and genuine. The inner life has the capacity to simplify the complexities of the outer life. The inner world and the outer world must go together. Otherwise, what will happen? The inner life will have to wait for millennia to offer God's Truth to the world at large and the outer life will remain a barren desert for millennia.

There is definitely a link between these two worlds. We have to consciously feel this link and finally, we have to touch and strengthen the link with our soul's determination and our body's dedicated service and willingness. Now the body listens to the mind. When the mind says, "Go this way," the body goes. But the moment the mind says, "No, no, no! That is the wrong way to take. Follow some other direction," the body follows. In this way the body is caught by limitations. But far beyond the domain of the mind is the soul. The soul is flooded with light. If we consciously try to have a free access to the inner being, to the soul, then naturally the light of the soul will come to the fore and help us at every moment to deal with the tenebrous darkness in and around us. Finally we will see that either we have transformed this darkness into light or we have come millions and millions of miles away from darkness and are bathing in the sea of infinite Light.

So, if the physical body listens to the soul and not to the doubtful, doubting, sophisticated, complex, destructive and unaspiring mind, at every moment the link between the two worlds will be strengthened and one will complete the other. That is to say, the inner world will have the outer world as its chariot and the outer world will have the inner world as its charioteer. If there is a chariot without a charioteer, it is useless, for without a charioteer the chariot cannot move. Again, if there is a charioteer without a chariot, he is also useless. So both the charioteer and the chariot are necessary. They are of equal importance. Similarly, the outer life and the inner life are of equal importance.

* * *

A warrior in the outer world shines in his armour.
A warrior in the inner world shines in his meditation.

* * *

The inner world belongs to the soul's illumination.
The outer world belongs to life's determination.

* * *

SERVICE

WORK AND SERVICE

Why do we work? We work to support ourselves, to support our dear ones. We may also work to keep our bodies in perfect condition. But a true aspirant looks upon work differently. He sees work as a veritable blessing. To him, each difficult and apparently painful job is a blessing in disguise. To him, work is nothing short of a dedicated service. He has discovered the truth that by offering the results of what he says, does and thinks, he will be able to realise God. He works for the sake of God. He lives for the sake of God. He realises Divinity for the sake of God.

Fate is our building. We had the power to build it; we have the power to demolish it. Whether to demolish the building, or build a new one or transform the present one is a question of paramount importance. But to do any of the three, we shall have to work physically, vitally, mentally, psychically and spiritually. Not without purpose has God so graciously granted us the body, vital, mind, heart and soul.

Each human being must find his own work, the work that helps him grow in his soul. Nothing can be more encouraging, inspiring and fulfilling than to discover one's true inner work, which is the work of Self-realisation. Carlyle touched a deep truth when he said, "Blessed is he who has found his work; let him ask no other blessedness."

Each soul is a chosen instrument of God. Each soul has a particular mission here on earth. Each person has to realise and fulfil himself, not in his own way, but in God's way. God, out of His infinite Love, and by virtue of His self-imposed divine Duty, gives to each aspirant what he needs. At the same time, God does not expect an iota more than the aspirant can offer. It was a great human voice that said, "From each according to his abilities, to each according to his needs."

There is a common complaint which is voiced by all human beings irrespective of age, caste or creed. What is it? "I have no time." With a poetic sigh, they tell the world, "So much to do, so little is done." Here, time is acting as our worst foe. Time is able to cause worry, fear and frustration in us because we are working through our ego and for the ego. There is always a constant battle between our ego's injudicious intensity and time's inscrutable and merciless flow.

But if we work with our soul and for the soul, then time not only helps us, but at each moment it appears before us as a golden opportunity: for our soul knows unmistakably how to throw itself into the cosmic rhythm of the infinite Time.

True, each human being is an instrument of God, chosen to do a particular work, to fulfil a divine mission here on earth. But nobody should imagine, even in his wildest dream, that he is indispensable. God gives us an unparalleled opportunity in each distinct job to enter into His Heart's absolute Infinitude. If we do not avail ourselves of this constant opportunity, God the Compassionate Father cannot help saying, "Sleep, my child, sleep. You are the child of My eternal Patience. I wanted you to be in My all-transforming Light. Since you do not want that, I shall have to be in your eyeless night."

***

DUTY SUPREME

The poet sang:

> I slept and dreamed that life was Beauty.
> I woke and found that life was Duty.

Duty and beauty are like the North Pole and the South Pole.

What is beauty? Beauty is the oneness of the finite and the Infinite. Beauty is the expression of the Infinite through man the finite. Beauty is man's embodiment of God, the Infinite. In the material world, in the physical world, it is through beauty that God reveals Himself.

The beauty of the soul is beauty unparalleled in the physical world. This beauty inspires the outer world and fulfils the inner world. This beauty makes us one with God's Soul, the Light infinite. This beauty makes us one with God's Body, the universe. When we live in the world of aspiration, we come to realise that the transcendental Duty and the universal Beauty are the perfect expressions of one and the same reality.

God thinks of His Duty. God meditates on His Duty. Man loves his reward. Man cries for his reward.

Duty performed unconditionally makes God happy, and that is what He does at every moment.

Reward gained effortlessly and constantly makes man happy, and that is what he always expects and lives for.

In our human duty we think of man in man. In our human duty we see man in man. That is to say, we love bondage in ignorance.

Our divine duty is to meditate on God in man. Our divine duty is to see God in man. That is to say, to love Divinity in Immortality.

Human duty begins with compulsion and very often ends in frustration and repulsion. Divine duty begins with inner necessity and ends in a flood of ecstasy.

In our day-to-day life, duty is something unpleasant, demanding and discouraging. When we are reminded of our duty, we lose all our inner spontaneous joy. We feel miserable. We feel that we could have used our life-energy for a better purpose. Duty is painful, tedious and monotonous simply because we do it with ego, pride and vanity. Duty is pleasant, encouraging and inspiring when we do it for God's sake. What we need is to change our attitude toward duty. If we work for the sake of God, then there is no duty. It is all joy, all beauty. Each action has to be performed and offered at the Feet of God. Duty for God's sake is the duty supreme.

In our unaspiring life we perform duties and feel that duty is another name for labour. We also feel that duty is an imposition, while reward is a most coveted pleasure. In our aspiring life, duty is voluntary. No, never is it obligatory. And reward is the energising joy of selfless service. In our life of realisation, duty is our divine pride and reward is our glorious, transcendental height.

No right have we to undertake any other duty before we work out our own spiritual salvation. Did God not entrust us with this wonderful task at the time of our very birth? The supreme duty is to constantly strive for God-realisation. Time is short, but our soul's mission on earth is lofty. How can we waste time?

Love your family much. This is your great duty. Love mankind more. This is your greater duty. Love God most. This is your greatest duty, the duty supreme.

There are two things: one is remembrance, the other is forgetfulness. All of us know that it is our duty to collect our salary. Indeed, it is our duty. And we always remember it. But there is another duty. We have to work. That duty we forget. In order to get our salary, we have to work. Somehow we manage to forget this. In the spiritual world also, there is a duty. This duty is to enjoy the fruits of God-realisation. We all know it and we are extremely eager to perform this duty. But unfortunately we forget the other duty: meditation. One duty is to enjoy the fruits; the other duty is to acquire the fruits. But we are clever enough to cry for the fruits of realisation long before we have entered into the field of meditation. No meditation, no realisation. Without meditation, God-realisation is nothing but self-deception.

Duty and reward, from the spiritual point of view, go together. It is like the obverse and reverse of the same spiritual coin. Duty is man the aspiration, and reward is God the Realisation and God the Liberation. Again, in reward is man's eternal journey, his ever-transcending journey; and in duty is God the ever-transforming, ever-manifesting, ever-fulfilling Reality here on earth and there in Heaven.

In our unaspiring life, and even in our aspiring life, we see that duty precedes reward. Duty comes first; then it is followed by reward. In the life of realisation it is otherwise: reward first, then duty. How? When God offers His transcendental Height, His highest Illumination to someone, it means that God has already granted him full realisation. God has accepted him as His chosen instrument. The very fact that God has accepted him as His chosen instrument indicates that he has already received the highest reward from God. Later God tells him about his duty: to love mankind, to help mankind, to serve the divinity in humanity, to reveal God the eternal Compassion and to manifest God the eternal Concern on earth, here and now.

* * *

SPIRITUALITY: THE FOUNT OF WORLD PEACE

Spirituality is aspiration. Spirituality is Yoga. When we have learned what we can expect from aspiration and what we can expect from Yoga, world peace will no longer remain a far cry. Aspiration is an aspirant's conscious longing for the deeper reality. Yoga is a seeker's conscious oneness with God.

Aspiration leads man to God-Consciousness. Yoga offers God-Consciousness to man. Aspiration takes man back to the Source. Yoga inundates man's consciousness with the Light, Peace, Bliss and Power of the Beyond.

Why do we aspire? We aspire because we love God and want God to love us. Why do we practise Yoga? We practise Yoga in order to feel consciously that God is our very own. We practise Yoga because we feel that our fulfilment on earth can take place only when we have revealed and manifested God's Divinity and Reality here on earth.

When we aspire, we go far beyond the domain of the physical mind and sit at the Feet of God the Light. When we practise Yoga, we dive deep within, and there we see God and talk to Him face to face.

He who has no aspiration can never free himself from stark ignorance, and he who does not practise Yoga can neither receive nor achieve boundless Light.

Here on earth we have two major instruments: one is the mind, the other is the heart. Very often the mind that we use is the doubtful mind, and the heart we use is the fearful heart. But, unfortunately, the doubtful mind can never aspire, and the fearful heart can never practise Yoga.

True aspiration and teeming human limitations never go together. True Yoga and the life of unlit pleasure cannot go together. Constant aspiration and all-fulfilling divinity can and must go together. The highest type of Yoga, which is conscious surrender to God's Will, always goes together with the Life of God.

Aspiration tells man that he will be able to see the truth of the Beyond. Yoga goes one step ahead. Yoga tells man that the truth of the Beyond is within him. Finally, God comes and tells man, "My child, you are the truth of the Beyond. You are My Beyond."

Spirituality is the fount of world peace. Spirituality is the fulfilment of all responsibilities. This is because divinity is the birthright of spirituality. When an individual touches the foot of a tree, his consciousness enters into the tree: into the branches, into the leaves, into the fruits and into the flowers. In the spiritual sense, God is the tree and the leaves, fruit, branches and flowers are human beings. When you touch the Feet of God, your very consciousness enters into His universal Consciousness and the infinite beings of His manifestation.

Each individual has his own way of defining peace. A child finds peace in noise and activity. That is his fulfilment and in his fulfilment is his peace. An adult finds his peace somewhere else. He finds his peace when he feels that he can lord it over the world. And in the evening of life, an old man thinks that he will get peace if the world recognises his greatness, or if Mother Earth offers her gratitude to him. He feels that he has done much for humanity and Mother Earth, and he expects something in return. He will have peace only if his expectation is fulfilled.

But peace can never dawn on any individual if it is not properly sought. The child cannot get true peace by running around in the street. He soon finds frustration in his so-called fulfilment. A day will come when he will pray to God for a calm and quiet·life. Then he will have peace.

If an adult wants to have peace, real peace, he has to realise that he cannot get it by possessing the world or governing the world. It is only by offering what he has and what he is, consciously and unreservedly, to the world at large, that he will have peace.

The old man who will soon pass behind the curtain of Eternity can have peace only if he cherishes the idea that he is not a beggar, but a king. He was a king and he still is a king. He has offered his inner and outer wealth to mankind and Mother Earth. If, in the evening of his life, he does not expect anything from the world, then his inner consciousness and outer being will be flooded with peace.

World peace will begin when the so-called human expectation ends. World peace can dawn only when each individual realises the supreme Truth:

Love is the revelation of life and
Life is the manifestation of love.

World peace will come into existence when each individual nation consciously feels that the other human beings, the other nations, need not depend on it. No nation is indispensable; but if one nation helps another devotedly and unconditionally, then the world will be inundated with fulfilling peace.

Spirituality is the fulfilment of all responsibility. To love the world is our responsibility. To please the world is our responsibility. We know our own teeming responsibilities; but when we think of the world, unfortunately we do not think of it in a divine or proper way. The world immediately misunderstands us, and we find it impossible to have an inner connection with the world. It is like a mother and her son. In spite of her best intentions, the mother finds it difficult to please the son. She thinks of him in her own way and likewise, the son understands the mother in his own way. Because of this lack of communication, the mother and the son get no joy in fulfilling their responsibilities toward one another.

We love the world; we have to love the world; it is our responsibility. What happens when we try to love the world or when we attempt to fulfil our responsibility to the world? We try to possess and bind the world, and while we are doing this we see that we have already been bound and possessed by the world. We had a sublime opportunity to fulfil our responsibility to the world, but we have badly misused it.

We want to please the world, but how can we please the world if we are not pleased with our own lives? It is sheer absurdity to try to please others if we are not pleased with our inner and outer existence. God has given us big mouths and we try to please others with our mouths, but inside our hearts there is a barren desert. If we have no aspiration, how can we offer the world peace, joy and love? How can we offer anything divine when we don't practise what we preach? If we don't follow the path of spirituality, we shall only preach; it will be a one-sided game. But if we really practise Yoga we shall also *live* the truth. Our preaching will bear fruit only when it is practised.

How can we fulfil all our responsibilities? We have tried in human ways, but we have failed. We think of the world with good thoughts and ideas, but the world remains exactly the same as it was yesterday. We love the world, but the world still remains full of cruelty and hatred. We try to please the world, but the world doesn't want to be pleased. It is as if the world has taken a vow that it won't allow itself to be pleased. And why does all this happen? It is because we have not pleased our Inner Pilot, the One we have to please first. If we have no aspiration to please our Inner Pilot, how can we offer the world peace, joy and love? Unless and until we have pleased the Inner Pilot, the world will always remain a battlefield where the soldiers of fear, doubt, anxiety, worry, imperfection, limitation and bondage will fight; and consciously or unconsciously we will play with these undivine soldiers. Fear, doubt, anxiety, worry and animal propensities can never offer us world peace.

Again, deep within us divinity is crying to come to the fore. There the divine soldiers are our simplicity, sincerity, purity, humility and feeling of oneness. These soldiers are more than ready and eager to fight with fear, doubt, anxiety and worry. Unfortunately, we are not consciously identifying ourselves with the divine soldiers; we are consciously or unconsciously identifying ourselves with the undivine soldiers. That is why world peace is still a far cry. World peace can be achieved, revealed, offered and manifested on earth only when the divine power of love replaces the undivine love of power.

* * *

Question: In practical terms, how can we give the world love and concern?

Sri Chinmoy: A practical thing is something that comes spontaneously from within and not from without. When you get up in the morning, if the thought comes to your mind to show love or concern for the world, that is a practical idea. How can you transform this practical idea into fruitful reality? In the morning or in the evening, during your regular prayer, you can add to your prayer this: "O Lord, I wish this world to be better, more illumining and more fulfilling, by Your infinite Grace." God is the creator and sustainer of the world. If your prayer reaches the Creator, which it will certainly do if it is sincere and intense, He can easily carry your concern and love for the world into the field of manifestation.

As an individual you are here; you cannot be somewhere else at the same time. But your prayer, your aspiration, can approach Someone Who is omnipresent. All of us have been praying and meditating here in this room, but spiritually we have been spreading peace and love into the world. Physically we are bound in this tiny room, but spiritually we are flying like birds; our wings are widespread with peace, joy and love.

When you feel something, when you see something, you may call it a practical experience. Here we have been meditating for fifteen or twenty minutes. During that time, our experience of inner peace and love was absolutely practical. To us these things were most tangible. While you are praying or meditating here next week, look at yourself. Is it not a reality—the peace, the joy, the love that you are getting?

What we get we can easily give to others. But the process is an inner process. And the best way to carry out this inner process is to approach the Source. We know that we cannot go everywhere and we cannot approach everyone during our prayer. But there is Someone who can do this on our behalf, and that is God. During our prayer, if we ask Him to offer peace, concern and love to the world at large, He can do it. If He is pleased with our request, naturally He will do it. So our daily communion with God is the best way for us to offer the world our love and concern.

* * *

THE HERO MARCHES ALONG

He who has loved this world
Has only got excruciating pangs.
The world has thrown on him
All ugliness, filth, dirt and impurity.
Yet the hero marches along
Carrying the burden of the entire world.
At the end of his teeming struggles
He will go and stand at the Feet of the Lord Supreme.

* * *

HOW TO CHANGE HUMANITY

To change humanity
First your own erring shape of soul recast.
Anon your eyes shall find
Nothing around remains unchanged at last.

* * *

Question: Do you not feel that national boundaries and political dogma divide human beings into different camps, creating unspiritual environments and making peace, for an individual as well as for a nation, a distant star?

Sri Chinmoy: I do strongly feel that national boundaries and dogma are really impairing the growth of our evolving human consciousness. But it is the elevation of the individual's mind and spirit that must precede the awakening of our social institutions such as churches and governments. It is the spiritual and mental elite who can infuse the general mass with their illumining light. As we know, the policies of institutions and nations are usually embodiments of the general consciousness. These policies can be influenced considerably by enlightened individuals. Mother India in particular has not lacked in such enlightened souls, nor does she lack them now.

It is only a matter of time until Time itself will create an opening so the spiritual consciousness may permeate the individual and his society. On our part, a conscious spiritual effort has to be made so that the higher forces from above can come down and touch the very depths of our seeking hearts. When this occurs, the gap that we now see between our aspiration and its fulfilment in society will no longer exist.

Question: If man, when dissatisfied with the world, escapes the world and seeks out higher planes of existence, how will humanity ever be able to establish peace and happiness on earth?

Sri Chinmoy: The world is all imperfection. Life stands as a huge question. Evil is seen everywhere. These are the problems that we face every day. Moreover, the more spiritually advanced a man is, the greater is his suffering from the present conditions of the world. He sees the disease, he feels the disease; but he has no proper medicine. Even if he has a remedy, it is not enough to cure all earthly ailments. So he often feels that his fight will be of no avail and therefore takes the easier path, the path of escape into the Bliss of the higher planes.

But this can never be the case with the divine warrior. He will fight until the victory is won. Now, what do we mean by his "victory?" It is the establishment of the Kingdom of God here on earth, and not just in some higher world. As he knows that the Divine is omnipresent, he seeks to reveal Him in everyday life. If we are not satisfied with the world as it is, that is no reason for leaving it. On the contrary, we should try to change it — physically or intellectually or spiritually — depending on our own development and capacities.

God is perfect Perfection. This Perfection can be achieved only when there is an inseparable union between matter and spirit, between the outer and the inner life.

Some people want only to meditate. They do not want to give anything to the world. They have acquired some inner wealth, but they are afraid that the moment they try to offer it to the ignorant world, the world will misunderstand or misuse them. So they act like misers. This is selfishness. Again, there are some who want to give but do not want to meditate. This is foolishness. If we do not meditate, if we do not possess something, then how are we going to give? There are many people on earth who are ready to give, but what do they have? So we have to play our part. First we have to achieve; then we have to offer. In this way we can please God and fulfil mankind.

Question: What is the relationship between silence and action?

Sri Chinmoy: There are two kinds of silence. One silence is dynamic; the other is static. Static silence is found in deep meditation, which is preparation. Dynamic silence is found in action, which is manifestation. The inner silence guides and illumines us. The outer silence reveals and manifests us. Prayer, meditation, concentration and contemplation are inner silence. Dedication, service and action are outer silence. Dedicate yourself; fulfil the Will of God — but only after knowing the Will of God. You can know the Will of God only by practising inner silence. Otherwise, if you try to help mankind in your own way, you think that you are serving God but really you are just aggrandising your own ego. You say, "I have done this; I have done that." But the important thing is: Were you inspired by God? Were you commissioned by God? If your actions are not inspired by God, they are inspired by your ego. Then the service that you offer to the world will be full of darkness and imperfections.

Question: How can one accept and love one's fellow man?

Sri Chinmoy: First of all you must feel that your fellow man is part and parcel of your own existence. I have two eyes. If my left eye does not function as well as my right eye, what do I do? Do I become angry with my left eye? Do I take it out of my body? Do I keep my left eye closed or cover it with my hand and say, "I won't let you see"? No. At that time I have the feeling of oneness. I simply accept my left eye as less capable than my right eye, but still as a part of me. If my left eye does not see well, I use my right eye also. Whenever I have to use my eyes, I use both eyes, and the eye that is more powerful naturally does more work.

You must regard the persons around you as limbs of your own body. Without them you are incomplete. You may feel that they are less developed, but they also have their role to play. Your thumb is much more powerful than your little finger. But the little finger also has its job. God has created five fingers. Although some are shorter and weaker than others, you know that only when you have five fingers are you perfect. Now your middle finger is the tallest. If you feel that for this reason you don't need your shorter fingers, then you are sadly mistaken. If you want to play the piano or if you want to type, then you need all five fingers.

You can love the people around you only when you feel the necessity of real perfection. If you remain isolated as an individual, then your achievement will be limited. Your very sense of perfection will be limited, very limited. But when you think in terms of unlimited perfection, then you have to love humanity. For it is only by accepting humanity as part and parcel of your own life, and by perfecting humanity with your own illumination, that you can fulfil yourself.

* * *

When I am all devotion to service-light, I am with the active and for the active.

* * *

DO NOT CONVERT
AND DO NOT BE CONVERTED

Do not convert.
Let him go in his own way.

Do not be converted.
You must go in your own way.

Do not convert.
His resistance-night
Will devour your inner joy.

Do not be converted.
Your resistance-night
Will devour his inner joy.

God will ask his freedom
To love you.

God will ask your freedom
To feed him.

Do not convert,
Do not be converted.

* * *

THE GOAL OF THE BEYOND

Obey and trust,
Trust and obey.
  Indeed, this is the short way
    To the Goal of the Beyond.

Love and serve,
Serve and love.
  Indeed, this is the shorter way
    To the Goal of the Beyond.

Surrender and offer,
Offer and surrender.
  Indeed,this is the shortest way
    To the Goal of the Beyond.

* * *

MEDITATION

MEDITATION

MEDITATION: AN INTRODUCTION

Why do we meditate? We meditate precisely because we need something. And what is that something? That something is the conscious feeling of oneness with the Supreme. This conscious feeling must be spontaneous and, at the same time, soulful.

Let me start with the ABC of meditation. The spine and the neck must be kept erect. The best way to meditate is to sit cross-legged on the floor. If it is not possible for some of you to sit on the floor, please try to sit on a chair with your whole back straight and erect. If you want to meditate at home, which you should do faithfully and devotedly every day, please try to keep a sacred place, a corner of your room which is absolutely pure and sanctified. You may sit on a small cushion or rug. Please wear clean and light clothes. If possible, please burn incense at the time of your meditation, and place some flowers in front of you. Those of you who are my disciples will keep my picture right in front of you. Others will keep a picture of their spiritual Master, the Christ or some other beloved spiritual figure. You may begin your meditation by repeating the name of the Supreme or the name of your spiritual Master. This I am telling you in general, but a day will come when you yourselves will discover a few inner secrets. Perhaps you have already discovered some by this time.

Please be careful to breathe properly. Try to breathe in as slowly and quietly as possible; and try to breathe out more slowly than you breathe in. If possible, leave a short gap between your first exhalation and your second inhalation. But if it is not possible, never do anything that strains your breathing system or any of your organs.

Each time you breathe in, try to feel that you are bringing into your body peace, infinite peace. Now, what is the opposite of peace? Restlessness. When you breathe out, please try to feel that you are giving out nothing but the restlessness of your body and mind and the restlessness that you see around you. When you breathe this way, restlessness will leave you. After practising this a few times, please try to feel that you are breathing in strength and power from the universe. And when you exhale, try to give out fear. When you breathe out, all your fear will come out of your body. Next try to feel that you are breathing in joy, infinite joy, and breathing out sorrow, suffering, melancholy.

This is spiritual breathing, which in Sanskrit is called *pranayama. Prana* is the vital energy, the Life-Breath; *yama* means control. So *pranayama* is control of the Life-Breath. The very first exercise you can practise is to repeat once, as you breathe in, the name of God, or the Supreme, or the Christ, or whomever you adore. Then hold your breath and count to four while calling for your Supreme Beloved. When you breathe out, call twice for Him. So the rhythm will be one, four, two.

Gradually an aspirant can increase his capacity to four, sixteen, eight. But I wish you to practise only *one, four, two* right now.

This you can do to try to purify your mind. But if you want to have more purity, you can do one more spiritual exercise which is most effective. You all know the significance of *Aum*, the name of God. To start with, on Sunday you will repeat this sacred name of the Supreme one hundred times; Monday, two hundred; Tuesday, three hundred; Wednesday, four hundred; Thursday, five hundred; Friday, six hundred; Saturday, seven hundred. Then on the following Sunday you come down to six hundred; Monday, five hundred; and so on, to four hundred, three hundred, two hundred, one hundred. If you want to establish purity all around you, within and without, then this is the most effective spiritual exercise. In New York some of my disciples have done this. They have achieved, I must say, considerable purification of their nature and their emotional problems. Without purity no divine quality can remain permanently in our nature, in our body, in our system, in our life. If one lacks purity, then no divine truth can stay within him permanently. But whenever there is purity, then peace, light, bliss and power will be able to function most successfully. This does not mean that I am telling you that you are all impure—far from it. But the purest nature, the purest life, will always have the deepest blessings of the Supreme. The more pure we are, the closer we are to the Supreme.

Now let us come to the problem of thought. Most of us become a victim to thoughts—ugly thoughts, uncomely thoughts, silly thoughts, fearful thoughts—the moment we enter into meditation. How can we be freed from this attack? The first thing we have to know is whether the thoughts that are attacking us are coming from the outer world or from deep inside ourselves. In the beginning it is difficult, I must say, to distinguish the thoughts that are coming from the outside and those that are arising from within. But gradually we will be able to know that some thoughts are coming from outside, and these thoughts can be driven back faster than the thoughts that come from within.

Suppose you have started your meditation and suddenly a flood of thoughts and impure ideas enters into you from outside. Now, when you see that a thought is about to enter, you have to know whether it is a good thought or a bad thought, a divine thought or an undivine thought. If it is a divine thought, please welcome the divine thought. If it is a thought of God or a thought of divine joy, divine love, beauty or purity, then allow that thought to come inside you and let it play, let it expand. Or try to follow the thought. If it is something about Grace, something about Divinity, Infinity, Eternity, Immortality, please try to see where the thought goes. Try to follow that thought like a faithful dog. But if it is a bad thought, counter it immediately with your soul's will. Please try to collect your soul's will from your heart and bring it right in front of your forehead. The moment your soul's will is seen by the thought, the thought is bound to disappear.

Now I wish to speak about the thoughts that we have already accumulated within us. When we see a thought arising from deep within us that is not divine, that is absolutely impure and unlit, immediately we shall try to rid ourselves of it. One way is to feel that there is a hole right at the top of our head and that the thought is like a channel or river which flows out and does not come back; it is gone and we have lost it. The other method is to feel that we are a boundless ocean and that these thoughts are like fish. We represent the very depths of the ocean, with its calm, quiet feeling of tranquility. The play of the fish on the surface can never disturb us.

I wish to say that it would be advisable for each of you to fight with the outer thoughts right now and to deal with the inner thoughts later on. But if you have inner thoughts which are divine, progressive, encouraging and inspiring, please try to grow with them and feel that they are like feet, feet of Infinity, of infinite Light, infinite Bliss, that can carry your body, mind, heart and soul to a higher realm.

Now, about the still deeper meditation. Those who are meditating on the *ajna chakra* (the third eye) should also practise concentrating on the heart. If the heart remains barren — that is to say, if the heart centre is not opened up and the third eye *is* opened — then there will be a great deal of confusion in our human nature. If the third eye is not flooded with the purity of the heart, then you will have vision and, at the same time, you will be the victim of merciless temptation. You will try to enter into somebody to see what is happening in his nature. There are a thousand and one things which will eventually lead you far, far away from the path of spirituality. There are people who have opened up their third eye without having opened the heart centre and who, by the Grace of the Supreme, have not misused their vision; but it is always safer to concentrate first on the heart centre. Unless and until the emotional part of our human nature is totally purified, it is very dangerous for us to open the third eye.

So please concentrate on the heart centre first. This centre is called *anahata*. You will get all joy here; you will get all love here. In this world, what do we need? Joy. What else do we need? Love. When we have achieved joy and love, then we can have vision or wisdom in our third eye. Women, without exception, should try to meditate on the heart centre. It is easier for them to open the heart centre than it is for men. For men, it is easier to open up the third eye.

When you are meditating at home, if possible, please meditate all alone. This rule does not apply to a husband and wife if they have the same spiritual Master. The closest spiritual friends who understand each other thoroughly in their inner lives can also meditate together. In our Centre, the disciples should meditate collectively. But for individual daily meditation, I feel it is better if one meditates in one's own room privately, in secret.

The best hour for meditation, according to Indian seers, sages and spiritual Masters, is between three and four o'clock in the morning. That is called *Brahma Muhurta*, the time of the Brahman, the best time. But here in the West, if you go to bed late, the best hour for you is five-thirty or six in the morning. The precise hour is to be settled according to the individual case and the individual capacity.

Now, that is the first time in the day. If you can meditate again between twelve and twelve-thirty, for ten or fifteen minutes, it is wonderful. This meditation you have to do inside, not in the street. A day will come when you will be able to meditate anywhere, while driving or doing anything else, but now it is advisable to meditate indoors, in a proper place.

Then, when the sun is about to set, you can look at the sun and meditate. For ten minutes try to meditate. At that time, please try to feel that you have become totally one with the sun, with the cosmic nature. You have played your part during the day most satisfactorily and now you are going to retire. That will be your feeling.

Then meditate when you retire for the night—nine o'clock, ten o'clock, or whenever you go to bed. It is always better to go to bed by eleven o'clock at night. But necessity knows no law; if you are compelled to work at night, it is all right for you.

Each one should meditate in his own way. Sometimes people ask me what they should do if they do not have a good meditation, if they feel restless. If any of you find it difficult to meditate on a particular day, then do not try to force yourselves. Those who are my disciples, just look at my picture, at a picture taken of me in a high consciousness. Do not try to meditate, do not try to concentrate. Only look at my picture, at my eyes or at my forehead or at my nose—just look. If you follow some other path, or if you have no Guru but you have a picture of something spiritual to concentrate on, please concentrate on that and do not try to force yourself to meditate. Then, when you get up for your daily work, do not even once feel miserable that you could not meditate. If you feel that your inner being is displeased with you or if you are displeased with yourself, then you are making a great mistake. If you cannot meditate on a particular day, try to leave the responsibility to your Master or to God. Never feel sorry. If you feel sorry, the progress that you made yesterday or the day before will be diminished.

There are some who want to meditate while lying down. I wish to tell you that that kind of meditation is not at all advisable for the beginners, nor even for those who have been meditating for quite a few years. It is only for the most advanced disciples and for realised souls. Otherwise, you will lie down and immediately you will enter into the world of sleep or a kind of inner drift or doze. Furthermore, while you are lying down your breathing is not as satisfactory as it is when you are meditating in a sitting position.

Please do not take a heavy meal before your meditation. A minimum of two hours should elapse between your mealtime and your meditation. Again, suppose you are pinched with hunger and you know that if you eat right now then you will have to wait for two hours before you can meditate. In that case, please drink a small quantity of water or juice. You have to know that when you are extremely hungry you should not meditate. If the hunger-monkey is pinching you, you have to feed him a little and make him quiet for a few minutes. If you want to eat after meditation, please wait for half an hour so that your system can assimilate the results of the meditation. During that half-hour you can move around, you can read if you like. You may have a very small quantity of milk, water or juice, but not a proper meal.

* * *

Concentration makes us perceptive. Meditation makes us receptive. Contemplation makes us intuitive.

* * *

A moment of gratitude offered to God is an hour of most intense meditation on God.

* * *

Question: I have never been to your Centre before. I have read a few books but I'm a beginner in meditation.

Sri Chinmoy: You are coming here for the first time, and you have read many books, but have not meditated before. Books have given you the inspiration to enter into the field of aspiration. Here we are all aspiring to reach the Highest and fulfil the Highest.

In the spiritual life when you are in the presence of a spiritual Master you receive according to your capacity of receptivity. You are a beginner, but that does not mean you will be denied something. Everybody was a beginner once upon a time. A beginner in any school cannot sit together with someone who is far advanced because their lessons will clash. But in the spiritual life we have to feel our inner oneness with those who are ahead of us. We also have to feel how far and how deep we want to go.

Those who are my disciples do not need special meditations because I have taken the responsibility for their meditation. How? I have simplified the matter. There is a photograph of me in my highest transcendental Consciousness. A seeker should always meditate on what inspires him most. Just because I am their Master, my disciples get abundant inspiration from meditating on this picture. If anybody looks at it with love, joy and devotion, no matter how much of a beginner he is, no matter which path he followed

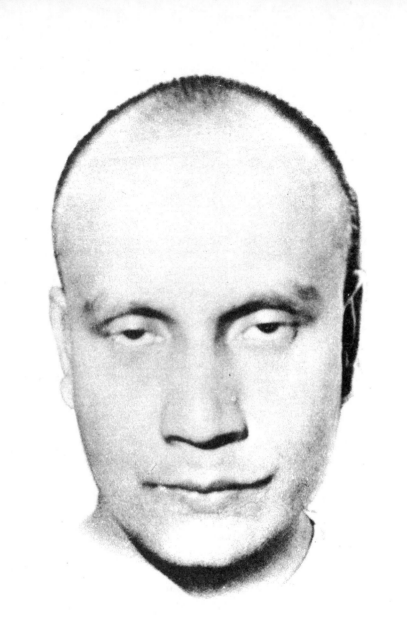

Sri Chinmoy in his highest Transcendental
Consciousness.

before, just because the person is a seeker, my inner consciousness will open its door to him. On our path if anyone devotedly concentrates a few minutes each day and enters into my third eye, then I take the responsibility for his meditation. During his meditation at home, if the seeker is attuned to me, I will immediately feel that a voice is coming from within and telling me that that person meditated at this hour and so forth.

You are a beginner, but you do not have to be doomed to disappointment. Your sincere cry can make you swim in the sea of aspiration. The easiest way to meditate for my disciples is to concentrate on my picture. You can try it just for a couple of days. If you have faith in me, which is of paramount importance, I can assure you that your life of real aspiration can immediately begin. It is your own sincerity that will easily expedite your inner search for ultimate realisation.

Question: How can we learn to meditate? I believe in God, but it is very hard for me to meditate.

Sri Chinmoy: The best way to begin to learn how to meditate is to associate with people who have been meditating for some time. These people are not in a position to teach you, but they are in a position to inspire you. If you have some friends who know how to meditate, just sit beside them while they are meditating. Unconsciously your inner being will be able to derive some meditative power from them. You are not stealing anything from them, but your inner being is taking help from them without your outer knowledge.

If you want to be under the guidance of a spiritual Master, the Master's silent gaze will teach you how to meditate. The Master does not have to explain outwardly how to meditate or give you a special form of meditation or a *mantra*. He will simply meditate on you and inwardly teach you how to meditate. Your soul will enter into the Master's soul and bring the message, the knowledge of how you should meditate, from his soul.

Outwardly, I have given very few disciples a specific way of meditation. But I have a few hundred disciples and most of them know how to meditate. How do they learn? When I meditate at the Centres or at public meetings, they see something and feel something in me. And what part of them actually sees this? It is their souls. Their souls enter into my soul and learn from my soul, and then with this wisdom they teach the disciples how to meditate. All real spiritual Masters teach meditation to the disciples and admirers in silence. When a genuine spiritual Master meditates, Peace, Light and Bliss descend from above and enter into the sincere seeker. Then automatically he learns how to meditate from within.

If you have a Master, it is easier to learn how to meditate because you get additional help from the Master's conscious Concern. But if you do not want to follow a specific path, or if you do not want to be under the guidance of a spiritual Master, if you just want to learn how to meditate a little and not go to God-realisation, then the best thing is to associate with spiritual people in whom you have faith. Unconsciously they will help you. But this process will not take you to your Goal. You will learn to walk, but you will not be able to walk fast. You will not be able to run fast, faster, fastest toward your

Goal. For that you will need higher lessons, inner and deeper lessons, from some spiritual Master.

* * *

CONCENTRATION

Concentration is the arrow.
Meditation is the bow.

If you want to sharpen your faculties, concentrate. If you want to lose yourself, meditate.

It is the work of concentration to clear the roads when meditation wants to go either deep within or high above.

Concentration wants to seize the knowledge it aims at. Meditation wants to identify itself with the knowledge it seeks for.

An aspirant has two genuine teachers: concentration and meditation. Concentration is always strict with the student; meditation is strict at times. But both of them are solemnly interested in their students' progress.

Concentration says to God: "Father, I am coming to You."

Meditation says to God: "Father, do come to me."

Concentration is the commander who orders the dispersed consciousness to come to attention.

Concentration and absolute firmness are not only inseparable but also interdependent divine warriors.

Concentration does not allow Disturbance, the thief, to enter into his armory. Meditation lets him in. Why? Just to catch the thief red-handed.

Concentration challenges the enemy to a duel and fights him out. Meditation, with its silent smile, diminishes the challenge of the enemy.

* * *

Sri Chinmoy demonstrates concentration.

Question: What is the difference between concentration, meditation and contemplation?

Sri Chinmoy: When we concentrate we do not allow any thought to enter into our mind, whether it is divine or undivine, earthly or heavenly, good or bad. The mind, the entire mind, has to be focused on a particular object or subject. If you are concentrating on the petal of a flower, try to feel that only you and the petal exist, that nothing else exists in the entire world but you and the petal. You will look neither forward nor backward, upward nor inward. You will just try to pierce the object that you are focusing on with your one-pointed concentration. But this concentration is not an aggressive way of looking into a thing or entering into an object. Far from it! This concentration comes directly from the soul's indomitable will, or will power.

Very often I hear aspirants say that they cannot concentrate for more than five minutes. After five minutes they get a headache or feel that their head is on fire. Why? It is because the power of their concentration is coming from the intellectual mind or, you can say, the disciplined mind. The mind knows that it must not wander; that much knowledge the mind has. But if the mind is to be utilised properly, in an illumined way, then the light of the soul has to come into it. When the light of the soul has entered the mind, it is extremely easy to concentrate on something for two or three hours or as long as you want. During this time there can be no thoughts or doubts or fears. No negative forces can enter into your mind if it is surcharged with the soul's light.

So when you concentrate, try to feel that the power of concentration comes from here, the heart centre, and

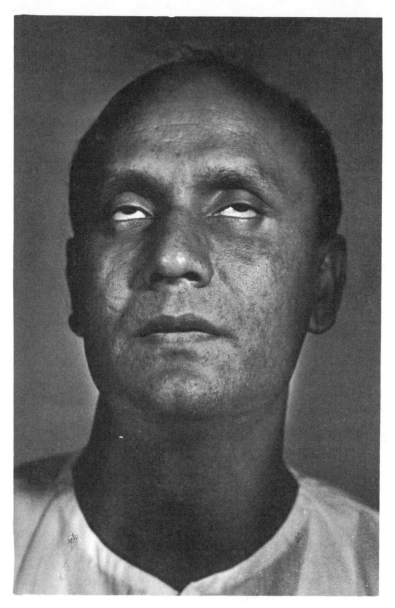

Sri Chinmoy demonstrates contemplation.

then goes up to the third eye. The heart centre is where the soul is located. The physical heart is tiny, but the spiritual heart—your true home—is vaster than the universe. When you think of your soul at this time, please do not form any specific idea of it or try to think what it looks like. Just think of it as God's representative, as boundless Light and Delight, which is in your heart. The Light comes from your heart and passes through your third eye, and then you enter into the object of your concentration and have your identification with it. The final stage of concentration is to discover the hidden ultimate truth in the object of concentration.

What concentration can do in our day-to-day life is unimaginable. Concentration is the surest way to reach our goal, whether the goal is God-realisation or merely the fulfilment of human desires. It is concentration that acts like an arrow and enters into the target. He who is wanting in the power of concentration is no better than a monkey. A real aspirant sooner or later acquires the power of concentration either through the Grace of God, through constant practice or through his aspiration. Each seeker can declare that he has a divine hero, a divine warrior, within himself. And what is that divine warrior? It is his concentration.

When we concentrate, we have to concentrate on one particular thing. If I am concentrating on a certain disciple, then he will be the only thing in my mind. He becomes, at that time, the sole object of my attention. But when we meditate, we feel that we have the capacity deep within us to see many, deal with many, welcome many—all at the same time. When we meditate, we try to expand our consciousness to encompass the vast sea or the vast, blue sky. We have to expand ourselves like a bird spreading its wings. We have to expand our finite consciousness and enter into the universal Consciousness where there is no fear, no jealousy, no doubt, but all joy, peace and divine power.

When we meditate, what we actually do is enter into a vacant, calm, still, silent mind. We go deep within and approach our true existence, which is our soul. When we live in the soul, we feel that we are actually meditating spontaneously. On the surface of the sea are multitudes of waves, but the sea is not affected below. In the deepest depths, at the bottom of the sea, it is all tranquility. So when you start meditating, try to feel your own inner existence first. That is to say, the bottom of the sea: calm and quiet. Feel that your whole being is surcharged with peace and tranquility.

Then let the waves come from the outside world. Fear, doubt, worry—the earthly turmoils—will all be washed away, because inside is solid peace. You cannot be afraid of anything when you are in your highest meditation. Your mind is all peace, all silence, all oneness. If thoughts or ideas want to come in, you control them with your inner peace, for they will not be able to affect you. Like fish in the sea, they jump and swim but leave no mark on the water. Like birds flying in the sky, they leave no trace behind them. So when you meditate, feel that you are the sea, and all the animals in the sea do not affect you. Feel that you are the sky, and all the birds flying past do not affect you. Feel that your mind is the sky and your heart is the infinite ocean. This is meditation.

When we are in meditation, we want only to commune with God. Now I am speaking in English and you are able to understand me because you know English well. Similarly, when you know how to meditate well, you will be able to commune with God, for meditation is the language we use to speak to God.

Through concentration we become one-pointed and through meditation we expand our consciousness into the vast. But in contemplation we grow into the vast itself. We have seen the Truth. We have felt the Truth. But the most important thing is to grow into the Truth and become totally one with the Truth. If we are concentrating on God, we may feel God right in front of us or beside us. When we are meditating, we are bound to feel Infinity, Eternity, Immortality within us. But when we are contemplating, we will see that we ourselves are God, that we ourselves are Infinity, Eternity, Immortality. Contemplation means our conscious oneness with the infinite, eternal Absolute. In contemplation we discover ourselves. When we contemplate, Creator and creation become one. We become one with the Creator and see the whole universe at our feet, the whole universe inside us. At that time, when we look at our own existence, we don't see a human being. We see something like a dynamo of Light, Peace and Bliss.

One should concentrate for a few minutes each day before entering into meditation. You are like a runner who has to clear the track—see if there are any obstacles and then remove them. Then, when you begin meditating, feel that you are running very fast, with all obstacles out of your way. You are like an express train, an inner train, that only stops at the final destination. Then, when you reach the Goal, you have to become the Goal. This is the last stage, contemplation. Seekers who are just entering onto the spiritual path should start with concentration, for a few months at least, and then enter into meditation. Then they must meditate for a few years and finally enter into contemplation.

Question: Could you please discuss how contemplation differs from meditation?

Sri Chinmoy: If you meditate on a specific divine quality, such as Light, Beauty, Peace, or Bliss in an unshaped form, or if you meditate in an abstract way on Infinity, Eternity or Immortality, then constantly you will feel an express train going forward inside you. You are meditating on Peace, Light or Bliss while the express train is constantly moving. Your mind is calm and quiet in the vastness of Infinity; but there is a movement: a train is going endlessly toward your goal. You are envisioning a goal and meditation takes you there.

In contemplation it is not like that. The entire universe, the farthest Goal, is deep inside you. When you are contemplating, you are holding within yourself the entire universe with all its infinite Light, Peace, Bliss and Truth. There is no thought, no form, no idea, nothing. Everything is merged in contemplation; all is one. In your highest contemplation, you are one with the Absolute. But in your highest meditation there is a dynamic movement. That movement is not aggressive; you are not beating or striking anyone. Far from it! But a dynamic movement is going on in your alert consciousness. You are fully aware of what is happening in the inner world and in the outer world and, at the same time, you are not affected. In contemplation you are also not affected, but there you and your whole existence have become part and parcel of the universe, which you are holding deep inside you. This is the main difference between contemplation and meditation.

Question: How do I know that while meditating I am entering into a higher plane and that it is not just my imagination?

Sri Chinmoy: There is a very easy way to know. If you are actually entering into a higher plane, you will feel that your body is becoming very light. Although you don't have wings, you will feel that you can fly. In fact, when you have reached a very high world, you will actually see a bird inside you that can easily fly in the sky as real birds do.

When it is your imagination, you will get a very sweet feeling for a few minutes and then immediately dark or frustrating thoughts will come into you. You will say, "I studied so hard, but I did not do well in my examination," or "I worked so hard in my office today, but I could not please my boss." These negative forces in the form of frustration will immediately come in. Or doubt will enter and you may say, "How can I meditate so well? Yesterday I did so many wrong things; I told so many lies. How can God be pleased with me? How can I be having such a high meditation?" But if it is really a high meditation, you will feel that your whole existence, like a divine bird, is soaring up and flying. While you have this feeling, there is no sad thought, no negative thought, no frustrating thought, no doubt. It is all joy, all bliss, all peace. You are flying in the skies of delight.

Right after our meditation, if we have a good feeling for the world, then we know our meditation was good. If we see the world in a loving way in spite of its imperfections, then we know that our meditation was good. And if we have a dynamic feeling right after meditation, if we feel that we came into the world to do something, to become something, this indicates that we have done a good meditation. This feeling that we have to do something does not mean that we are feeding our human ambition. No! The moment we try to feed our ambition, it will entangle us like a serpent. What we have come into the world to do is what God wants us to do. What we have come into the world to become is what God wants us to become. What God wants us to do is to grow into His very image. What God wants us to be is His dedicated instrument. During our meditation if we get the feeling that God wants us to grow into His very image and wants us to be His dedicated instrument, and if this feeling is translated into action after our meditation, then we can be sure that we were meditating well.

But the easiest way to know if we have had a good meditation is to feel whether peace, light, love and delight are coming to the fore from within. Each time light comes forward, or love comes forward, or peace or delight comes forward, the whole body will be surcharged with that divine quality. When we have this experience, we know that we have done a very good meditation. Each time they come to the fore, we are bound to feel that we are remembering a forgotten story. It is only through meditation that we can remember our forgotten story. This story was written by the seeker in us; it was not written by somebody else. It is our own creation, but we have forgotten it, and it is meditation that brings it back. When we remember this story, we are overjoyed that we have created such a beautiful story and that this is our life story.

Question: When you have a personal problem which you wish to solve through your meditation, how can you resolve it and know that the answer you get comes directly from the soul and not from the emotional vital?

Sri Chinmoy: One way to know the difference is to feel that the emotional vital has one voice and the soul has another voice. Let us take the vital as one runner and the soul as another runner. In the case of the vital runner, he runs very fast at the very beginning, with excessive excitement and enthusiasm, but he does not reach the goal. He runs about thirty metres out of a hundred and then cannot run any more. The other type of runner also runs very fast at the beginning. He is confident and once the starter fires the gun, he does not stop until he reaches his goal.

When you get a voice, immediately try to see which type of runner this voice represents. Is this the runner who will stop only when the goal is reached, or is this the runner who runs thirty metres and then loses all his energy? The soul knows its capacity and will go to the goal with utmost confidence. If it comes from the emotional vital, you will feel that the answer you get will not take you to your goal. But if it comes from the soul, you will feel confident that it will take you to the goal. If this is the case, then rest assured that it is your soul speaking.

Here is another way. When you have a voice which is offering you a solution to your problem, imagine that a vessel is being filled. If this voice gives you the feeling of a vessel being filled drop by drop, slowly and steadily with utmost inner security, then you will know that it is the soul's voice. Otherwise, you will feel that the vessel is being filled with a tumbler or a glass in a hurried manner. It will fill up quickly, but very soon it will begin to spill over the top. The other way, with utmost confidence and inner poise, the soul will fill the vessel. If you have had that kind of patient feeling, then it is the soul's voice.

A third way is to imagine a flame inside your heart. Now, there are two types of flame. One is steady; the other is flickering. The steady flame inside your heart is not disturbed by any inner wind. But the flickering flame is disturbed by fear, doubt, anxiety, worry. If you feel that your answer is a flickering flame, then it is the voice of the emotional vital. But if it is a very steady flame rising toward the highest, then you know it is your soul's voice you have heard. Once you know it is your soul's voice, you can rest assured that your problems will be solved, because the soul's voice has much strength, while the vital's voice has no strength.

Question: Why doesn't God make all our meditations equally good?

Sri Chinmoy: You don't have a good meditation every day, in spite of your best intentions. Some days you get up and meditate early in the morning at your proper time but real meditation does not come. Then, instead of cursing yourself or cursing your Master, you should simply say: "Oh, perhaps this is what the Supreme wants. Perhaps the Supreme wants me to have this experience." You must feel this consciously. You are trying your best to meditate well, but unfortunately your meditation is not at all satisfactory. So you have to feel, "I am trying my best. Now it is up to Him to give me the best meditation." But please remember that your own aspiration and your will to meditate regularly and punctually at a particular hour are still of greatest importance.

You know that is is necessary for the body to eat, but you can't eat the most delicious food every day. Your wife may cook extremely well, but if she does not give you the most delicious food every day, what will you do? Should you get angry? No! At that time you feel that she had something more important to do for you than cook. Similarly, you should feel that if the Supreme has not given you a good meditation on a particular day, He is thinking of doing something very great for you in some other way. Instead of getting angry with Him, have faith in Him and feel that He will give you some different experience.

In your wife's case, her whole existence is inside you. If she cannot give you the most delicious food, she will do something else to please you, to make you happy. In God's case, if God does not give you a good meditation today, He will give you something else which is equally important or more important. A person we love has every right to please us in various ways; otherwise we become bored. Today, through meditation God is pleasing you, tomorrow through dedication He will please you, and the day after tomorrow, He will please you in still another way. He wants to fulfil Himself in and through you every day. But He has every right to change His means of doing it. If you have a fixed menu and say, "This meal is good; I will eat it every day," after a few days you will be sick of it. It is the same thing with divine food. There should always be variety.

Question: You say we should meditate in the heart, but I find it easier to meditate in the mind.

Sri Chinmoy: If you find it easier in the mind, then meditate in the mind. But if you do so, you will be able to meditate for perhaps five minutes, and out of that five minutes, for one minute you may meditate very powerfully. After that you will feel your whole head getting tense. First you get joy, satisfaction, but then you may feel a barren desert. For five minutes you will get something, but if you want to go on beyond that, you may feel nothing. If you meditate here (in the heart) a day will come when you start getting satisfaction. If you meditate in the heart, you are meditating where the soul is. True, the soul is everywhere — in the mind, in the body, everywhere. But it is like my situation now. I am here at the United Nations. If someone asks, "Where is Chinmoy?" you can say that I am at the United Nations, or you can say that I am in Conference Room 10. My presence is spiritually pervading the entire United Nations, but my living consciousness is right here in this room. If you come here, I will be able to do more for you than for others who are elsewhere in the building. Similarly, when you focus your concentration in the heart, you get much more inner satisfaction than when you meditate in the mind, because the heart is the seat of the soul. But it is difficult for some people to meditate in the heart because they are not used to doing it.

You have to be wise. There is a vast difference between what you can get from the mind and what you can get from the heart. The mind is limited; the heart is unlimited. Deep within us is infinite Peace, Light and Bliss. To get a limited quantity is an easy task. Meditation in the mind can give it to you. But you can get more if you meditate in the heart. Suppose you have the opportunity to work at two places. At one place you will earn two hundred dollars, and at the other place five hundred dollars. If you are wise, you will not waste your time at the first place. But you have to know that the source and the reality is in the heart. Reality is everywhere, but the actual manifestation of the reality has to be in a particular place. Inside the heart is the soul, and if you meditate in the heart the result is infinitely more fulfilling.

Let us not be satisfied with the things that we get very easily. Let us cry for something which is more difficult to get, but which is infinite and everlasting. If you get something from the mind, tomorrow doubt may come and tell you that it is not real. But once you get something from the heart you will never be able to doubt it or forget it. An experience on the psychic plane can never be erased from the heart.

Question: In meditation, sometimes the mind stops functioning and there seems to be little information coming.

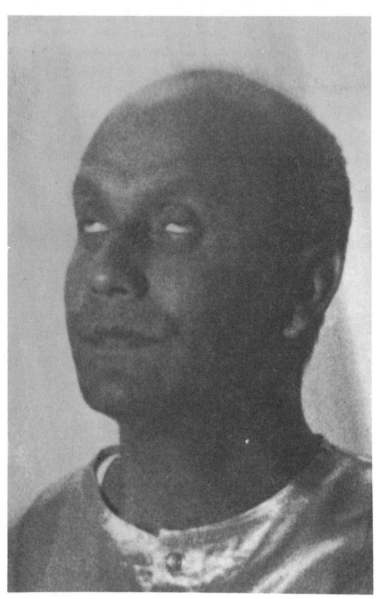

(Photo by Sarama)

Sri Chinmoy demonstrates meditation.

Sri Chinmoy: In meditation we should not give importance to the mind. If there is no information coming in, it is good. Real meditation is not information; it is identification. The mind tries to create oneness by grabbing and capturing you and this may easily make you revolt. But the heart creates oneness through identification. The mind tries to possess. The heart just expands and, while expanding, it embraces. With the mind we only divide ourselves. The mind may try to do something and immediately the body or the vital may try to prevent it. But if the heart wants to do something, no matter how difficult, it will be done. This is because when the mind gets no satisfaction when it tries something, it just says that there is no reality there and gives up. But when the heart does not get satisfaction, it feels that it has not done the thing properly. So it tries again, and continues trying until satisfaction dawns at last.

* * *

When a seeker meditates on himself, he feels his inner potentiality and sees his outer possibility.

When a seeker meditates on God, he feels his inner divinity and sees his outer reality.

* * *

Question: When I first began meditating at three o'clock in the morning, I used to have very good meditations and I was very inspired. But after a few days, I didn't have the same inspiration and it became very difficult.

337

Sri Chinmoy: When we start something for the first time, we get inspiration. Anything that is new gives us tremendous inspiration, just because it is something new. But if we continue doing it, we do not have the same enthusiasm, the same impetus, the same inspiration. We want to get something very deep, very high and very sublime, something most illumining, from our early morning meditation. We are like a long distance runner. When the starter fires the gun, at the very beginning he is really inspired and he starts running very fast. But after two or three miles, he becomes very tired; running becomes tedious and difficult. Now, if he gives up running just because he is tired and because his inspiration is gone, he does not reach the goal. But if he continues running, he will finally reach the goal. Then he will definitely feel that it was worth the struggle and suffering of the body.

It is like that in the spiritual life also. When you start your journey at three o'clock in the morning, feel that tomorrow is the continuation of that journey. Do not take it as a new beginning. Every day you have travelled another mile. By taking one step at a time you reach the Goal.

In order to maintain the same level of meditation, you have to be very spiritually advanced. I am not throwing cold water on you; far from it. I wish to say that in the beginning you should be very happy if at times you get very good, very high, sublime meditation. When you don't have a good meditation, don't allow yourself to become a victim to frustration. If you get frustrated, you are losing your capacity to an even greater extent. Then on the following day, at that time also, it will be impossible for you to meditate deeply.

If you don't have a good meditation today, then try to forget about it. Tomorrow if you have a meditation that is a little better, try to remember it. The past is dust. The past has not given you realisation; that is why you are still praying and meditating. So why should you think of the past? You have to forget all that did not inspire you or encourage you to go farther. So if today's meditation does not inspire you or has not given you most satisfactory results, try to forget it altogether.

You have aspiration and then you lose it. Then you cry for it, but you may not get the same aspiration back again. But here you have to realise that you are not an expert in meditation. Now your meditation is at the mercy of your inspiration or aspiration. When you are inspired, you have aspiration and you are ready to meditate. But this aspiration, this inner urge, will last only for a day or a few weeks and then it disappears. But when you become an expert, meditation will be at your command.

How can we become an expert in anything? If we want to become a singer or a poet or a dancer, we have to practise daily. It is the same with meditation. When we practise meditation daily, there comes a time when it becomes spontaneous. If we regularly meditate once or twice a day, then we develop a kind of inner habit. After a while, at such and such an hour, we will feel compelled to meditate. We will feel that meditation is our soul's necessity and the inner urge to meditate will never be able to leave us. It will always inspire and energise us. Early every morning when it is time for our meditation, our inner being will come and knock at our heart's door.

Question: Sometimes after meditation I lose the joy that I have received from my meditation. Is there a method that would be helpful in holding onto that joy?

Sri Chinmoy: There are two reasons why you lose your joy. One reason is that your mind starts functioning most powerfully and vehemently. While functioning in this way it allows obscure, impure, undivine thoughts to come in either consciously or unconsciously and then your joy has to disappear. But if purity is well-established in the mind, then the joy will last for a long time.

Another reason you might lose your joy is because your vessel is small and you have taken light, which is joy itself, beyond the capacity of your vessel. The quantity of light that you have gotten during your meditation has satisfied you, but the excess you were not in a position to hold in your vessel; so you felt miserable.

Question: What do you mean by highest meditation?

Sri Chinmoy: The highest meditation is when you do not have any thought at all. Now, while we are meditating, we are victims to many thoughts, undivine thoughts, ugly thoughts, bad thoughts, evil thoughts and so forth. Then we may do a kind of meditation where we get fairly good thoughts, divine thoughts, fulfilling thoughts and illumining thoughts. This is a higher state. But when we are in the highest, there will be no thoughts, either good or bad. There is only Light. In Light, vision and reality are together. You are sitting there and I am standing here. You are the reality; I am the vision. I have to look at you. Then, I have to enter into you in order to know that you are the reality. But when we do the highest meditation, at that time it is not like that. The reality and the vision are together. Where you are, I have to also be; where I am, you have to be, because we are one. So, in the highest meditation, reality and vision go together. That is why we do not need thoughts or ideas or anything. First a thought enters into us. Then we give it form. Then we come to understand what is going on, or what we are thinking about. But when we see that the Knowledge, the Knower and the thing that is to be known are all together, at that time we are having the highest type of meditation.

Question: How can one make meditation practical?

Sri Chinmoy: We say somebody is practical only when we see that in the outer life he does the right thing at the right moment. He thinks and acts in a specific way so that he will not be deceived by others, and so that his outer life will run smoothly, without any major catastrophes. But no matter how clever, how sincere, or how conscious we are, at times we are at a loss in the outer life. We do not know what to say. We do not know what to do. We do not know how to behave. Or, despite our saying and doing the right thing, everything goes wrong. We do not know how to cope with our outer existence; we cannot manage our lives. We sincerely want to do something or become something, but we cannot do it.

Why does this happen? It happens because our outer capacity is always bound by something, and that something is our inner awareness. If we are practical in the inner life, if we are doing the right thing in the inner world, we will not be bound by anything, because we will have inner awareness. One who has inner awareness has free access to infinite truth and everlasting joy, and he is able to control his outer life. What gives us inner awareness? Meditation. We are practical in our inner life when we pray and meditate. A practical thing should always be natural, and what can be more natural and spontaneous than seeking to fulfil God? How do we fulfil God? Through meditation.

The inner life constantly carries the message of Love, Truth and God. The outer life does not do this. Where the Truth is, there is a seed. Let us allow the seed to germinate, to grow into a plant, to become a tree. When the tree bears fruit, we can eat it. And while we are eating, we will know that this fruit belongs to the outer world although its source is the inner world. We will see the capacity of the inner world being manifested in the outer world. We always grow from within, not from without. It is from the seed under the ground that a plant grows. From inside we grow out.

No matter how many hours we work, no matter how many hours we talk, no matter what we do or what we say, we are not nearing the Truth-Light. But if we meditate first, and afterwards act and speak, then we are doing the right thing and becoming the right thing. The inner life, the inner practicality, must guide the outer life, and not the other way around. It is not that the outer life will have a separate existence. No! The life-breath of the outer life has to come from the inner life. The inner practicality must enter into the outer life of each individual seeker on earth. Only then can he be really practical in the outer life.

Question: Through meditation is one able to create or master psychic powers?

Sri Chinmoy: Through meditation it is possible to get psychic powers, but it depends on the soul whether an individual will actually get them. Sometimes an aspirant will acquire psychic powers and then not want to pray or meditate anymore. Instead, he will want to help people. Unfortunately, the ignorance of these people will capture and infect him and finally he may leave the spiritual path. So acquiring psychic powers may be dangerous. But when one becomes perfect, when one realises God, at that time if one starts using psychic powers, it is safe.

Psychic powers do not necessarily help one in realising God, but they may come to a seeker on the way to realisation. Psychic powers are like beautiful trees or delicious fruits on the way to the Goal. If somebody walks along a road where there are no trees, no flowers, nothing, then he is not tempted to stop on his journey. Psychic powers will very often take sincere seekers away from the path. Once you have realised the Goal, the psychic powers are bound to come. So it is better not to pay any attention to the psychic powers now. Only pay attention to your aspiration and inner cry. When it is time, God Himself will give you all the psychic powers. But right now what He wants is for you to realise Him.

Question: During a meditation, if something external to the meditation occurs—such as noise or something unforeseen—is it better to include it in the meditation or to try to shut it out and pursue the meditation?

Sri Chinmoy: Each seeker has to know his own standard of meditation. If we are a beginner, we should feel that anything that is not part of the meditation is like an intruder. We should not allow an intruder, a foreigner, to enter into us and disturb us. But if we are very advanced, and there is a disturbing sound or a noise during your meditation, we can go deep into the sound itself and try to assimilate it. If we have the capacity, then in our own consciousness we can transform the attack of a most powerful, most challenging foreign element into an inner music, a thrilling or haunting music, which will really add to our meditation. But we have to develop this capacity to transform a disturbing, annoying noise into soothing, thrilling and soul-stirring music. When we have this capacity, we shall include the disturbance in our meditation. As long as we don't have the capacity, we shall always exclude it.

Question: Sometimes when I get into meditation I feel peace and light all around me. Then someone calls me from the kitchen or some other place and I have to stop my meditation. Then I feel frustrated.

Sri Chinmoy: If somebody calls you during your meditation, do not be upset. Feel that the experience that you had a few moments ago was most sublime. Then, if you can bring this peace, love or light to the person who has called you or distracted you, you will see, instead of frustration, the extension of the light you have received. Then you will feel more joy because of the expansion of your achievement.

What you are doing is separating your life of meditation from the world of reality. Instead, try to feel that you are bringing the flow of your meditation into the new situation which is the cause of the disturbance. By extending your meditation in this way, you will see it inside the situation also. Meditation is not only in silence but also in the hustle and bustle of the world. You will find that you can be happy there also.

* * *

WHAT IT HAS

His concentration has given him
     What is has: Power.
With Power he has changed
     The lives of multitudes.

His meditation has given him
     What it has: Love.
With Love he has changed
     The face of humanity.

His contemplation has given him
     What it has: Oneness.
With his Oneness he has become man
          The lover divine.
With his Oneness he has become God
          The Beloved Supreme.

* * *

Question: Should a person shut himself away all alone and reject humanity in order to meditate?

Sri Chinmoy: He who meditates has to act like a divine hero amidst humanity. Humanity is part and parcel of God. By throwing aside humanity, how are we going to reach divinity? We have to accept the world as it is now. If we don't accept a thing, how can we transform it? If a potter does not touch the lump of clay, how is he going to shape it into a pot? The world around us is not perfect, but we also are not perfect. Perfect Perfection has not yet dawned. We have to know that humanity at present is far, far from perfection. But we are also members of that humanity. How are we going to discard our brothers and sisters who are our veritable limbs? I cannot discard my arm. It is impossible. Similarly, when we meditate soulfully, devotedly, we have to accept humanity as our very own. We have to take it with us. If we are in a position to inspire others, if we are one step ahead, then we have the opportunity to serve the divinity in the ones who are following us.

So we must not enter into the Himalayan caves. We have to face the world here and now. We have to transform the face of the world on the strength of our dedication to the divinity in humanity. Meditation is not an escape. Meditation is the acceptance of life in its totality with a view to transforming it for the highest manifestation of the divine Truth here on earth.

Question: If meditation is the only way of seeing God face to face, what advice would you give to the man who has a family to look after?

Sri Chinmoy: When the family man gets up early in the morning, what does he think of? He thinks of the members of his family, the education of his children and so forth. But before he allows these thoughts to enter into him, before he enters into activities, if he can meditate, if he can think of God for five minutes or ten minutes, these few minutes will be of great benefit to him. Yes, he shoulders responsibilities; he has to think of his whole earthly family. But again, who shoulders the responsibility of the entire universe? Not he, not the members of his family, but God, God Himself.

If the head of the family meditates on God, on Light — for God means Light — then Light descends. It starts to decrease his worries and anxieties. When one concentrates, whatever he wants to do becomes easier. Similarly, if an individual who has many family problems meditates for five or ten minutes before he thinks of his family, it will immediately help him by reducing the difficulties he faces; also, the Light that he receives will operate in him. He does not have to meditate for ten or twelve hours. He knows that his progress may not necessarily be very fast; but slow and steady wins the race.

If you try to feel God every day, the living God, inside your children and the members of your family, then gradually you will see and feel Light operating within them. But people do not do that. They look upon their children as their possessions, and feel they have every right to mould them and guide them according to their own sweet will. But if they can feel that they love their children and all the members of their family precisely because God is inside them, if they think of that and meditate on that, they are doing the best thing for their own and their family's progress.

Question: If we get Light from the soul during meditation, do we actually manifest it?

Sri Chinmoy: When we enter into our soul through meditation, we realise Peace, Light and Bliss. Then, through the physical, we offer these qualities to the world. When we look at someone or say something or do something, the physical is manifesting what the soul has experienced or realised. We have meditated here for about twenty minutes. All of us have entered into the realm of soul according to our capacity. Whatever we have achieved in the inner region will now be manifested by the body. About an hour ago when you came in here you did not bring Peace or Light in with you. After you came in you invoked Peace, Light and Bliss. Now this Peace, Light and Bliss have entered into you through the soul, and from the soul they have now entered into your physical consciousness. If you go and stand in front of a mirror you will see the difference between what you were an hour ago and what you are now. This obvious physical difference you will see is due to the fact that the physical consciousness is manifesting the Light that the soul has invoked.

* * *

PRAYER AND MEDITATION

Prayer and meditation are medicines to cure us. As we go to a doctor for medicine to cure our physical body, similarly prayer and meditation are the medicines which will cure us in our inner life.

With prayer we grow individually into the highest Divinity. But whenever we pray, often there is a subtle desire for something. We may call it an aspiration, because we pray to become good, to say or do something good, to have something divine which we do not have, or to be free from fear, jealousy, doubt and so on. In meditation we do not do that. We just allow ourselves consciously to enter into the effulgence of Light, or we invoke the universal Light to transform our ignorance into wisdom.

When we pray, we aspire toward the Highest and our whole existence goes upward like a flame. Prayer can come from the heart, but there is always a tendency in prayer to desire something. When we pray, we automatically act as if we are beggars who are crying to God to grant us a boon.

When a beggar comes and knocks at the door, he does not care whether the owner is a rich man or a poor man; he just knocks and knocks in order to get something. This is the way we pray to God, asking for this and that, looking up at Him and crying to Him. We feel God is high above while we are down below. We see a yawning gulf between His existence and ours. We do not know when or to what extent God is going to fulfil our desires. We just ask and then wait for one drop, two drops or three drops of Compassion, Light or Peace to descend upon us.

When we meditate, it is nothing like that. In meditation we dive into the vast sea of Consciousness. We do not have to ask God for Peace or Light because we are swimming in the sea of divine qualities. At that time, God gives us more than we can ever imagine. The deeper we go in meditation, the more we expand our own consciousness, the more abundantly the qualities of Light, Peace and Bliss grow inside us. Meditation itself is the fertile soil where the bumper crop of Light, Peace, Bliss and Power can grow.

In prayer we have nothing and God has everything. That is why we say, "God, give me this." When we meditate we know that whatever God has, either we also have it or we will someday have it. We feel that whatever God is, we also are, but we have not brought it forward.

In the West, many saints have realised God through prayer only; they did not care for meditation. In the Western world we hear more about prayer than about meditation. In the East we pay more attention to meditation. This is the difference between prayer and meditation: when I pray, I talk and God listens. When I meditate, God talks and I listen.

If we want to differentiate between prayer and meditation, we can say that prayer is the conscious ascent of the human consciousness and meditation is an invitation to the Infinite or an offering to the Infinite. It is the individual who will choose whether he would like to make rapid progress by praying or by meditating.

Aspiration is within both prayer and meditation. He who is praying feels an inner cry to realise God. When we pray, we go up, up, up. He who is meditating feels the need of bringing Consciousness right into his being, into his own consciousness. Aspiration is the only key for both prayer and meditation. Either we reach up to God or He comes down to us. Ultimately, it is the same. God lives on the third floor, but when He comes down to the first floor, He is still the same God. One aspirant may go up and get Him; another may bring Him down. When we pray we go up and touch Him; when we meditate we bring Him down into our consciousness.

If one wishes to help other people, the most important thing is to pray and meditate every day. You cannot really help people without first getting the inner capacity through your prayer and meditation. If you want to help people, then help people *after* you have received inner strength from your own prayer and meditation. Do the first thing first. If you pray you will get spiritual wealth; if you meditate you will get spiritual wealth. But if you try to help others without meditation, without your wealth, what will you be able to give them? At that time you yourself are a beggar too. Your prayer and meditation are your inner work. When you work in the morning by praying and meditating, God gives you your salary, your spiritual wealth. Once you have your money, you can give it to others.

Your prayers can help another person, but you have to know how. You are praying to God and that particular person has God within him. When you pray for his welfare, you are not touching him directly: you are touching the God in him. Your prayer is going to God, the Source.

What do you do if a plant is dry? You need not actually touch the plant itself. You pour water at the root and the plant again gets strength. As you would go to the root of a plant, go to man's Source. His Source is God. The person you are praying for will get the most benefit if you pray with this idea in mind.

To eliminate strain while meditating or praying, try to focus all your attention on the heart, not on the mind. First try to see the heart-source. From there you will feel a flow which will be going either upward or downward. Try to direct the flow so it moves upward from the heart. This flow, which is divine Grace, is like water. Each time you pray or meditate, feel that you are digging inside. Naturally, the all-nourishing water comes up, for this water is being supplied constantly from its infinite Source: God.

* * *

Question: If we give you everything on the physical plane, will we grow more into your soul?

Sri Chinmoy: Absolutely. Physical work is the body's prayer, the body's meditation. You can surrender while you are washing dishes, while you are providing any kind of service. If you are surrendered to me, then you become a perfect instrument.

In prayer you go to God and ask Him to please do this or that; and in meditation God comes and tells you what to do. During your prayer you go up so your Father can please and fulfil you; and during your meditation He comes down and asks you to manifest Him. This kind of prayer and meditation you can do in the physical plane while you work. Devoted service is a real form of prayer and meditation. When you do dedicated service, you are performing the task of your soul.

* * *

To converse with God, man has his throbbing prayer.
To converse with man, God has His illumining Bliss.

To commune with God, man has his silent meditation. To commune with man, God has His urgent Peace.

* * *

THE ABSOLUTE

No mind, no form, I only exist;
  Now ceased all will and thought.
The final end of Nature's dance,
  I am It whom I have sought.

A realm of Bliss bare, ultimate;
  Beyond both knower and known;
A rest immense I enjoy at last;
  I face the One alone.

I have crossed the secret ways of life,
  I have become the Goal.
The Truth immutable is revealed;
  I am the way, the God-Soul.

My spirit aware of all the heights,
  I am mute in the core of the Sun.
I barter nothing with time and deeds;
  My cosmic play is done.

* * *

THE INNER TREASURE:
PEACE, LIGHT
AND BLISS

(i) PEACE

OUTER   PEACE   AND   INNER   PEACE

The outer peace and the inner peace: the outer peace
is man's compromise; the inner peace is man's
fulfilment. The outer peace is man's satisfaction without
being satisfied at all. The inner peace is man's satisfaction in being totally and supremely fulfilled.

How can the outer peace have the same capacity as
the inner peace? The outer peace can have the same
capacity if and when man's creation and God's creation
become inseparably one.

What is man's creation? Man's creation is fear. Man's
creation is doubt. Man's creation is confusion. What is
God's creation? God's creation is Love. God's creation is
Compassion. God's creation is Concern.

Fear is the feeble ant in man. Doubt is the wild
elephant in man. Confusion is the devouring tiger in
man.

God's Love for man is man's aspiration. God's Compassion for man is man's salvation. God's Concern for
man is man's perfection.

Man's fulfilling and fulfilled search for the Real is peace. God the Love is man's eternal Guest in the inmost recesses of his heart. God the Peace is man's eternal Host in the inmost recesses of his heart. That is why we can unfalteringly and unmistakably claim that the loving and fulfilling peace is our birthright.

How can we have peace, even an iota of peace, in our outer life, amid the hustle and bustle of our multifarious activities? Easy: we have to choose the inner voice. Easy: we have to control our binding thoughts. Easy: we have to purify our impure emotions.

The inner voice is our guide. The binding thoughts are the dark and unpredictable weather. The impure emotion is the inner storm. We have to listen to the inner voice always. It is our sure protection. We have to be cautious of the binding thoughts. These thoughts have tremendous vitality. We must never allow them to swell into mountains. We have to face them and then dominate them. These thoughts are absolutely non-essentials. We have to refrain from the luxury of the emotional storm. Impure emotion is immediate frustration, and frustration is the harbinger of total destruction within and without.

How can we choose the inner voice? To choose the inner voice, we have to meditate early in the morning. To control and dominate our undivine thoughts, we have to meditate at noon. To purify our unlit, impure emotions, we have to meditate in the evening.

What is meditation? Meditation is man's constant awareness and conscious acceptance of God. Meditation is God's unconditional offering to man.

Peace is the beginning of love. Peace is the completion of truth. Peace is the return to the Source.

* * *

Man invents war. Man discovers peace. He invents war from without. He discovers peace from within.

* * *

World peace will begin when the so-called human expectation ends. World peace can dawn only when each individual realises the Supreme Truth: Love is the revelation of Life and Life is the manifestation of Love.

* * *

World peace can be achieved, revealed, offered and manifested on earth when the divine Power of Love replaces the undivine love of power.

* * *

What are the things that prevent us from acquiring peace in the outer world? Our self-indulgence in the world of the body; our self-aggrandisement in the world of the vital; our self-doubt in the world of the mind; and our sense of self-insufficiency in the world of the heart.

What are the things that can inspire us to have peace in the outer world? Simplicity can inspire our body, humility can inspire our vital, sincerity can inspire our mind and purity can inspire our heart.

* * *

Peace conquers the animal in me.
Aspiration illumines the human in me.
Realisation immortalises the divine in me.

* * *

Peace begins when expectation ends.

* * *

Peace begins when the mind is powerfully captured.

* * *

OUR PEACE IS WITHIN

No price is too great to pay for inner peace. Peace is the harmonious control of life. It is vibrant with life-energy. It is a power that easily transcends all our worldly knowledge. Yet it is not separate from our earthly existence. If we open the right avenues within, this peace can be felt here and now.

Peace is eternal. It is never too late to have peace. Time is always ripe for that. We can make our life truly fruitful if we are not cut off from our Source, which is the peace of Eternity.

The greatest misfortune that can come to a human being is to lose his inner peace. No outer force can rob him of it. It is his own thoughts, his own actions, that rob him of it.

Our greatest protection lies not in our material achievements and resources. All the treasure of the world is emptiness to our divine soul. Our greatest protection lies in our soul's communion with the all-nourishing and all-fulfilling peace. Our soul lives in peace and lives for peace. If we live a life of peace, we are ever enriched and never impoverished. Unhorizoned is our inner peace; like the boundless sky, it encompasses all.

Long have we struggled, much have we suffered, far have we travelled. But the face of peace is still hidden from us. We can discover it if ever the train of our desires loses itself in the Will of the Lord Supreme.

Peace is life. Peace is bliss eternal. Worries — mental, vital and physical — do exist. But it is up to us whether to accept them or reject them. To be sure, they are not inevitable facts of life. Since our Almighty Father is All-Peace, our common heritage is peace. It is a Himalayan blunder to widen the broadway of future repentance by misusing and neglecting the golden opportunities that are presented to us. We must resolve here and now, amidst all our daily activities, to throw ourselves, heart and soul, into the sea of peace. He is mistaken who thinks that peace will, on its own, enter into him near the end of his life's journey. To hope to achieve peace without spirituality or meditation is to expect water in the desert.

For peace of mind, prayer is essential. To pray to God for peace with full concentration and singleness of devotion even for five minutes is more important than to spend long hours in carefree and easy-going meditation. Now, how to pray? With tears in our hearts. Where to pray? In a lonely place. When to pray? The moment our inner being wants us to pray. Why to pray? This is the question of questions. We have to pray if we want our aspirations to be fulfilled by God. What can we expect from God beyond this? We can expect Him to make us understand everything: everything in nothing and nothing in everything, the Full in the Void and the Void in the Full.

We must always discriminate. We have to feel that the outer world which attracts our attention is ephemeral. To have something everlasting, to attain to a rocklike foundation in life, we have to turn toward God. There is no alternative. And there is no better moment to take that turn than when we feel most helpless.

> To feel oneself helpless is good.
> Better to cultivate the spirit of self-surrender.
> Best to be the conscious instrument of God.

In the human life everything depends on the acceptance or rejection of the mind, including the search for peace. The function of purity in the mind is to remove the clouds of doubt and confusion and the ties of ignorance in the mind. If there is no purity in the mind, there can be no sustained success in the spiritual life.

We own peace only after we have totally stopped finding fault with others. We have to feel the whole world as our very own. When we observe others' mistakes, we enter into their imperfections. This does not help us in the least. Strangely enough, the deeper we plunge, the clearer it becomes to us that the imperfections of others are our own imperfections, but in different bodies and minds. Whereas if we think of

God, His Compassion and His Divinity enlarge our inner vision of Truth. We must come in the fulness of our spiritual realisation to accept humanity as one family.

We must not allow our past to torment and destroy the peace of our heart. Our present good and divine actions can easily counteract our bad and undivine actions of the past. If sin has the power to make us weep, meditation has undoubtedly the power to give us joy, to endow us with the divine wisdom.

Our peace is within, and this peace is the basis of our life. So beginning today let us resolve to fill our minds and hearts with tears of devotion, the foundation of peace. If our foundation is solid, then no matter how high we raise the superstructure, danger can never threaten us. For peace is below, peace is above, peace is within, peace is without.

* * *

Question: How can we attain lasting inner peace?

Sri Chinmoy: We can attain lasting inner peace only when we feel that our Supreme Pilot is in the many as one and in the one as many. When we consciously feel this truth in our life, we get lasting peace in whatever we say, whatever we do, whatever we offer and whatever we receive.

The day I feel my existence and my illumining heart in everyone is the day I immediately become one in many. When I receive or bring down Peace from above, immediately I feel that I am many, not one. Then when I assimilate the Peace in myself, I see the Peace has been assimilated in all of us. Then I have a conscious feeling of oneness, of the oneness in the many and the many as one.

Peace comes in and we lose it because we feel that we are not responsible for humanity, or that we are not part and parcel of humanity. We have to feel that God and humanity are like a great tree. God is the tree, and the branches are His manifestation. We are branches, and there are many other branches. All these branches are part of the tree and are one with each other and with the tree. If we can feel that we have the same relationship with God and with humanity as the branch has with its fellow branches and with the tree as a whole, we are bound to get everlasting peace.

Question: How can a person really find inner peace?

Sri Chinmoy: On a practical level, do not expect anything from others on the physical plane. Just give and give and give, like a mother who gives everything to her child thinking that the child is not in a position to give her anything in return. Do not expect anything from the world; only love the world and offer your capacity, your inner wealth, your joy. Everything that you have, give to the world unconditionally. If you expect anything from the world, then you will feel miserable because the world does not understand you, the world does not care for you. If you can do anything unconditionally, then you will have peace of mind. This is one way.

The other way is to meditate on the heart, where there is constant joy, constant love. At that time you will not cry for appreciation from others. You will all the time depend on your inner Source, where there is infinite Joy, infinite Love, infinite Peace. The best thing is to meditate on the heart. This second way is most effective.

Question: There is so much injustice and nothing we can do to help ourselves.

Sri Chinmoy: You say that there is nothing you can do, but I am giving you a way to protect yourself. We have been meditating here for five or ten minutes. This meditation has real power. In your office there is much injustice. Injustice itself is a kind of negative power, a destructive power. True, you cannot change the minds of the people who are causing this injustice, but you can protect yourself against them. They are striking you inwardly and because of your fear or your incapacity you don't strike them back. But if you become very strong, very powerful inwardly, your strength will take you to some other place or will give them some illumination. God's Compassion will save you from this kind of injustice if you enter into the spiritual life seriously.

Another way of protecting yourself, which is quicker, is to have peace of mind. At our Tuesday meditation we bring down Peace, which is very solid. It is not something imaginary. You can feel Peace; you can swim in the sea of Peace when you meditate with us on Tuesdays. Injustice is an undivine power, but Peace is an infinitely more powerful divine weapon. It is solid power. When you are in Peace, no human power can upset you.

When you have to defend yourself or protect yourself, try to use a higher weapon. If people say something and you retaliate on the same level, there will be no end to it. Again, if you simply swallow your anger, they will continue to take advantage of you. But when they see and feel tremendous inner peace in you, they will see something in you which can never be conquered. They will see a change in you, and this change will not only puzzle them but also threaten and frighten them. They will feel that their weapons are useless.

Peace is the most effective weapon with which to conquer injustice. When you pray and meditate, your whole being becomes flooded with Peace. Then, no matter what other people do, you will just feel that they are your own children playing in front of you. You will say, "These are all children. What more can I expect from them?" But right now, because they are grown up in terms of years, you become angry and upset instead. If you pray and meditate regularly, you will soon feel that your peace is infinitely stronger, more fulfilling and more energising than the unfortunate situation that they create.

* * *

The presence of Peace in the heart is divine oneness.

The presence of Peace in the mind is divine illumination.

The presence of Peace in the vital is divine dynamism.

The presence of Peace in the body is divine satisfaction.

* * *

Question: I have an experience here at your Dag Hammarskjold lectures which I never am aware of at your other talks. I know you are bringing down tremendous Peace, which I feel in both places, but here at these lectures I have a feeling that I am falling asleep. Yet I hear what you are saying.

Sri Chinmoy: When I give talks I bring down Peace, and this Peace is something tangible for the seekers. When the seeker is eager to swim in the sea of Peace, he is allowed by the Supreme to do so. During this experience, the mind does not operate; only the heart operates. The activity of the mind is totally silenced, and the heart starts functioning in its place. The function of the heart is to identify with anything that is around it or before it or inside it. Your heart is identifying with Peace and this Peace is silencing the mind. It is not inertia; it is not an experience of useless futility or something bad. No, in this Peace you are cultivating the inner truth and growing into the Light which illumines the darkness that you faced or the ignorance that you cherished before you entered into meditation.

I bring down Peace, Light and Bliss in boundless measure, and according to his receptivity each seeker receives this Peace, Light and Bliss. This Peace is not an unconscious way of putting you to sleep. No, this Peace silences the outgoing energy of the mind and, at the same time, illumines the inflow of the heart. And when you are in the heart, the aspiring heart, you become one with the Peace that sustains the divine Reality in you.

* * *

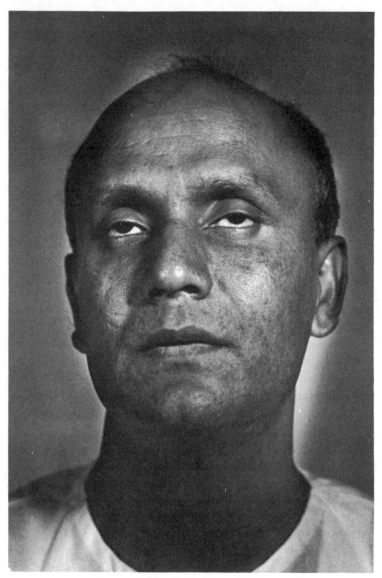

(*Photo by Manohar John Summer*)

Sri Chinmoy brings down Peace

WITHIN, ONLY PEACE

Many foes have I without;
Within, only Peace.
The outer world has turned me mad.
The inner world has smashed the
    mountain of my errors.
The outer world, coming near me,
    has opened the door of destruction.
In my inner world, the ever-beautiful,
    the eternal Infinite, is dancing.

* * *

Aspiration can be raised to meet the Peace above; but Peace must be brought down to remove one's difficulties.

* * *

(ii) LIGHT

Of all the divine qualities, unfortunately Light is
wanted least, even though it is needed most by all.
People want Peace, Joy and Power, but very rarely do
they want Light. Unconsciously or consciously they are
afraid of Light. They feel that the effulgence of Light
will uproot the ignorance-tree which they embody. They
feel that the divine Light will expose their imperfections,
limitations and bondage. This is not true. The divine
Light embraces the world in all its ignorance.
Something more, the divine Light feels that it is its
bounden duty to elevate the human consciousness into
the plenitude of the Life Divine.

* * *

THE INNER EXPERIENCE OF LIGHT

The outer experience of Light is immediate inspiration.
The inner experience of Light is eternal aspiration.

With inspiration, we run toward the farthest Beyond. With aspiration, we become the Goal of the ever-transcending Beyond.

The outer experience of Light is the transformation of binding desires into liberating freedom. The inner experience of Light is the transformation of earth's fate into God's Face.

The outer experience of Light is necessary in order to build the Palace of transcendental Truth on earth. The inner experience of Light is essential in order to watch and enjoy the cosmic Dance of Reality, Divinity and Immortality.

Reality is the dreamer in us. Divinity is the lover in us. Immortality is the fulfiller in us.

The dreamer dreams and acts. The lover loves and becomes. The fulfiller fulfils and transcends.

In our spiritual existence we find that quite a few parts of our being cry for the inner experience of Light, but among these there are two which are really trying to have the inner experience of Light. These two members of our inner existence, are the mind and the heart—the searching mind and the aspiring heart. The searching mind and the aspiring heart come together to the transcendental Light, the Light Supreme, and say, "O Light of the Supreme, save us, illumine us. We are far apart, but we want to live together. We want to become inseparable."

Light answers, "That is quite easy. I shall fulfil your wish. But I wish to ask each of you one thing. Mind, tell me, what is your best quality?"

The mind hesitates and says, "You want me to tell you my best quality, but I have no good qualities! My best quality is my stupidity."

Light consoles the mind, saying, "Oh no! Your best quality is your sense of boundless vastness. Your sense of boundless vastness, O mind, is your best quality."

Then Light asks the heart, "What is your best quality?"

The heart spontaneously says, "I, too, have no good qualities. If I have to tell you what my best quality is, then I feel that it is my insecurity. For I always feel insecure."

Light consoles the heart and says, "No! Your best quality is your universal oneness. Your universal oneness, O heart, is your best quality."

Then Light asks the mind, "Have you any idea how far you are from your Goal?"

The mind replies, "I have no idea at all. But I feel that I am far from my Goal, farther than the farthest."

Light says, "O searching mind, your farthest Goal you can bring right into you if you once can make yourself feel that your very existence on earth is for the supreme Reality and the absolute Truth."

Light asks the heart, "Heart, how far are you from your Goal?"

The heart answers, "I feel that my Goal is very near, right in front of me. But alas, to my utter astonishment and sorrow, I do not see it. If I do not see my Goal face to face, then my feeling has no conviction. First I want to actually see my Goal right in front of me, and then I want to grow into my Goal."

Light says to the heart, "Heart, you can see your Goal right in front of you and you can grow into your Goal immediately if you can discover the eternal truth that your existence on earth has come directly from the eternal Existence of the Supreme, and that you are part and parcel of the Supreme. O heart, when you have discovered this truth—that you are of the Supreme—then you are bound to see your Goal right in front of you."

Now the mind asks Light, "O Light, please tell me if there is anything I have done that has displeased you."

Light says, "Yes, you have misused time. When you foolishly misuse time, you displease me deeply."

"How can I stop misusing time?"

"You can stop misusing time if you believe in my illumining Reality and if you believe that I need your service unreservedly for my full manifestation on earth. If you believe in my illumination and if you believe that I badly need your assistance, then you will stop misusing time."

The heart asks Light, "O Light, is there anything I have done that has displeased you?"

"Yes, you have displeased me by wasting time, and you are still wasting time mercilessly. That is why I am displeased with you. You can stop wasting your time if you believe in my illumining Reality and if you believe that I need your dedicated service, your soulful service, for my immediate and permanent manifestation on earth."

"O mind, O heart, if you listen to me, if you fulfil my needs, then both of you can stay together permanently, inseparably."

The mind says to Light, "O Light, I give you my word of honour: I shall serve you; I shall fulfil your manifestation."

The heart says to Light, "O Light, I shall serve you unreservedly and unconditionally for your immediate and permanent manifestation on earth."

When we have the inner experience of Light, we realise that the finite can embody and reveal the Infinite and, at the same time, the Infinite can manifest its Infinity, Eternity and Immortality in and through the finite. When we have the inner experience of Light, we feel the constant necessity of knowing whether we are working for God, whether we are constantly taking God's side or whether God is taking our side. After we have had the inner experience of Light, we always want to take God's side. We do not want and do not allow God to take our side. This is the experience that transcends all other experiences. A seeker of the highest order, and even a Yogi or spiritual Master of the highest order may at times ask the Supreme to take his side. But when one has had the full inner experience of infinite Light, one always takes the side of the Supreme.

In the ordinary life there are many people who feel that there is no happiness on earth, and so the best thing is to live without happiness. But a spiritual Master does not see eye to eye with them. He asks them to have the inner experience of Light just once. If one has the inner experience of Light, then his life is all happiness. For him every day is happiness, every hour is happiness, every minute is happiness, every second is happiness.

In the ordinary life there are many people who think that there is no fulfilling love on earth. They claim that there is only one kind of love, the love that binds us, the love that chains our hands and shackles our hearts. But a spiritual Master tells them, "No, there is something called real love, divine love, the love that liberates, the love that perfects human imperfections, the love that fulfils. You can have this love if you have had an iota of the inner experience of Light. The inner experience of Light tells us that human life is a constant unfulfilling want whereas the divine life is a constant fulfilling and fulfilled achievement. Before we have the inner experience of Light, we try to live on earth and hope to live in Heaven in the future. But once we have had the inner experience of Light, we actually do live in Heaven on earth: we live in the heart of eternal Time and in the lap of Immortality."

* * *

Question: During concentration and meditation, what kind of practical things can I do to see the divine Light?

Sri Chinmoy: You are using the word "practical." Here I wish to say that concentration *is* practical; meditation *is* practical. We have to know that God, who is all Light, is natural. Only what is natural can be practical plus practicable. So from now on, please feel that concentration is something natural in your life. Meditation is also something natural in your life. Feel that when you do not meditate, you are doing something unnatural, abnormal, unusual, because inside you is God and the effulgence of divine Light.

You want to see the Light. Either you are trying to enter into the vastness of this Light or you are trying to bring to the fore the Light that you already have. Wonderful! But there are many people who are afraid of Light. They say, "Yes, we want Light." But the moment Light comes to them, they feel that they are going to be exposed. People feel that if they can hide themselves in a dark room, then they will be in a position to see the world and pass judgement, but that nobody will be able to see them. This is their hope. So their darkness, they feel, is a kind of safety and security. When Light comes and is ready to enter into them, they feel that all their weaknesses and limitation, all their negative ideas and negative thoughts, will be exposed. But the very function of Light is to illumine, not to expose; to transform our negative and destructive thoughts into positive and affirmative thoughts.

You want to know how you can receive Light or how you can bring Light to the fore. For that you need preparation, and what is that preparation? The preparation is your pure concentration, your pure meditation. When you start your meditation or concentration, try to feel that you have come from Light and you are inside Light. This is not your imagination; this is not your mental hallucination. Far from it! It is a real, solid, concrete truth that you embody Light and that you are Light itself. You will see that there is a spontaneous flow of Light from within. First you will feel it inside your heart. Then you will feel it in your forehead, in the third eye; and finally you will feel it all over.

There is another way of seeing Light. While breathing, when you draw in the breath, please feel that you are breathing in something that is purifying all that has to be purified inside you and, at the same time, energising all that is unfed. In the beginning, there are quite a few things inside you that have to be purified. There are quite a few things which are hungry. So when you feel that you are feeding, energising and, at the same time, purifying, then you will see that Light becomes absolutely natural.

Since you have accepted our path, please look at my forehead in my transcendental picture. You will see Light and that Light you will feel inside you also, because there is only one Light, and that is God. He is operating inside me, inside you, inside everyone. But, in my case, I can consciously see it and make others feel it. So if you concentrate on my transcendental picture and soulfully repeat the word "Light" fifty, sixty, one hundred times, then I assure you that you are bound to see Light — either blue or white or gold or red or green — because from my transcendental consciousness I am ready to offer Light to anybody who sincerely wants it. This is the secret that I am telling you.

On Thursday at the New York Centre, when you sit in front of me, you can concentrate on my forehead when I am in deep meditation. Take your time and say the word "Light" silently, and while you are saying it, try to feel that you have formed a bridge between yourself and me. Then you will feel continually that you are entering into me and that I am entering into you. You don't have to meditate for four hours or ten hours. No! In a matter of a few minutes, if you have a soulful feeling of oneness with me, you are bound to see Light. This I will be able to do for you, and for other sincere seekers who are my students and disciples. But for others I will not be able to do this, because they have not accepted me as their own.

It is not at all a difficult thing for a sincere seeker to see Light. But those who want to see Light out of curiosity may be denied by God, because they only want to see, and not to grow into, Light. However, if God wants me to show them Light, in spite of their unwillingness, in spite of their disbelief in God, I can show them. It is God who knows what is best for us. In your case, today you will see the Light and tomorrow you will aspire to grow into it. This is what a seeker does: today he sees the Goal, tomorrow he reaches the Goal, and the day after tomorrow he grows into the Goal. So you try; I shall help you.

* * *

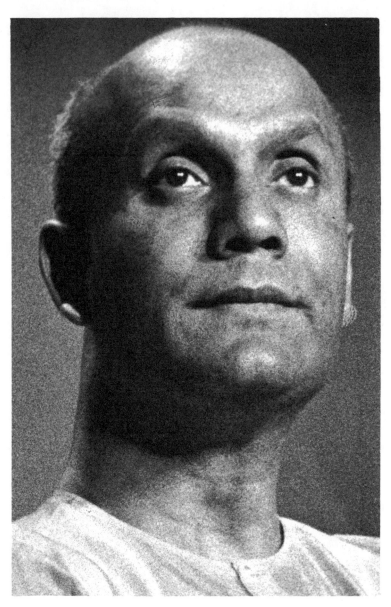

Sri Chinmoy manifests divine Light.

BLISS

Man's unseen strength lies in his hope. His hope's strength lies in his sacrifice. His sacrifice's strength lies in God's Grace. His Grace's strength is the all-fulfilling Delight.

"Please tell me, my real Lord, how I can live without
   trouble and without pleasure."
"My son, to live without trouble,
   what you need is your soul's light.
To live without pleasure,
   what you need is your soul's joy."

DELIGHT

Delight is the source of existence. Delight is the meaning of existence. Delight is the language of Infinity, Eternity and Immortality.

Delight was our inner past. Delight is our inner present. Delight shall be our inner future. No matter if our outer mind understands not or cares not to understand this self-revealing truth.

Delight is not satisfaction of the mind, the vital and the body. It is something deeper, higher and purer. Delight needs no outer help for its existence. It is self-existent, self-revealing and self-fulfilling.

Delight is the divine bridge between Peace and Power, between Light and Truth, between God's unmanifested Dream and His manifested Reality.

The aggressive, dynamic and apparently conquering vital excitement is not Delight. Delight is surcharged with a creative consciousness which is at once energising, fulfilling and itself fulfilled.

God and I are one when I reach Him through Delight in the plane of Delight. God is the whole, and I am a portion of Him when I reach Him through my soul's Delight. God is the Boatman and I am the boat when I reach God through Delight here on earth.

In Delight alone can an aspirant be true to his inmost self. In Delight alone can he feel and understand what God is like. Men speak of God twenty-four hours a day, but not even for a fleeting second do they feel Him, not to speak of understanding Him. If the outer life of an individual can swim in the sea of his soul's Delight, then only will he feel God's Presence and understand Him in His cosmic Vision and absolute Reality.

High, higher and highest is the plane of Delight. With our illumined consciousness, we rise into that plane and become self-enraptured. Having crossed the corridors of sublime silence and trance, we become one with the Supreme.

Infinity without Delight means the creation without a Creator. Indeed, this is absurd.

Delight without Infinity means the Creator without the creation. Indeed, this is equally absurd.

Delight is self-creation and self-experience. Delight in the Highest, absolute Highest, is known as *Ananda Purusha.* There the Delight is Infinity, Eternity and Immortality. There is another type of delight which is called *ananda atma*, when from infinite Delight, Delight takes shape and form. In the earth-bound consciousness, Delight is called *ananda atma*.

When Delight gradually descends into the obscure, impure, unlit, imperfect nature of man to transform human nature, it finds constant resistance. Then we see that Delight loses its power because of teeming ignorance, and short-lived pleasure looms large. In the Highest, the triple consciousness of *Sat-Chit-Ananda,* Existence, Consciousness and Delight go together. But when they want to manifest themselves, they do it only through Delight.

When Delight descends, the first rung that it steps on is called the supermind. The supermind is not something a little superior to the mind. No. It is infinitely higher than the mind. It is not 'mind' at all, although the word is used. It is the consciousness that has already transcended the limitations of the finite. There creation starts. Form begins one rung below. This rung is called the overmind. Here multiplicity starts in an individual form. The next rung is the intuitive mind. With the intuitive mind we see multiplicity in a collective form. With intuition we see all at a glance. We can see many things at a time. From the intuitive mind, Delight enters into the mind proper. This mind sees each object separately. But although it sees everything separately, it does not try to doubt the existence of each object. Next, Delight enters into the physical mind — that is, the mind that is governed by the physical. This mind sees each object separately; plus, it doubts the existence of each object. Real doubt starts here in the physical mind.

After it has descended through all the levels of the mind, Delight enters into the vital. In the vital we see the dynamic force or the aggressive force. The force that we see in the inner or subtle vital is the dynamic, and the force that we see in the outer vital is the aggressive. From the vital, Delight enters into the physical. There are two types of physical: the subtle physical and the physical proper. In the subtle physical, Delight is still descending, and we may still be conscious of it. But in the subtle physical we cannot possess or utilise the truth; we can only see it, like a beggar looking at a multi-millionaire. Finally, when we come to the gross physical, there is no Delight at all.

Delight descends, but we do not see even an iota of it in the gross physical. What can we do then? We can enter into the soul on the strength of our aspiration and the soul will consciously take us to the highest plane, to Existence-Consciousness-Bliss. At that time, our journey can become conscious. We have entered into the triple consciousness, and we can begin descending consciously into the supermind, the overmind, the intuitive mind, the mind proper, the physical mind, the vital and the physical. When we are successful in the physical, that is to say, when we can bring down Delight from the highest plane and the physical can absorb and utilise this Delight, the life of pleasure ends. At that time we come to realise the difference between the life of pleasure and the life of Delight. The life of pleasure is followed by frustration and destruction. The life of Delight is a continuous growth, continuous fulfilment, continuous achievement and continuous God-manifestation in God's own way.

Without Bliss, man is an external superficiality. With Bliss, man is a fulfilling inner and outer reality. Without Bliss, man is a song of frustration and destruction. With Bliss, man is constant fulfilment and constant perfection.

* * *

Question: You have said that it is very difficult to bring down Delight for the disciple. Is there any particular reason for this?

Sri Chinmoy: There are two reasons. One reason is that some disciples don't aspire most sincerely, and the other reason is that the physical and vital impurity of the disciples unconsciously or consciously resists the descent of Delight.

Question: Once you said that transcendental Delight is one of the divine qualities not manifested on earth. Why is that?

Sri Chinmoy: On the highest plane there is Existence-Consciousness-Bliss; we call it *Sat-Chit-Ananda*. *Sat* is Existence; *Chit* is Consciousness; *Ananda* is Delight. Consciousness is the source of everything, but Consciousness cannot stay without Delight and Existence. If there is no Existence, there can be no Consciousness. If there is Existence and Consciousness, Bliss is required for Self-fulfilment.

Great spiritual Masters from time immemorial have brought down the *Sat* and *Chit* aspects. But *Ananda* is much more difficult to bring down. Some could not bring it down at all. Some brought it, but it lasted for only a few seconds or a few minutes and then went back up again. Peace is accessible; we can bring down Peace. Light and Power can easily be brought down. But the Delight which immortalises our inner and outer consciousness has not yet been established on earth. It comes and then goes away because it sees so much imperfection in the earth-atmosphere that it cannot remain.

Even spiritually advanced people are often confused. They feel an inner ecstasy which comes from the vital world, and they think that this is the real Delight. But it is not so. Real Delight comes from the highest world to the soul, and from the soul it saturates the whole being.

This *Ananda* is absorbed differently from physical delight, or what we call pleasure or enjoyment. The supramental Delight is totally different from the world of pleasure and enjoyment. Once you get even an iota of it, you feel your entire being dancing for joy like a child with utmost purity, and your outer being feels true Immortality in its outer existence. If you get this Delight even for a second, you will remember it all your life.

All around us is the cosmic Game, the cosmic Play. The universe is full of joy, inner and outer joy. When realisation takes place, we have to feel the necessity of manifesting this constant Delight in our heart. This Delight glows, but it does not actually burn. It has tremendous intensity, but it is all softness and absolutely sweet-flowing Nectar.

One day I brought it down into my gross physical, so that when I was smiling, at that time I was scattering the highest Delight to each of you. But I must say that it has all disappeared. There is nobody among the disciples who has kept any of it.

Question: Do children sometimes experience this kind of Delight?

Sri Chinmoy: No. Children do not have the highest Delight. They get psychic delight. They get some delight from the psychic being, from the inner being, or from the soul, which they express spontaneously. And very often children express their joy through their pure, un-corrupted vital. But the highest Delight, which comes from the plane of *Sat-Chit-Ananda*, children do not get. One can feel it only in one's deepest, highest meditation. Children also have to go through meditation, concentration and contemplation in order to experience this quality.

[*Sri Chinmoy then asked his disciples to try to invoke* Ananda]. Please place your hand on your heart. Try to feel the most beautiful child on earth and in Heaven inside your heart. This is the soul. The men will naturally see the child as masculine, and the women will naturally see the child as feminine. The soul is neither masculine nor feminine, but when it takes human incarnation, it takes a form. Try to see the child as only seven days old. In terms of spiritual evolution, some of you do not have even that seven-day-old child, forgive me to say. Although the souls started their journey millions of years ago, there are one or two individuals here who have had only one or two human incarnations. Naturally their souls' evolution is perhaps only a few hours old or a few minutes old in purely spiritual terms. Now, please think of the seven-day-old child. Then in absolute silence, please say *Ananda* seven times.

Question: Guru, could you tell me the difference between joy, Bliss and Delight?

Sri Chinmoy: Joy is in the physical plane. Bliss is in the inner place, but it is centered around something specific. Delight, with its immortal Light, runs throughout the entire being.

An unaspiring person can have joy, but he cannot have divine Bliss or Delight. Only a seeker can experience Bliss and Delight. Bliss is intensity. Delight is Immortality's freedom flying constantly in Infinity's sky.

Question: What is the difference between ecstasy, Bliss and Delight?

Sri Chinmoy: Ecstasy is something which we usually feel in our higher emotional or illumined vital. Bliss is something we feel in our aspiring, devoted heart. We also feel Bliss in the searching mind. Delight is something we feel from the soles of our feet to the crown of our head; it is the entire being that enjoys Delight. Delight we feel throughout the body when we are totally dedicated and when we listen unconditionally to the dictates of the Supreme.

Sri Chinmoy manifests divine Bliss.

Question: Is Delight the highest aspect of the Supreme?

Sri Chinmoy: Peace, Light and Delight fall into the same category. These three qualities are the highest aspects of the Supreme. Peace spreads; Light illumines; Delight immortalises. These are their destined roles.

Question: What is the relationship between Light and Delight?

Sri Chinmoy: Light and Delight are inseparable. Both embody the Truth, but each contains particular aspects of the Truth which we can invoke. When we invoke Light, we feel that our life of ignorance, which has lasted for millennia, will be removed; we try to illumine our life of darkness. When we invoke Delight, we feel that our suffering of millennia will be removed; we try to transform our pangs and suffering into Delight.

* * *

FROM
HUMAN   PERSONALITY
TO
DIVINE   INDIVIDUALITY

EGO

THE HUMAN EGO

The ego is that very thing which limits us in every sphere of life. We are God's children; we are one with God. But the ego makes us feel that we do not belong to God, that we are perfect strangers to Him. At best, it makes us feel that we are going to God, not that we are *in* God.

The ordinary human ego gives us a sense of separate identity, separate consciousness. No doubt, a sense of individuality and self-importance are necessary at a certain stage in man's development. But the ego separates our individual consciousness from the universal Consciousness. The very function of the ego is separation. It cannot feel satisfaction in viewing two things at a time on the same level. It always feels that one must be superior to the other. So the ego makes us feel that we are all separate weaklings, that it will never be possible for us to be or to have the infinite Consciousness. The ego, finally, is limitation. This limitation is ignorance, and ignorance is death. So ego ultimately ends in death.

There are many thieves, but the worst of all these thieves is undoubtedly our ego. This thief can steal away all our divinity. Not only are our experiences afraid of this ego-thief, but even our realisation, our partial realisation, is afraid of it. We have to be very careful of the ego-thief.

Our human ego wants to do something great, grand and magnificent, but this unique thing need not be the thing that God wants us to do. It is always nice to be able to do great things, but perhaps God has not chosen us to do that particular thing. God may have chosen us to do something insignificant in the outer world. In the Eye of God, he is the greatest devotee who performs his God-ordained duty soulfully and devotedly, no matter how insignificant it may seem. Each man is a chosen child of God. Similarly, each man is destined to play a significant part in God's divine Game. When God sees a particular person performing the role that He chose for him, then only will He be filled with divine Pride. Our ego will try to achieve and perform great things, but in God's Eye we can never be great unless and until we do what God wants us to do.

The ordinary, common human ego feels that it has achieved everything and that it knows everything. This reminds me of an anecdote which Swami Vivekananda related to the Parliament of Religions in Chicago in 1893. It is called "The Frog in the Well." It happened that a frog was born and brought up in a well. One day a frog from the field jumped into the well. The first frog said to the other, "Where do you come from?"

The second frog said, "I come from the field."

"Field? How big is it?" said the first frog.

"Oh, it is very big," said the second.

So the frog from the well stretched and stretched its legs and said, "Is it as big as this?"

"No, bigger! Much bigger!" said the frog from the field.

The other frog jumped from one end of the well to the other and said, "This must be as big as the length of the field."

The second frog said, "No, the field is infinitely vaster."

"You are a liar!" said the first frog. "I am throwing you out of here."

This shows the tendency of our human ego. Great spiritual Masters and sages speak of Infinity, Eternity and Immortality. The beginner who is just starting his spiritual life will immediately ask, "Is Infinity a little larger than the sky?" The sage will say, "No, Infinity is infinitely larger than your imagination, larger than your conception." Immediately the sage will be criticised because ego makes us feel that what we have realised can never be surpassed by the realisation and experience of others. The ego does not like to feel that someone else has more capacity or that someone else can do something which it cannot do.

At one time ego will make us feel that we are nothing and at another time ego will make us feel that we are everything. We have to be very careful of both our feelings of importance and our feelings of unimportance. We have to say that if God wants us to be nothing, then we will gladly be nothing and if God wants us to be everything, we will be everything gladly. We have to surrender unconditionally and cheerfully to the Will of God.

If He wants us to be His peers, we shall be. If He wants us to be His slaves, we shall be. If He wants us to be His true representatives on earth, we shall be. "Let Thy Will be done." This is the greatest prayer that we can offer to God. In the sincere depths of this prayer is the transformation of ego.

* * *

BETWEEN NOTHINGNESS AND ETERNITY

Barren of events,
Rich in pretentions
My earthly life.
Obscurity,
My real name.
Wholly unto myself
I exist.
I wrap no soul
In my embrace.
No mentor worthy
Of my calibre
Have I.
I am all alone
Between failure
And frustration.
I am the red thread
Between Nothingness
And Eternity.

* * *

Question: How can I conquer ego?

Sri Chinmoy: Feel that your ego is a thief inside you. When you see a thief, what do you do? You chase him. Feel that a thief has entered into you, into your room of aspiration. Start chasing your ego, the thief, early in the morning. In the evening you will be able to catch it. If you can really feel that your ego is a thief, a day will come when you will be able to catch it. It may not come all at once, but if you know that something is stolen and you have seen the thief, you will continue searching. Your search is bound to be rewarded one day. When you catch the ego, what will happen? Your sword of universal oneness will transform it.

Ego is separativity and individuality. Separativity and human individuality cannot live in the sea of oneness and universality. If we want to maintain our separate individuality, our life will end in destruction. A drop, before entering the ocean, says, "Here is the mighty ocean, the vast ocean. When I enter into it, I will be totally lost; I will be totally destroyed; I will have no existence!" But this is the wrong way of thinking. The drop should be spiritually wise. It should feel, "When I enter into this vast sea, my existence will merge with it inseparably. Then I will be able to claim the infinite ocean as part of myself." Who can deny this? The moment the drop enters into the ocean, it becomes one with the ocean; it becomes the ocean itself. At that time who can separate the consciousness of the drop from the consciousness of the entire vast ocean?

The human ego is constantly bothering us. But if we have the divine ego which makes us feel, "I am God's son, I am God's daughter," we will not tend to separate our existence from the rest of God's creation. God is Omniscient, Omnipotent, Omnipresent. If He is all, He is everywhere, and if I am His son, how can I be limited to one particular place? This divine ego or divine pride is absolutely necessary. "I cannot wallow in the pleasures of ignorance. I am God's child. To realise Him, to discover Him in myself and in everyone, is my birthright. He is my Father. If He can be so divine, then what is wrong with me? I came from Him, from the Absolute, from the Supreme; therefore, I should be divine too." This kind of divine pride has to come forward. The ordinary ego that binds us constantly has to be transformed. The divine ego, the divine pride which claims the universe as its very own, should be our only choice.

The ego deals only with the person and his possessions. If we deal with the universal Consciousness, we become the entire universe. In this consciousness we do not act like a tiny individual who can only claim himself and feel, "This is my property. This is my capacity. This is my achievement." No, at that time we will say, "All achievements are mine. There is nothing that I cannot claim as my very own."

In the spiritual life the easiest way to conquer ego is to offer gratitude to God for five minutes daily. Then you will feel that inside you a sweet, fragrant and beautiful flower is growing. That is the flower of humility. When you offer Him your gratitude, God gives you something most beautiful, which is humility. Once it has seen the flower of humility, the ego goes away because it feels that it can become something better: universal oneness.

The more we give, the more we are appreciated. Think of a growing tree. A tree has flowers, fruits, leaves, branches and a trunk. But the tree gets real satisfaction not by possessing its capacity but by offering its capacity. Only in self-giving does it get satisfaction. When it offers its fruit to the world, it bows down with utmost humility. When it offers shade or protection it offers them to everyone without regard for wealth or rank or capacity. We also get real satisfaction by self-giving and not by keeping everything for our own use.

The ego always tries to possess things for itself. But when we transcend ego, we try to give everything for God's Satisfaction, for the world's satisfaction and for our soul's satisfaction. On the human level the ego tries to get satisfaction by using things for its own purpose. In the spiritual life, we transcend the human ego and then we use those things for a divine purpose, for the satisfaction of the entire world.

Question: I feel that I am always competing with others. How can I overcome this?

Sri Chinmoy: Try to feel your oneness with everybody. When you do, immediately you will expand your consciousness. If someone does something well, immediately you have to feel that it is you who have done it. He should also do the same when you do something significant. Whenever any individual does something very well, others have to feel that it is their conscious inspiration and aspiration that have enabled that individual to achieve this success. If we always have an attitude of teamwork, then we will be able to conquer the ego.

But the competitive ego should not be confused with divine pride. Sometimes we feel, "I am God's son, so how can I be so bad? How can I tell a lie? How can I be insincere? I am God's instrument, so how can I do this kind of thing?" This is also a type of ego, but this ego is not the challenging and destructive ego that makes us want to defeat everyone by hook or by crook and lord it over the whole world with our invincible superiority. The divine ego comes from our divinised consciousness, from our inner oneness with God. If we feel in a divine way that we are God's chosen instrument, then there can be no undivine ego in our life. First we have to feel this inwardly. Then in our actions we have to manifest it.

So whenever somebody else does something good, please feel that it is you who have done it. This is not wrong at all. You are not fooling yourself. Do not think, "Oh, I have not done it. My name is not so-and-so." Your name is the universal Consciousness. There is only one Being and that is the infinite and all-pervading 'I'. So when any inhabitant of the universe achieves something, you can easily and most legitimately claim that you have achieved it, if you can just identify yourself with the universal Consciousness.

My disciples accomplish many things on the physical plane which outwardly I have never done. But I immediately feel that it is I who have done these things, on the strength of my sincere and total identification with my disciples. When they do physical work or mental work, they accomplish so many things. At that time I give them credit. I appreciate them, I thank them and offer my heart's sincere gratitude to them. But in my inner being I immediately feel that it is I who have done it with an extended part of my consciousness. These are my spiritual children. Naturally, whatever my children have done is also my achievement. Then again, on the spiritual level, when I bring down Peace, Light and Bliss from above, my children have every right to feel it is with their conscious aspiration that I was able to bring these things down. It was not that they have nothing to do with it. They are not just passive recipients. They have to feel that together we have brought down this Peace, Light and Bliss.

Ego comes from separativity; therefore, how can there be any ego when we feel our true inner oneness? Where is the consciousness of 'I' if, when I do something, you can claim it? Where is the consciousness of 'you' if, when you do something, I can claim it? Where is the ego? It is gone — vanished within our mutual, divine and universal feeling of oneness.

So our ego is conquered in these two ways. When we identify ourselves with other human beings, at that time we feel our oneness with them and the competitive spirit disappears from our life. Then there can be no ego. And if we can feel that we have come from God, we are in God, we are for God and we are of God, that is another way to conquer human ego and transform it into divine pride.

Question: Once the human ego is transcended, is it possible to slip again into egocentricity?

Sri Chinmoy: No. Once the human ego is transcended, one will never fall back into it. It is only when the partial overcoming of the human ego takes place that one may slip back into egocentricity. Once a student passes his examination, he will never fail that examination. He will not have to sit for it again.

Question: I understand that preparatory to realisation, it is necessary for the ego to die.

Sri Chinmoy: If the ego dies or becomes extinguished, then we get nothing out of it. Only if we transform the ego, do we get something out of it. If we try to kill the ego, it is like taking some animal's life. This is not the right thing to do. We must tame the ego. The ego says, "I, mine, my husband, wife, children, etc." That ego is binding. But if we say, "I am everywhere, I am universal, I am God's son," this kind of feeling liberates us.

Try to expand yourself, and the more you expand your consciousness the wider will be your vision. Your limited consciousness is your ego, but when it is expanded it becomes universal. Then you are one with the Source totally.

Suppose that you have a knife. With this knife you can come and stab me, but if you use the same knife to cut a fruit and give me a portion, then you are doing the right thing. Similarly, when you can utilise the ego for a divine purpose, immediately it changes its face into a fulfilling reality. Even when your ego is unlit and impure, use it for the service of God and don't use it to destroy the world. While you are serving God, your ego becomes purified and in its complete purification your expansion of consciousness takes place. In ego's purification and transformation is man's conscious evolution and true satisfaction.

You have to know that nothing dies. In the spiritual life death means limitation, nothing else. When a tiny drop enters into the ocean, we think that the tiny drop is lost in the vastness and dies. But if we identify ourselves with the drop and, at the same time, with the vast ocean, we see that the personality of the drop is not lost; it is enlarged into the vast Infinity of the ocean. This is the so-called death of ego and human personality. With our ordinary human eyes we may see it as death; but with our heart's eye, with our inner eye, we see the transformation of the tiny drop into the infinite ocean.

DIVINE INDIVIDUALITY
AND ONENESS

WHO IS CALLED, WHO IS CHOSEN?

Who is called?
  He alone is called
  Who is ready
    To fight,
  Fight against teeming ignorance.

Who is chosen?
  He alone is chosen
  Who wants
    To win,
  Win the Victory supreme.

Who is called?
  He alone is called
  Who is prepared
    To love,
  Love the entire world.

Who is chosen?
  He alone is chosen
    Who embraces,
  Embraces the life
Of universal oneness.

* * *

NOT POWER, BUT ONENESS

Man has countless desires. He thinks that by fulfilling his desires he will be able to prove himself superior to others. When his desires are not fulfilled, he curses himself; he feels that he is a failure, hopeless and helpless. But God comes to him and says, "My child, you have not failed. You are not hopeless. You are not helpless. How can you be hopeless? I am growing in you with My ever-luminous and ever-fulfilling Dream. How can you be helpless? I am inside you as infinite Power."

Then man tries to discover something else in order to prove his superiority. He tries to exercise his power violently, aggressively. He wants to prove to the world that he is important. In order to prove his eminence he adopts any means, and his conscience does not bother him. God, out of His infinite Bounty, again comes to him and says, "This is a wrong choice. You cannot prove to the world that you are matchless, unique. What you actually crave from your superiority is joy, boundless joy. But this boundless joy will never be yours unless you know the secret of secrets. And that secret is your indivisible oneness with each human being on earth."

Then God continues. He says that He is strong, He is happy, He is fulfilled just because He is totally one with each human being, with the entire universe. Only when one is totally united with the rest of the world can he be truly happy. And this happiness makes a man unparalleled on earth. It is not power that makes us superior or makes us feel that we are priceless; it is our matchless oneness with God and the world. Others do not need us because we have power. No, others badly need our soul's oneness. We are great, we are greater, we are greatest only when we consciously feel our oneness with the entire world.

* * *

Question: I would like to know what the demands of my soul are when I accept a spiritual Master? Do I have to give all my life, all my intelligence, all my love?

Sri Chinmoy: When you say 'give', what do you really mean: give or give up? You need not give up anything when you accept a spiritual Master. Only you have to feel that what you call 'yourself' is another name for your Master. A feeling of indivisible oneness must be established between the Guru's consciousness and the disciple's consciousness. If you feel that you are giving up something, then there will be no end to your frustration.

As the disciple need not give up anything, so also he does not have to give anything to the Guru. The disciple just comes to the Guru and enters into the Guru with what he has and what he is. What do you have? You have a soul. What are you? You are the soul. There is no difference between what you have and what you are. If you enter into your Master with that knowledge, with that wisdom, with that understanding, then you will see, feel, and become totally one with your Master's existence. When the disciple's soul and the Guru's consciousness and soul are one, at that time you are not giving him anything. Your achievement is not at all different from what you are. There will be no more difference between the two than between your fingers and your hand.

So if you are asking what a Guru will demand of you, I wish to tell you that it is your soul, which is precisely what you have and what you are. You may *say* that what you have, both your wisdom and your ignorance, you are giving to your Guru; but if you see that you are inside your Guru, then there is no giving and taking. There is nothing to give and nothing to take; there is only growth inside the Guru's heart. Please stay inside your Guru as long as you can — forever. There is no time when a disciple's soul should be separated from his Master's consciousness. Remain inside the Master with what you have and what you are — not in the sense that you are giving anything to him but in the sense that you belong to each other. Feel that you are growing inside your Master. It is not a question of your giving him something and his having to give you something else in return. Again, there is no sacrifice in the feeling of oneness. When you feel that you and he are one, when you feel that you both have the same consciousness, the same existence, the same love; then there can be no sense of sacrifice.

* * *

INDIVIDUALITY AND PERSONALITY

Human individuality is a self-torturing personality. Divine individuality is a self-discovering personality.

Man does not have to lose his individuality and personality. Man has to feel and realise his all-pervading divine individuality and all-serving divine personality.

When we speak of individuality, we immediately see that it is composed of pride, vanity, desires, frustrations, fear, anxieties, worries and so forth. This kind of individuality can be observed in our ordinary day-to-day life. But there is another kind of individuality, which we call the divine individuality. Divine individuality is totally different from the individuality of pride, vanity, ego, earthbound desires, limited achievements and limited fulfilment. Divine individuality is a direct expression of the Divine in us.

God is one. At the same time, He is many. He is one in His highest transcendental Consciousness. He is many here on earth in the field of manifestation. At the highest, He is unity. Here on earth, He is multiplicity. God is the lotus, and He has many, many petals, each representing an individual aspect of Himself. He is manifesting Himself in infinite ways and in infinite forms.

When we speak of human personality, we immediately think of something coming from our physical consciousness or the physical body. A man, with his inborn capacities, tendencies and talents and all his characteristics, forms a kind of personality. When a man stands in front of me, his personality spreads like water flowing onto a flat surface. When we think of a person or a thing, immediately our own individuality enters into the personality of that person or thing. Right now I am here with you. But if my mind carries me to someone in India, my own individuality immediately becomes one with the person there. I have entered into the person who is now in India, and I can use his personality on the strength of my union with him. I have not lost my individuality. I feel that my individuality has been transformed into an all-pervading and all-serving personality.

The moment I think of anybody, my consciousness enters into him and pervades him. When my consciousness takes me into a person, I become part and parcel of him. Then I expand my consciousness there. When my consciousness expands, his consciousness also expands. We always serve the moment we consciously enter into something other than ourselves.

In our true Self we are all one. But in our outer self, we are many. Among the 'many,' we see that one is serving the other; and the 'other' may not take an active or even a conscious part in the process. For example, I am giving a talk here. You may feel that I am serving you with my knowledge and spiritual light, but I wish to tell you that you are also serving the Supreme in me through your communion with me and your understanding and appreciation of my offering to you. This is what we call the all-serving personality. The moment we stand before a person, even if he does not take an active or dynamic part in the interchange, our very presence constitutes an important part of the consciousness of that person. An ordinary person does not understand the language of a flower, but when he stands in front of a flower, what actually happens? He appreciates its beauty, and the beauty of the flower appreciates his consciousness. There is mutual appreciation, mutual love, mutual service.

I am serving you with all that I am and all that I have. You are serving me by becoming totally one with my consciousness. That is true service. In this kind of service we do not lose our individuality. My individuality remains inside you, and your individuality remains inside me. It is the extension of our personality in the form of this widened individuality which the Supreme expresses in infinite ways. Although a tiny drop of water can be taken as an individual drop, when it merges into the infinite ocean it does not lose its so-called individuality. On the contrary, its individuality is expanded into an infinite expanse of ocean. When we look at the ocean, we see the ocean as an immense being, a huge personality that has inside it billions and billions of living beings. It is a living being itself. By merging into the ocean, the drop becomes as great as the ocean. Similarly, when we enter with our individuality into our divine personality, we see that our individuality is transformed into the infinitely vast and all-pervading personality of the Divine.

Universality does not and cannot mean an utter extinction of the mounting individual flame in the human heart. On the contrary, when the individual transcends himself in the continuous process of universalisation, then he will have the full assurance to abide in the deeper, vaster and higher realms of Light, Peace and Power, and then only will he eventually grow into his own true self, his Self eternal.

* * *

Question: Will we retain individuality or shall we lose individuality when we realise God?

Sri Chinmoy: God does not want us to discard our individuality, but ordinary individuality and real, divine individuality are two different things. God Himself is, at the same time, one and many. He is one, but in the field of manifestation He has become many. He has selected each person as His chosen instrument; that is to say, each human soul is His chosen instrument. This kind of divine individuality which God has given to us is not the ordinary individuality which is determined by the ego: "I am this, you are that." God's individuality is a unique manifestation of His Reality. There is no clash, there is no jealousy, there is no battle, no fight. God Himself is manifesting Himself in a unique manner in you, in me and in others. That kind of individuality is a unique expression of the Divine in His multiplicity. It is just like the petals of the lotus; each petal has its own beauty and its own uniqueness.

* * *

MY NECESSITIES

A fatal necessity:
The whisper of my temptation.

A promising necessity:
The whisper of my prayers.

A fruitful necessity:
The whisper of my surrender.

A fulfilled necessity:
The whisper of my oneness.

* * *

THE SUNLIT PATH: LOVE, DEVOTION AND SURRENDER

LOVE

LOVE HUMAN AND DIVINE

Divine love is a flowering of delight and self-giving.
Human love is the gambol of sufferings and limitations.

Love is a bird. When we encage it, we call it human
love. When we allow love to fly in the all-pervading
Consciousness, we call it divine love.

Ordinary human love with its fears, accusations, mis-
understandings, jealousies and quarrels is a fire clouding
its own brightness by a pall of smoke. The same human
love, arising from the meeting of two souls, is a pure and
radiant flame. Instead of smoke, it emits the rays of
self-surrender, sacrifice, selflessness, joy and fulfilment.

Human love is often the terrible attraction of bodies
and nerves; divine love is the ever-blossoming affinity of
souls.

Divine love is detachment; human love is attachment.
Detachment is real satisfaction; attachment is quench-
less thirst.

Ascending love, arising from the soul's joy, is the smile
of God. Descending love, carrying with it the passion of
the senses, is the kiss of death.

413

Human love is usually self-embracing and self-persistent. Divine love is all-embracing and self-existent.

Love can be as brittle as glass or as strong as Eternity, depending upon whether it is founded in the vital or in the Soul.

Our higher emotions, taken away from their human objects and offered to God, are turned into divine nectar by His magic. Our lower emotions, if not transmuted and transformed, are turned into poison by our own hand.

Disappointment skillfully dogs vital love. Satisfaction divinely consummates psychic love.

When our vital wants to see something, it has to look through self-love. When our psychic being wants to see something, it sees through self-giving.

Human love says to divine love: "I can't tolerate you." Divine love says to human love: "Well, that is no reason for me to leave you."

* * *

Question: I believe that love is always the same, whether human or divine. Is this true?

Sri Chinmoy: No! Human love and divine love are two completely different things. If I give you fifteen cents and you give me a piece of candy, that is called human love. In divine love, you don't wait for my fifteen cents. You give me the piece of candy cheerfully of your own accord. Divine love is sacrifice, and in this sacrifice we are fulfilling God's Will, consciously or unconsciously. In human love, we display the buyer's and the seller's love, which is synonymous with self-interest. Mind you, I am not saying that human beings cannot express divine love. They can and sometimes do. But consistent divine love is, at present, rare in human beings.

* * *

Human love begins in false delight and ends in uncertain wisdom. Divine love begins in infallible wisdom and ends in perpetual delight.

* * *

If love means to possess someone or something, then that is not real love, not pure love. If love means to give oneself, to become one with everything and with humanity, then that is real love. Real love is total oneness with the object loved and with the Possessor of love. Who is the Possessor of love? God. Without love, we cannot become one with God. Love is the inner bond, the inner connection, the inner link between man and God. We must always approach God through love. The first step is love; the second step is devotion; the third step is surrender. First let us love God; then we have to devote ourselves to Him alone; third we have to surrender ourselves at His Feet and fulfil ourselves. Love, devotion and surrender are the secret keys to open the Door of God.

* * *

Marriage is at the mercy of love. At times love allows itself to be caught by marriage; at times it does not.

* * *

Love is the unique combination of Heaven's freedom and earth's discipline. In Heaven's freedom is earth's emancipation. In earth's discipline is Heaven's manifestation.

* * *

Love is always expensive, whether heavenly or earthly.

* * *

Question: How can we teach ourselves to love humanity, not just as a collective whole, but also specifically, when a person's defects and bad qualities are so obvious?

Sri Chinmoy: When you see that a person's defects and bad qualities are so obvious, try to feel immediately that his defects and bad qualities do not represent him totally. His real self is infinitely better than what you see now. On the other hand, if you really want to love humanity, then you have to love humanity as it stands now and not expect it to come to a specific standard. If humanity had to become perfect before it could be accepted by you, then it would not need your love, affection and concern. But right now, in its imperfect state of consciousness, humanity *does* need your love. Give humanity unreservedly even the most insignificant and limited love that you have at your disposal. This is the golden opportunity. Once you miss this opportunity, your future suffering will be beyond your endurance, because a day will come when you will realise that humanity's imperfection is your own imperfection. You are God's creation; so is humanity. Humanity is only an expression of your universal heart. You can and must love humanity, not just as a whole, but also specifically, for unless and until humanity has realised its supreme Goal, your own divine perfection will not be complete.

* * *

To have love is to have reality. Love is reality expressed and manifested.

* * *

Pure Love and untold misery do not and cannot live together. Pure Love is the body's constant oneness with the soul's flood of delight.

* * *

My definition of love is man's conscious manifestation of God's Light.

* * *

Love is sacrifice. Sacrifice is bloom and doom: bloom of the soul, doom of the ego.

* * *

Love will outlive the destructive mind. Devotion will outlive the uncertain heart. Surrender will outlive the negative life.

* * *

LOVE

Lord, what is animal love?
  Animal love is brute instinct.

Lord, what is human love?
  Human love is striking disappointment.

Lord, what is divine love?
  Divine love is an illumining experience.

Lord, what is transcendental Love?
  Ah, that is My Love.
  Transcendental Love
        Is
  My fulfilled universal Oneness.

* * *

Question: What is the relationship between divine Love and divine Compassion?

Sri Chinmoy: Divine Love is for everybody. It is like the sun. A person has only to keep open the window of his heart to receive the divine Love. Divine Compassion is for the selected few. God's Compassion is like a magnet that pulls the aspirant toward his goal. It is a mighty force that guides, pushes and pulls the aspirant constantly and does not allow him to slip on the path of Self-realisation. Divine Love comforts and helps the aspirant, but if the aspirant falls asleep, the divine Love will not force him to awaken and compel him to resume his journey.

Divine Compassion is not like human compassion. In a human way we can have compassion and pity for somebody, but this compassion does not have the strength to change the person and make him run from his ignorant condition toward the Light. In the case of God's Compassion, it is a force that changes and transforms the aspirant and keeps him from making major mistakes in his spiritual life. If it were not for God's Compassion, none of my disciples would be treading the path of Self-realisation. It is this Compassion that prevents them from committing serious mistakes and falling off the path. God's Compassion comes to the disciples through their Master's Grace. When God shows Compassion through the spiritual Master, He expects that the seeker will immediately come close, closer, closest to Him. Through Compassion alone, the disciple can become closest to God.

Love can be very often misunderstood. If one shows love, people may think that there is some motive behind it. They think, "He is showing me extra love, so he wants an extra favour." In the feeling of love between Guru and disciple, the disciple may be fifty percent loving and the Guru may be fifty percent loving. But in Compassion, the Guru may be offering ninety-nine percent and the disciple one percent, and even with his one percent the disciple is trying to enter into the field of ignorance. When Compassion comes, it flies like an arrow and tears down the veil of ignorance.

Love can stay even with ignorance, but Compassion will not. Compassion has to be successful; otherwise it will be withdrawn. It will stay for a few seconds, or for a few minutes or a few years; but it has to send a report to the highest Authority and say whether it has been successful or not. Eventually a time comes when the highest Authority says, "It is a barren desert. Come back." Then Compassion has to fly back to the highest Authority, the Supreme.

A true spiritual Master tries to approach his disciples with snow-white, purest love. But often he fails because his love gets no response. Then he changes his policy and tries Compassion. Again, often his Compassion is refused and misunderstood to the extent of actually being misused and abused. People ascribe motives to the Master's purest Love and purest Compassion. When the Master appreciates someone, that person doubts his motives. "How can the Master be so good? How can he be so nice? Perhaps he wants something more, something important, from me."

With his Love he has failed and with his Compassion he has failed. What remains? Unavoidable strictness! Love will still continue and Compassion will continue, but along with these two divine qualities, the Master adds strict inner and outer discipline. Finally, if he fails to see inner and outer discipline in an aspirant's life, he is compelled to tell the aspirant that his path is not for him. His mission can grow and fulfil itself only on the strength of the seeker's real inner devotion and selfless, dedicated service.

Question: I don't understand why God's Love doesn't enter into me even though I keep the doors shut.

Sri Chinmoy: If God's Love enters into you when you are not receptive to it, then you will regard it as a foreign element. You will not appreciate it or care for it. If somebody brings most delicious food right in front of you but you do not appreciate it, then why should he bring it to you? It would be a waste of time. You will just discard it and feel that it has no value.

An unaspiring person, a desiring person, will wallow in the pleasure of ignorance. Is it God's bounden duty to come down and offer His infinite Peace, Light and Bliss to this type of person? No! But if one is crying and struggling to get an iota of Peace, Light and Bliss, then God will feel that that one deserves it.

We know how to cry at every moment. We cry for the things that desert us and disappoint us; for the ego and its children: fear, doubt, anxiety and worry. We cry for name and fame, for money, wealth and possessions; but we do not cry to God for His Light and Delight. We do not cry for that which we are meant to cry for; we do not cry for the wealth which we all had once upon a time.

We cannot just play games with the eternal Truth and the highest Reality; we have to value them. In this world, if we value something, then we work very hard to acquire it. If we don't work hard, we get nothing. If we don't value wisdom, will wisdom dawn on us? Only when we have worked hard for it does wisdom dawn. For everything we get, we have to offer something of ourselves; but we see that what we give is next to nothing in comparison to what we get. It takes a second to open the door; and the person who comes in, the Eternal Guest, brings us Eternity. But if we don't take the trouble to open the door, then why should He come? We won't value Him; we will feel that He is bringing us rubbish and things that we don't need.

At every moment in the spiritual life we have to value Peace, Light and Bliss and cry for them. Then only can we expect to get them from God. Otherwise, even if He brings Peace, Light and Bliss in abundant measure, we will say that we don't need it. We will feel God's Grace operating through our prayer and meditation, but we won't want to accept it. If we don't appreciate what God gives, God is not displeased with us. He just waits until we are ready to receive His inner Wealth.

* * *

When we follow the path of love, we see that God is dearest to us, not because He is Omnipotent, Omnipresent or Omniscient, but because He is all Love. A child feels that his father is dearest to him precisely because he feels that inside his father is all love. He does not care to know how great his father is, whether his father is the magistrate or barrister or president. Just because his father is all love to him, his father is dearest.

Similarly, God, our eternal Father, can be approached most successfully and convincingly with love.

* * *

It is here on earth that we shall hear the message of the soul-stirring flute of Infinity. We do not have to go to Heaven; we do not have to go to any other realm of consciousness. Right here, here and now, we can hear the message of liberation, enlightenment and divine fulfilment if we follow the inner teaching, which is love divine: love for love's sake, love for God's sake.

* * *

The Life Divine is not a far cry here on earth. The fulfilment of Divinity here on earth can never remain a far cry if we know the secret of secrets. And that secret is to grow into the divine love, where the lover and the Beloved become one, the creation and the Creator become one, the finite and the Infinite become one.

* * *

DEVOTION

DEVOTION TO GOD

Devotion is the complete submission of the individual will to the Will divine. Devotion is adoration. Adoration is the spontaneous delight that springs from the heart. Who can be the object of our adoration? God. How can we adore Him? Through our self-surrender.

Man loves. He expects love in return. A devotee loves. But he loves human beings for the sake of his sweet Lord who abides in all. His love breathes in humility, spontaneous joy and selfless service.

Devotion is the feminine aspect of love. It is sweet, energising and complete.

A devotee sees a circle which is God. He enters into it with his soul's cry. He then silently comes and stands at the centre of the circle and grows into a tree of ecstasy.

A child does not care to know what his mother is. He just wants his mother's constant presence of love before him. Similar is the devotee's feeling for his Lord. Many come forward to help him in his life's journey. But he cares not for their help. God's Grace is his sole help and refuge. The tortures of hell are too weak to torment him while he is there with his Lord. His life in hell is a life of perfect bliss. His sufferings and tribulations in Heaven know no bounds if he is there without his Lord beside him.

Devotion is a soul-stirring emotion. It dynamically permeates the entire consciousness of the devotee. Devotion is action. This action is always inspired by the devotee's inner being.

Devotion brings in renunciation. True renunciation is never a life of isolation. Renunciation is an utter distaste for the animal life of the flesh. It is also a total absence of the ego. A life of true renunciation is a life that lives in the world but does not derive its values from the world.

Devotion is dedication. Dedication gives a devotee his self-fulfilment. Self-fulfilment is God's infinitude.

Unlike others, a devotee sincerely feels that he has nothing else in his possession save his desire for God. His desire is his jewel. God's Grace is His jewel. In offering his jewel to God, the devotee binds God. In giving His jewel to His devotee, God liberates and fulfils His devotee.

Devotion is our inner sweetness. Devotion is our divine intensity. Devotion is our supreme dynamism. God loves our snow-white sweetness. God appreciates our divine intensity. God admires our supreme dynamism.

A heart of devotion is purer than the purest flame. A heart of devotion is faster than the fastest deer. A heart of devotion is wiser than the wisest sage.

Purity's soulful permanence lives in devotion. Speed's truthful assurance lives in devotion. Wisdom's fruitful illumination lives in devotion.

* * *

Question: What is devotion? Just a desire to do everything possible for one's Guru?

Sri Chinmoy: For a disciple, devotion means his purified, simplified, intensified, devoted, consecrated, conscious and constant oneness with his Guru. The disciple must feel that the Guru is the spiritual magnet constantly pulling him toward the infinite Light of the Supreme. Devotion does not mean just a desire to do everything possible for one's Guru. Devotion is something infinitely deeper than desire. Devotion is the conscious awareness of Light in operation. In this Light the aspirant will discover that when he does something for the Guru or the Guru asks him to do something for him, he has already been given more than the necessary capacity by the Guru.

The manifestations of devotion are simplicity, sincerity, spontaneity, beauty and purity. The manifestations of devotion are one's intense, devoted feeling for one's object of adoration and one's consecrated oneness with the Inner Pilot.

Question: What is the difference between devotion and surrender?

Sri Chinmoy: In a seeker's devotion, there is a kind of give and take. The seeker says, "I devote my entire life to you, but you have to give me inner realisation, illumination or something else." This is conditional self-offering.

After devotion comes the stage we can call selfless love. Selfless love is when we love and don't care for anything in return; we become one with the object of our adoration. In this love there is a subtle feeling that the Beloved will give us the best fruit because we will not bother Him with silly emotional problems or desires, with "Give me this," or "Give me that." In selfless love, desire or demand has been done away with. The seeker knows that the Supreme will give him something nice, something worth possessing; he has not to ask for anything. This is selfless love.

Surrender is the last stage. In surrender we feel the absolute acceptance of the Divine and the Supreme. If we surrender our life totally and say, "God, I place my life entirely at Your Feet," then our whole existence enters into God. God is Omniscient, God is Omnipotent, God is Infinite, so our surrender immediately becomes the Omniscient, the Omnipotent and the Infinite. Surrender is the quickest road to oneness with God. If we just jump into the ocean of Peace and Bliss, then we will become one with God.

In surrender we say, "No matter what God wants to give me, no matter what He wants to do with my life, I am ready. I fully surrender with my very breath, my very existence. Even if God does not want my help, my life or my existence, I will be happy." At that time the disciple wants only the Will of God, the Supreme. This is true surrender.

It is very easy to say, "Let Thy Will be done." But when we say this, we have to identify ourselves with God's Will. How? Through surrender. If we really surrender, then we become one with God's Will. In the spiritual life, there can be no better achievement and no more powerful weapon than surrender.

* * *

DEVOTION

When you love
  With devotion,
You are divinely great.

When you surrender
  With devotion,
You are divinely good.

When you pray
  With devotion,
You are supremely great.

When you meditate
  With devotion,
You are supremely good.

Devotion, devotion, devotion.

* * *

SURRENDER

THE STRENGTH OF SURRENDER

The present-day world wants individuality. It demands freedom. But true individuality and freedom can breathe only in the Divine.

Human individuality shouts in the dark. Earthly freedom cries out in the deserts of life. But absolute surrender universally sings the song of divine individuality and freedom in the Lap of the Supreme. Surrender is the untiring breath of the soul in the Heart of God.

In surrender we discover the spiritual power through which we can become not only the seers but also the possessors of Truth. If we can surrender in absolute silence, we shall ourselves become the reality of the real, the life of the living, the centre of true love, peace and bliss.

A lovely child attracts our attention. We love him because he conquers our heart. But do we ask anything from him in return? No! We love him because he is the object of love; he is lovable. In the same way we can and should love God, for He is the most lovable Being.

Spontaneous love for the Divine is surrender, and this surrender is the greatest gift in life. For when we surrender, the Divine in no time gives us infinitely more than we would have ever dreamed of asking for.

Surrender is a spiritual miracle. It teaches us how to see God with our eyes closed, how to talk to Him with our mouth shut. Fear enters into our being only when we withdraw our surrender from the Absolute.

Surrender is an unfoldment. It is the unfoldment of our body, mind and heart into the sun of divine Plenitude within us. Surrender to this inner sun is the greatest triumph of life. The hound of failure cannot reach us when we are in that sun. The prince of evil fails to touch us when we have realised and established our oneness with that eternally life-giving sun.

Surrender knows that there is a guiding Hand and feels that this guiding Hand is ever present. This Hand may strike or bless the aspirant, but the surrendered aspirant has discovered the truth that whatever comes from the Supreme is always fruitful of good and light.

In life, everything may fail us, but not surrender. Surrender has a free access to God's Omnipotence. Hence, the path of surrender is the perfect perfection of protection.

Surrender has the strength to meet the Absolute and stay and play with Him eternally. God may at times play hide-and-seek with man's other divine qualities, but never with His devotee's genuine surrender.

Inner surrender transforms life into an infinite progress. It gives life the soulful assurance that life lives in God and God alone.

Surrender is the soul of the devotee's body. Surrender is the unparalleled fulfilment of the devotee's life. Surrender takes him to the Source. When he is in the Source, he becomes the Highest and reveals the Deepest.

Individuality hates surrender. Surrender illumines individuality. Individuality is self-will. Self-will is self-love. Surrender is God-Will. God-Will is God-Love.

God's all-fulfilling Grace descends only when man's unconditional surrender ascends.

Our surrender is a most precious thing. God alone deserves it. We can offer our surrender to another individual, but only for the sake of realising God. If that individual has reached his Goal, he can help us in our spiritual journey. However, if we offer ourselves to someone just to satisfy that person, then we are committing a Himalayan blunder. What we should do is offer ourselves unreservedly to the Lord in him.

Every action of ours should be to please God and not to gain applause. Our actions are too secret and sacred to display before others. They are meant for our own progress, achievement and realisation.

There is no limit to our surrender. The more we surrender, the more we have to surrender. God has given us capacity. According to our capacity He demands manifestation of us. Manifestation beyond our capacity God has never demanded and will never demand.

In man's complete and absolute surrender is his realisation: his realisation of the Self, his realisation of God the Infinite.

* * *

Surrender is the purest devotion that sees through the eye of intuition. Surrender is freedom, perpetual freedom, for it always stays with God, in God and for God.

The eye of surrender does not see the face of the hostile forces. It always sees the Face of God's Compassion, Protection and Divinity. The life of surrender divinely rings true. It is always filled with abiding inspiration, revealing aspiration and transcending realisation.

Surrender is the wisdom that sees and becomes the Truth. Surrender wishes nothing other than God. Surrender gets the very essence of God. Nothing is as practical as surrender, for it knows the supreme secret that to offer itself integrally to God is to possess God absolutely.

* * *

Surrender clings to God with all the might of the soul.
Surrender clings to God with all the love of the heart.
Surrender clings to God with all the will of the mind.
Surrender clings to God with all the dynamic energy of the vital.
Surrender clings to God with all the snow-white emotions of the body.

* * *

Question: Why is it that I find it so difficult to surrender to my inner life?

Sri Chinmoy: You constantly surrender to earthly things—noise, the traffic lights, the government. You feel that you are totally lost if you do not surrender to these things, whereas if you do surrender, at least you can maintain your existence on earth. You feel you have to be clever to stay on earth, that you have to make some compromise between your desires and the world that you actually see around you. So whatever the earth gives you, even if it is a form of torture, you feel that you have to accept it.

If you want to lead an aspiring life, then you have to have this same kind of feeling toward spiritual things. You have to feel that if you do not pray, if you do not meditate, then you will be totally lost; if you do not cry, if you do not surrender to the higher divinity, then your whole existence will be of no value. You have to feel that without the inner guidance you are totally helpless and lost. And this inner guidance comes only when you really want to surrender your ignorance to the Light within you.

There are millions and billions of people on earth who are not praying and meditating, but they still exist, although they may be living an animal life. But if you feel that it is not enough just to maintain your existence on earth, if you feel that your existence should have some meaning, some purpose, some fulfilment, then you have to go to the inner life, the spiritual life. If you see that only the inner life can offer you Peace, Light and Bliss, then naturally you will surrender to the inner life.

So aspiring people will try to go beyond earthly circumstances and events and surrender to their inner divinity. This is not the surrender of a slave to the master; it is not a helpless surrender. Here one surrenders his imperfections, limitations, bondage and ignorance to his highest Self, which is flooded with Peace, Light and Bliss.

Question: Is surrender a passive thing?

Sri Chinmoy: There is a great difference between the surrender of laziness or utter helplessness and dynamic surrender, which is surcharged with aspiration. If out of laziness or helplessness we say, "I have surrendered. Now I don't want to do anything," this is not enough. Our surrender has to be dynamic, constantly aspiring to grow into or merge into the Infinite. Our surrender has to be done consciously and spontaneously. When we surrender consciously and spontaneously to the infinite Truth, Peace, Light and Bliss, we become a perfect channel for these qualities to manifest in and through us on earth. In the West, surrender has been badly misunderstood. Here surrender is seen as submission to something or to somebody else. It is seen as a loss of individuality, an extinction of individuality. Then, where is the question of a perfect channel? But this view of spiritual surrender is a mistake. If we really want to be one with the infinite Ultimate, the Boundless, then we have to enter into it. When we enter into the Ultimate, we do not lose our so-called little individuality. On the contrary, we become the Infinite itself. On the strength of our total oneness, we and the Infinite become indivisible.

Question: Could you explain the difference between dependence and surrender?

Sri Chinmoy: In real surrender we feel that our darkest part is surrendering to our brightest part, that our unlit part is surrendering to our fully illumined part. Let us say that my feet are in darkness and my head is in light. My feet are surrendering to my head, knowing perfectly well that both the feet and the head are parts of the same body. This is the surrender of oneness. One enters into surrender knowing well that the brighter part is equally his.

We have to know what kind of dependence a seeker has. Some people are clever; they depend on the spiritual Master or on some higher authority, but only with a motive behind their dependence. But there is another type of dependence: a child's dependence. An innocent child feels that his father and mother will do everything for him. He feels that he is helpless. He has the sincere inner conviction that he cannot budge an inch or do anything without his mother's help, so he gets the mother's help.

To have true dependence, one has to feel that he is hopeless without the divine Grace of the Supreme. This kind of dependence helps us immensely. Some of my disciples feel that if they leave me even for one day, they will be totally lost, like children in the desert. Those who have that kind of sincere feeling will make real progress. They are dependent, but not like beggars. They depend on the higher light. When they depend on me, they feel that they are depending on something higher, which belongs to them.

If we have a free access to that higher plane and feel that the higher plane is also ours, then naturally we can depend on the higher plane. In that sense dependence is very good. Otherwise, most of the time people are telling a lie when they say they depend on God's Will or they depend on the Master's will. By saying this they only try to draw the attention of other disciples. They say, "Oh, Guru has said to do it? Then we will do it." Yet inwardly, two hundred times they have refused to do it. Outwardly they may do it, but with utmost inner unwillingness. So this kind of dependence is not good at all.

If your dependence is absolutely sincere, if you feel that without the help of the Supreme you cannot breathe, then this is surrender. When you breathe in, you depend on your life-breath. If your life-breath goes away, then you don't exist. Similarly, if you can feel that you are totally depending on the Will of the Supreme, which is far more important than your life-breath, then this dependence is true surrender.

* * *

I SHALL FLY ONLY
YOUR VICTORY-BANNER

I shall surrender my 'i'-ness at Your Feet.
I shall accept Your 'I'-ness in my dream.
I shall see the waves of Peace in Your Eyes.
I shall bind You with my sweet awakening.
O Beauty Supreme, in my life and death
I shall fly only Your Victory-Banner.

* * *

THE NECESSITY OF SURRENDER

There comes a time in our spiritual life when we realise that we are not satisfied with what we have, whether it is material wealth or inner wealth, or with what we are. At that time we are ready for surrender. How does one surrender? It is very easy. When we feel the need for surrender, automatically the means will come. If we are desperately in need of surrender, if we feel the soul's inner urge, if our entire being wants to surrender to God's Will, then automatically we will be given more than the necessary capacity, assurance, compassion and light from above and within. When we surrender, we empty all our impurity into God and He replaces it with His Purity and His Divinity.

Surrender to God's Will entirely depends on our necessity. If we feel that our life is meaningless, that we won't be satisfied or fulfilled without surrendering our earthly existence to God's Will, then surrender will be possible for us.

God can never compel us to surrender; it is we who have to feel the necessity of loving God and devoting ourselves to God at every second. We start with love. Even in the ordinary life, when we love someone, we gladly devote our life and our entire being to that person. In the spiritual life also, if we really love God, who is all Light and infinite Wisdom, then we have to devote ourselves to Him. So love and devotion must always go together.

When we devote ourselves to God we may have an ambition or a hankering for a personal way of getting the Truth. Some will say to the Supreme, "I am doing this for You; I have devoted all my life to You and expect You to give me something in return." This is quite natural, but from the highest spiritual point of view, it is wrong. Others will say, "I shall give what I have and what I am to God. If God does not like me or want me, then He may give me nothing; it is up to Him. My duty is to serve Him with what I have and what I am; it is His Duty to give to me or not to give to me, to utilise me or not to utilise me." A real seeker will try to please God in God's own Way.

Spiritual surrender is our absolute oneness with our own highest part, with the Supreme. We do not surrender to somebody other than ourselves. No! When our Master stands in front of us and bows down, to whom is he bowing? He is bowing to the Supreme in us. And when we bow down with folded hands to the Master, we are bowing to the Supreme in him. His Highest and our Highest can never be two different things; they are the same.

Our path of love, devotion and surrender will lead to the same goal as the path of *jnana*, wisdom. But we feel that the path of love is easier. The very word 'God' conquers our heart, not because God has infinite Power, but just because God is all Love. God is the mightiest on earth. But our human nature is so feeble that if we concentrate on God as infinite Power, we shall not be able to approach Him. If we say, 'God' and immediately feel that He is all Love, infinite Love, then we are right; His Love is His Power. If we approach God through Love, this is the easiest and quickest way.

* * *

Question: How can we surrender to the Supreme?

Sri Chinmoy: Let us say that as a child, when you were about three years old, you used to always listen to your mother. Perhaps you don't always listen to her now; but when you were a child, there were many things your mother asked you to do or not to do. Did you do anything wrong at that time by listening to her? No. Your mother asked you not to touch fire and you believed her. If you had touched the fire, it would have burnt your hand. But just because you were obedient and you surrendered to your mother's will, you escaped being burnt.

You have to have this same kind of faith in the spiritual life. You need to feel that your spiritual Master, like your mother, will not disappoint you or deceive you. You are now a child, a baby in the spiritual life. Your spiritual Master will not deceive you; your Inner Pilot will not deceive you. No! Surrender comes only when one has faith in somebody else, when one has more faith in that particular person then he has in himself.

You can also become a child just by unlearning. Ignorance and darkness have taught you many things which you have now to unlearn. A child knows practically nothing; he knows only how to love his mother and father, and that is more than everything for a child. Everyone has to unlearn things that the mind has taught him. So when we pray, when we meditate, the first thing we should do is get rid of doubts, suspicions and other negative qualities.

If you please your parents when they want you to do something, then if you ask them for money or for some other material help, immediately they will give it to you.

They will give it to you because they have much more money than you have, much more capacity in various fields. But if you don't please them, they will give you nothing.

When a child comes running to his father with a nickel he has just found in the street, he says, "Look, Father, I have found a nickel!" The father is so happy that his son has come to him. The child's sole possession, his only wealth, is a nickel. With this nickel he could have gone to a shop and bought candy or used it some other way, but he didn't do so. Instead, he came home to his father with this little nickel. Naturally the father is pleased and gives the child a quarter or dollar instead of the nickel.

In the spiritual life also, you give a little aspiration, which is your nickel, during your prayer or meditation for a few minutes early in the morning. Then immediately the spiritual Master will invoke so many things for you: Peace, Light, Bliss, Joy and Delight. But you have to give an iota of aspiration, for five minutes or half an hour of meditation in the morning.

God will never be indebted to you. You do have a little capacity; you meditate on God for a few minutes each day. The moment he sees that you are regular in your meditation, that you are sincere and earnest and have accepted the spiritual life wholeheartedly, God showers His boundless Compassion on you in the form of Light, Delight and Peace.

So give to God what you have: your childlike faith and inner cry. If you can give Him your inner cry and have implicit faith in Him, then surrender will automatically loom large in your life of aspiration.

* * *

JOY IN SURRENDER

When an aspirant is totally surrendered to God's Will, he will get abundant joy. He will feel all joy in his heart and he will live in constant joy. He will not be able to account for it or give any meaning to it. Early in the morning when he first gets up, he will get a very sweet feeling or sensation. If he touches a wall, he will get joy; if he touches a mirror, he will also get joy. His own joy enters into everything he sees. At times he may see that a solid wall is full of joy; a tree will be full of joy. If a taxi-cab goes by, he will see intense joy in the driver, even in the car itself. His inner joy will enter into each person, each object; and it will pervade everything.

If there is total surrender, then there can be no failure. Surrender means the greatest joy, deepest joy, most soulful joy, even in so-called failure. Success also brings the same joy. When we are successful in something, immediately we derive joy from our success. Similarly, if our inner and outer lives are surcharged with surrendering light, then at every moment we derive pure unalloyed joy from the highest Source. If we have this kind of spontaneous inner joy, then we can feel that it comes only from our total surrender to the inner Pilot, the Master, the Guru, God.

* * *

Question: I do not know what is going to happen to me in the future, and I worry a lot about my destiny. Is this right?

Sri Chinmoy: No, we should not worry. We should have implicit faith in God, in our Inner Pilot or in our spiritual Master. We have to feel that not only does God know what is best for us, but He will do what is best for us. We worry because we do not know what is going to happen to us tomorrow, or even the next minute. We feel that if we do not do something for ourselves, then who is going to do it? But if we can feel that there is someone who thinks of us infinitely more than we think of ourselves, and if we can consciously offer our responsibility to Him, saying, "You be responsible. Eternal Father, Eternal Mother, You be responsible for what I do and say and grow into," then our past, our present and our future become His problem. As long as we try to be responsible for our own life, we will be miserable. We will not be able to properly utilise even two minutes out of every twenty-four hours we have. When we can feel that we are God's conscious instruments and He is the Doer, then we will not worry about our destiny; we will not be afraid of our destiny. For we will know and feel that it is in the all-loving Hands of God, who will do everything in us, through us and for us.

Let us consciously offer our very existence—what we have and what we are—to God. What we have is aspiration to grow into the very image of God, into infinite Peace, Light and Bliss. And what we are right now is just ignorance, the ignorance-sea. If we can offer our aspiration-cry and our ignorance-sea to God, then our problem is solved. We should not and we need not ever worry about destiny. On the strength of our surrender, we become inseparably one with God's Cosmic Will.

Surrender is protection; surrender is illumination; surrender is perfection. We begin our journey at the

very commencement of our life. We surrender our existence to our parents and get, in return, protection. We
surrender to their will, to their advice and suggestions,
and we are well-protected. Joy boundless we feel in our
day-to-day life when we are children. Why? Because we
surrender our personal will, our own inner thinking, to
our parents, and immediately we receive joy plus protection. In protection is joy, and in joy is protection.

Then, when we walk along the path of spirituality, at
every moment we try to listen to the dictates of our inner
being. The more we listen to our inner being, the greater is our joy and the higher our fulfilment. And then,
when our term is over, when we have to enter into
another world for a short rest, we also surrender. To
whom? To the Inner Pilot, the Lord Supreme. At the
end of our journey we surrender our very breath to the
Supreme. Then we again get joy, perfect joy, unalloyed
joy.

*Question: What is involved in the surrender of the
vital, and of the physical body? Having surrendered with
the heart and soul, how can we best help the other recalcitrant members of our being to surrender?*

Sri Chinmoy: After surrendering the heart and the
soul, if you want your recalcitrant members, the vital
and the physical body, to surrender to God, you can do
two things. The first thing is to make them feel that they
are as important as the heart and soul in the fulfilment
of your mission on earth. The second thing is to threaten
them, saying that you will remain in the soul's region
and not care for their limited happiness, achievement

and fulfilment on earth. Your inspiration and aspiration and your threat of withdrawal will compel them to make a decision. Very often they do care for boundless joy, achievement and fulfilment and they do identify themselves consciously and sincerely with the heart and the soul. Then they become part and parcel of the integral surrender.

* * *

When the aspirant bitterly starves his questioning mind and feeds his surrender sumptuously, God says: "The time is ripe. I come."

* * *

THE MESSAGE OF SURRENDER

Today You have given me the message of surrender.
I have offered to You my very flower-heart.
In the dark night with tears,
In the unknown prison-cell of illusion,
In the house of the finite,
No longer shall I abide.
I know You are mine.
I have known this, Mother,
O Queen of the Eternal.

* * *

Question: Our path is the path of love, devotion and surrender. Can there be oneness with each of these qualities, or does real oneness come only in surrender?

Sri Chinmoy: It is like this: Stand in front of a tree, preferably at night, and look at the tree's foliage — its leaves and branches. Try gradually to feel that you are the tree — you are the branches, you are the leaves and you are the root. This is the outer tree.

Then you have to imagine for a couple of minutes that you have a tree inside you. This tree has only three branches. The names of these branches are love, devotion and surrender. You will sit on the branch that is called love, and there you and God are absolutely one.

Then you will sit on the branch called devotion. While sitting on the devotion branch you have to feel not only that God and you are one, but that there is a tremendous intimate concern and feeling of inseparable oneness between you and God. God devotes His infinite Light to your fulfilment and you devote your utmost capacity, whatever capacity you have, to the fulfilment of God's Will. On the branch of devotion your oneness is thickened and intensified.

Next comes the branch of surrender. When you sit on the branch of surrender, you have to feel that the oneness that was on the love branch, and the intimacy that you felt on the branch of devotion came to you only on the strength of your implicit surrender to God's Will. You had aspiration to become one with God, but it was not your aspiration that made you one with Him. Inside your aspiration you had surrendering light. "God, I am aspiring, but I have surrendered to You and it is up to You to fulfil my aspiration or leave me where I am." This was your prayer.

When you sit on the branch of surrender, you have to feel that your oneness on the love branch and your intimate oneness on the devotion branch came because of the implicit, unconditional surrender that you had inside your flaming, climbing aspiration.

* * *

LOVE, DEVOTION AND SURRENDER

Love is action. Devotion is practice. Surrender is experience.

Love is realisation. Devotion is revelation. Surrender is manifestation.

Love is the meaning of life. Devotion is the secret of life. Surrender is the Goal of life.

In my love, I see God the Mother. In my devotion, I see God the Father. In my surrender, I see God the Mother and God the Father together in one body.

Love without devotion is absurdity. Devotion without surrender is futility.

Love with devotion was my journey's start. Devotion with surrender is my journey's close.

I love the Supreme because I came from Him. I devote myself to the Supreme because I wish to go back to Him. I surrender myself to the Supreme because He lives in me and I in Him.

* * *

Love is sweet, devotion is sweeter, surrender is sweetest.

Love is sweet. I have felt this truth in my Mother's spontaneous love for me.

Devotion is sweeter. I have discovered this truth in my Mother's pure devotion toward the perfection of my life.

Surrender is sweetest. I have realised this truth in my Mother's constant surrender toward the fulfilment of my joy.

Again, love is mighty, devotion is mightier, surrender is mightiest.

Love is mighty. This truth I feel when I look at my Father's Face.

Devotion is mightier. This truth I discover when I sit at my Father's Feet.

Surrender is mightiest. This truth I realise when I live in the breath of my Father's Will.

Devotion is the intensity in love and surrender is the fulfilment of love. Why do we love? We love because at every moment we are pinched with hunger to realise the highest, to feel the inmost, to be consciously one with the universal Truth, Light, Peace and Bliss and to be completely fulfilled.

* * *

Surrender to God's Will is the highest realisation of our hidden power.

* * *

GOD, GRACE AND THE GURU

GOD AND DIVINE GRACE

THE FINITE AND THE INFINITE

God is at once finite and infinite.

He is space.
He is measured.
He can be measured.
He must needs be measured.

He is beyond space.
He is measureless.
He is boundless.
He is infinite.

God is infinite Consciousness, infinite Bliss; yet He can also assume a finite form. He is infinite, He is finite and, at the same time, He transcends both the Infinite and the finite. He is life, He is death; yet again, He is beyond both life and death. Many people cannot agree with the idea that God can be finite. But let us think of one of God's divine qualities called Omnipresence. According to our human feeling, when we think of Omnipresence, we immediately think of vastness. True, He is as vast as the world. But because He is in everything, God is also in the finite. Again, God is Omnipotent. Where is His Omnipotence if He cannot become a small child, a tiny insect or an atom? At our sweet will we can do practically nothing. But just because God is Omnipotent, He can do anything He wants to do at His sweet Will: He can be vast, He can be infinitesimal.

God the Infinite has entered into us, into these finite bodies, which last for fifty, sixty or seventy years. The Infinite gets the greatest joy only by making itself finite as well. We have to know, we have to feel and we have to realise this for ourselves; only then will we see God in His creation. Otherwise, we will think that God is in Heaven and, although we are His creation, we have no connection with Him.

Finite and Infinite, according to our outer understanding, are opposites of each other. But in God's Eye they are one. The finite and the Infinite always want to go together. The finite wants to reach the Absolute, the Highest, which is the Infinite. The Infinite wants to manifest itself in and through the finite. Then the game is complete. Otherwise, it will only be a one-sided game. There will be no true joy, no achievement, no fulfilment.

Inside the finite is the message of the Infinite; in the finite is first the revelation and then the manifestation of the Infinite. The finite is necessary because it is through the finite that the Infinite plays its role in the cosmic rhythm here on earth. At the same time, the Infinite is necessary because it is in the Infinite that the finite has its eternal shelter. There it finds protection and perfection.

God is everything, but each person has to feel for himself what God is for him. God can be infinite Light, infinite Consciousness, infinite Power, infinite Bliss, infinite Compassion, infinite Energy. He can be personal, with form; again, He can be impersonal, without form. At times we get joy when we see God with form; at times we get joy when we see God without form. We can see Him in His impersonal aspect as a vast expanse of Light. In His personal aspect He can appear in the form of a luminous human being. When He appears as a personal Being, we can have all kinds of intimate talks with Him face to face. Even spiritual Masters will not necessarily see the Supreme in the same way. For each Master, He may appear differently.

The Formless is necessary to realise the Highest, the Ultimate, the Infinite; and the form is necessary to reveal and manifest the Highest and the Inmost in an intimate way. That which is infinite in consciousness can be seen in the formless aspect. Again, it can house itself in form. That is why the heart can hold Infinity inside it. When you enter into the subtle physical, it is all formless; when you enter into the physical, it is all form.

If one starts his journey by thinking of God as a personal God with form, then he will realise Him as a personal God. If he starts his Yoga thinking of God as impersonal, then he will realise the impersonal aspect of God. It depends on how the seeker wants to approach God while he is in the process of aspiring. If someone practises Yoga while thinking of God's infinite Consciousness, then he will realise God as infinite Consciousness. A spiritual Master may first realise one aspect of God; but when he has his full realisation, he sees God in all His aspects.

If you meditate in order to achieve something in a most tangible and intimate way, it is helpful to approach the Supreme in the form of the Mother, the Mother Divine. But if you want to experience something abstract, such as Light or Bliss, then you will approach God as the formless Consciousness.

I see God as a luminous Being, the most luminous Being, who has infinite Love, Concern and Compassion for mankind. My disciples regard the Supreme as a personal God, like a human being. Although the Supreme has both personal and impersonal aspects, if you approach Him as a personal Being, especially in the beginning, your journey will be safer because the personal way is easier. If you want to see God's impersonal aspect, you may become confused or afraid of the vastness. A human being may be only six feet tall, but inside him the soul has boundless capacity. Let us take the soul as the impersonal God and the body as the personal God. In the beginning it is much easier for the seeker to identify with his body than with his soul. If my soul wants to manifest its beauty or its strength through the physical, then the soul will give my body luminous beauty or solid strength. So the seeker can think of the form as an expression or manifestation of the formless.

When the beginner meditates early in the morning, he should meditate on the Feet of the personal Supreme. Then, along with his own devoted love, he will feel God's Compassion and Concern. He will say, "Here is someone who is really great, infinitely greater than I.

454

That is why I am touching His Feet with such devotion." He will feel that there is some purpose behind what he is doing. By touching the Feet of the Supreme, he is trying to become one with the Supreme. If someone is very tall, I won't be able to touch his head. But I can touch his feet. Whether I touch his feet or his head, I can say that I have touched him. But when I touch his feet, immediately I get the feeling of purest joy and devotion.

Then, after touching the Feet of the personal God, we have to concentrate on the Heart of the personal God. Touching His Feet may give us a devotional feeling, but we have to ask ourselves, "Do I consider Him as my very own, or is it just because He is very great that I am touching His Feet?" We can touch the feet of a very great spiritual Master, but along with our veneration, we have to claim that person as our very own. If we feel that he is our very own, then our devotion gets dynamic power; it enters into activity. When we feel that the Supreme in human form is our very own and that we are His very own, only then can we have complete identification and inseparable oneness with Him. And from that oneness we get boundless joy.

When you feel that your spiritual Master is your very own, you want to give him something of yours. But there has to be an exchange. He will give you what he has and you will give him what you have. How do you actually exchange? It is through Light transmitted through the eyes. When the Master and the disciple look at each other, at that time what does each one do? The Master looks at the disciple with soulful compassion and the disciple looks at the Master with soulful adoration. The Master, who represents the personal Supreme, has all compassion, and the seeker has all adoration. So they exchange their offering and then they become inseparably one.

The eye is the place of vision and light. Adoration is a form of light, and compassion is also a form of light. Between the eyebrows, and a little above, is the third eye. This is the place through which we shall give what we have to the personal God, and the personal God will give us what He has. This form of meditation can be practised by any aspirant who is trying to go beyond his limited existence.

* * *

GOD'S NAME

There is one God called by many different names. I like the term 'Supreme'. Other Masters have used different names. Jesus Christ used the term 'Father'. He said, "I and my Father are one." His Father, your Father and my Father are the same, but I get a sweeter feeling from using the term 'Supreme' instead of saying 'God' or 'Father'.

All religious faiths have the same God, but they address Him differently. A man will be called 'Father' by one person, 'Brother' by another and 'Uncle' by someone else. Similarly, God is also addressed in various ways, according to one's sweetest, most affectionate feeling.

Instead of using the word 'God', I use the word 'Supreme' most of the time. I ask my disciples to do the same, for I feel it gives us a more intimate connection with Him. Although God and the Supreme are one, there is a subtle distinction between the two. The highest Supreme is different from what we call God. When we speak of God-realisation, here 'God' is synonymous with the Supreme. But usually when we say 'God', we feel that He embodies a height which is static. He is like a mountain that is high, but flat. When we use the term 'God', we feel that He has reached His Height and stopped. He does not have a constantly evolving Consciousness; He is something finished, a finished product. But when we say 'Supreme', we are speaking of the Supreme Lord who not only reaches the absolute Highest, but all the time goes beyond, beyond and constantly transcends His own highest Height. There is a constant upward movement.

* * *

MAN AND GOD

The aim of life is to become conscious of the supreme Reality. The aim of life is to be the conscious expression of the eternal Being.

God is not something to be obtained outside of ourselves. God is that very thing which can be unfolded from within.

In the ordinary life each human being has millions and millions of questions to ask. In the spiritual life a day dawns when the seeker feels that there is only one question worth asking: "Who am I?" The answer of answers is: "I am not the body, but I am the Inner Pilot."

How is it that a man does not know himself, something which ought to be the easiest of all his endeavours?

He does not know himself precisely because he identifies himself with the ego and not with his real self. What compels him to identify himself with this pseudo-self? It is ignorance. And what tells him that the real self is not and can never be the ego? It is his self-search. What he sees in the inmost recesses of his heart is his real self, his God. Eventually this seeing must transform itself into becoming.

What is the relationship between God and man? God has a living Breath, and that living Breath is man. Man has a Goal, and the name of that Goal is God. In God is man's satisfaction, achievement and fulfilment.

Man's necessity is God. God's necessity is man. Man needs God for his highest transcendental realisation, and he will have it in God. God needs man for His absolute Manifestation here on earth. We need God to realise our highest truth or highest existence. God needs us to manifest Him here on earth totally, divinely and supremely.

God and man are eternally one. God is man yet to be fulfilled in His Infinity, and man is God yet to realise his divinity. Like God, man is infinite; like man, God is finite. There is no yawning gulf between man and God. Man is the God of tomorrow; God, the man of yesterday.

I have to grow, and God has to flow. I grow as a human being into His highest Consciousness, and God flows into me and through me with His infinite Compassion.

God's Dream-Boat is man—man the aspiration, man the experience, man the realisation, man the total oneness with God the Omniscient and Omnipotent, God the all-loving Father.

Man's Life-Boat is God. Man's very existence is God.

Man realises God, man embodies God and man finally will manifest God here on earth.

God's Dream is man. God fulfils Himself in man, with man, through man and for man. What does it mean when we say that man is a Dream of God? First, we have to know that God's Dream is not like a human dream. There is a great difference between human dreams and God's divine Dream. Earth's dream is mental fantasy; God's Dream divine is the precursor of Reality. Each second God's Dreams are immediately being transformed into reality. Human dreams are often pensive thoughts and ideas which we sometimes try to realise. Very often when we dream, we feel miserable because our sweet dreams are never fulfilled. Sometimes we become victims of hostile forces which make us dream about all kinds of horrible incidents taking place in our life. Again, sometimes we create our own fantasies during the day and they come out at night in the form of a dream.

In God's case He does not have these kinds of dreams. His Dream is more like the lid on a box. If you just lift the lid, there is the world, there is the goal. So in God's Drama, today's Dream is tomorrow's Reality. When we become one with God, we see that everything in God's Dream already embodies the Reality itself. That is to say, when the Divine dreams in the seeker, then Reality is going to be manifested immediately in his life.

* * *

IS GOD'S POWER LIMITED?

The other day a young friend of mine asked me why God had not yet made the whole world spiritual after so many thousands of years. "Is God's Power limited?" he asked. "Does He not choose to make the world spiritual?" I wish to say that God's Power is unlimited, but it is we who do not want to become spiritual. That is to say, earth does not want God's Light.

God is wise, infinitely wiser than we are. Someone with less power than God can force another individual to do something that he does not want to do. But God does not force anyone to do anything. He feels that if He uses force, then we cannot get the ultimate Joy. You can force someone to eat, but inwardly he will curse you. God only says, "My child, I am telling you to eat this for your good. If you eat this food, you will get nourishment. Then you will be strong and you will be able to fight against ignorance." God offers His Light, His inner nourishment, but he does not force anyone to accept it. This is what His policy is.

God sees the past, the present and the future. He knows that the right thing is to constantly offer us His Wisdom and infinite Patience. Human beings do not have patience and they feel that by striking their child, by forcing him, they are doing the best thing. But when this child grows up, he will only want to strike his parents in return. Right now, he is innocent, he is helpless. If the father beats his son, the child will remember this very incident. He may leave home at an early age and have nothing to do with his parents. Or when he becomes an adolescent, he will play tit for tat: you struck me, now I will strike you. This is what happens when human parents misuse their power.

But God the Father will not act in this way. He will only show abundant Compassion, infinite Compassion. Then, in return, His child will eventually offer infinite gratitude to God for showing His infinite Compassion-Light. The child will receive this Light and he will try to become worthy of his Father. When Compassion works, when Light works, then Wisdom works. If you offer wisdom to someone, then in ten or twenty years that person will also want to offer you wisdom when he himself has achieved it.

God will never give anything untimely. That would be like plucking an unripe fruit from a tree, thinking that it will be most delicious. If you eat it before it is ripe, it will taste deplorable. You always have to wait for it to ripen. Similarly, if somebody is fast asleep and you go and tell him that it is time for him to get up, then he will just kick you and you will feel miserable. He will say, "What are you doing? It is all well and good for you to get up. You do whatever you want to do. It is time for me to sleep." Sleep is what is giving him joy. You are powerless at that time.

Look at the power of a Justice of the Supreme Court when he is in his office. Again, when this same man is with his wife and children, he cannot exercise this kind of power. His own son won't listen to him. He may ask his son to bring him a glass of water and his son won't do it. The Supreme Court Justice and the father are one and the same person. When he is in court, the whole nation listens to him; whereas at home his own children won't listen to him.

When in Heaven, the Supreme is really the Highest and, at the same time, He is constantly transcending Himself. The Supreme has that kind of supreme Power

Sri Chinmoy brings down divine Compassion.

in the inner world. But when He wants to operate here on earth with His children, He has infinite Patience. He becomes one with their ignorance. He says, "All right, if you want to disobey Me, if you want to play these kinds of silly games, then let Me also play a little with you."

You may ask how God manifests His Power in man. I wish to say that He manifests not only Power but all His other qualities through Love. God uses Power, but He prefers to manifest Himself through Love, Concern and Compassion.

* * *

GRACE AND COMPASSION

We turn to the Lord for Grace; He looks to us for sincerity.

A feeble prayer brings down God's omnipotent Grace. Such is the magnanimity of God's Compassion.

To a sincere heart, God's Grace is swifter than a weaver's shuttle. To an insincere heart, it is slower than laziness itself.

God may be unkindness to those who think, but He is all Kindness to those who feel.

Although man frequently loses faith in God, God never loses His Patience. For He knows well that His Grace is destined to save mankind from the tentacles of its own misery.

Our tears to God are our greatest strength to bring down His adamantine Protection.

If one wants to be illumined by one word from the lips of God, then that word is Compassion.

Although we are accountable to God for all our conscious and unconscious actions, God, being the Father, finds no better way of dealing with us than to accept, with His benign Compassion, our never-ending errors.

We may not see God personally. But if we can realise the relation between His Grace and His Power, it is as good as seeing Him.

We offer our surrendered helplessness to God from below. He showers blessings on us from above.

God's Grace and God's Justice have been rivals right from the birth of creation. But it goes without saying that His Justice can never keep pace with His Grace.

In season and out of season we crack venomous jokes, and God simply smiles. But if ever God cracks a joke — and needless to say, He does so with a set purpose and with the most benevolent intention — we immediately shed bitter tears or become violently angry.

If we think of God's Justice before we think of His Compassion, our hearts will be mistaken. His Justice wants man to be fully exposed, but His Compassion wants to drop a veil over man's follies and misdeeds.

The universe is not vast enough for God's Grace to be buried. Hence, it will never disappear.

Our enemy is anger. Anger's enemy is patience. Patience too has an enemy called ignorance. To be sure, eyeless ignorance also has an enemy, although unbelievable. What is it? God's Grace.

God's Compassion is that which comes to all, being fully beyond the touch of human wickedness.

God's descending Grace and man's ascending delight are part and parcel of earth's evolving consciousness.

* * *

IF I CAN

    If I can perfect my faith
Thy Grace is sure to come.
    The more I give to Thee
The more I absorb Thy Balm
    That heals my bosom's pangs.
Without Thy Love supreme,
    Nothingness all I am —
A dark and barren dream.

* * *

I AM THY SERVANT

I am Thy servant of servants, humble, low.
Truly I care not who Thou art, O Lord!
Thy Grace I invoke, only Thy Grace sublime.
In Thee alone I find my bosom's cord.

My mind craves not for fame, O Thou Unknown,
Nor for Thy boundless Power, Knowledge-Sun.
My Lord, my first and last desire serene —
Make me Thy Vision's golden, deathless son.

* * *

Question: Which is more important: God's Grace or God's Justice?

Sri Chinmoy: To him who wants to love God, God's

Grace is more important. To him who wants God to love him, God's Justice is more important.

* * *

PERSONAL EFFORT AND GOD'S GRACE

To make the fastest progress, God's Grace plus personal effort is required. Some seekers say, "If we care for God's Grace, then what is the necessity of personal effort here on earth?" They are mistaken because personal effort will never stand in the way of God's descending Grace; personal effort expedites the descent of God's Grace to earth.

Surrender is not something we can suddenly offer to God. Total surrender requires personal effort; again, total surrender can play the part of personal effort. God can give us all that He wants without even an iota of personal effort from us. He says, "It is for your own satisfaction that I ask you to make this little personal effort." When we can make this personal effort, our whole life will be surcharged with divine pride: "See what I have done for God?" Our conscious oneness with God, who is infinite, who is eternally immortal, who is our Dearest prompts us to do something for Him.

If we sincerely make personal effort, then God is bound to be pleased with us. Why? Because He can tell the world, "My child, my chosen instrument, has done many things for Me." We can prove ourselves worthy of our existence on earth and, at the same time, we can make God proud of us through our personal effort. But while making our personal effort, we have to know that in God there is infinite Grace. When Grace descends, there is no more personal effort; it is only dynamic self-surrender. When we offer the results of our aspiration and inner urge to God, that is called true surrender. If we do not offer the results to God, but just lie like a dead body at His Feet, letting Him work for us, in us and through us, it is wrong. God does not want an inactive body, a dead soul. He wants someone who is active, dynamic and aspiring; someone who wants to be energised so that he can do something for God; someone who wants to realise God and manifest all the divine qualities here on earth.

Divine surrender, from the spiritual point of view, comes from will power. If we have an adamantine will, then we will get the capacity to make unconditional surrender. Again, if we can surrender unconditionally to God, then we will get the capacity to develop will power. Inner will power, which is the soul's light, and surrender, which is the oneness of our heart with the Absolute, always go together. They are inseparable. There can be no difference between the soul's will power and the unconditional surrender of our entire being to the Will of the Supreme. Both are equally strong.

* * *

God's Grace can and will blot out the past if and when you are ready to face and transcend the facts of your present life.

* * *

Self-effort is necessary.
God's Grace is indispensable.

* * *

THE HOUR CAME

The hour came.
I was not ready.
God descended,
 Smiled
And
 Departed.

The hour came again.
I was not ready.
God ascended,
 Pushed
And
 Barked.

The hour came not.
I was ready.
God slept.
 I cried.
Ignorance sang.
 Satan danced.

* * *

A temptation is nothing but a kind of test. If we pass these tests, we become one with God. At first, God will only watch and observe. If, on the one hand, we say outwardly that we don't want to stay with ignorance, but on the other hand, we secretly enjoy wallowing in earthly pleasures, then God simply keeps quiet. We may say that we don't want to eat ignorance-food, but at the same time we continue eating it. Here we are acting like a camel. A camel eats thorns and his mouth bleeds. He will say to himself that he will never eat these thorns again, but soon afterwards he does the same thing. Like this, some of us say we don't want to stay with ignorance, but the next moment we again become most intimate friends with ignorance.

But if God sees that we are sincerely trying to pass our examination, then immediately He will give us the capacity. When He feels that we really don't want to mix with ignorance, that we no longer want to have anything to do with it, then He gives us infinite inner power and strength to come out of ignorance.

God never tests; God never tempts. He will just give us the inner strength to conquer temptations. God's Compassion itself is our greatest power. But we receive His Power only when we are sincere. God's help, just like sunlight, is there for everyone. If somebody keeps his doors and windows open, then he receives sunlight in his room. But if he keeps the doors and windows shut, then sunlight cannot enter. So God's divine Compassion is constantly raining down, but we have to keep our heart's door open. Only then will we be able to come out of ignorance.

* * *

The river enters into the ocean and immediately its functioning ceases.

The doubting mind of the really sincere seeker enters into the Light of the Master and it immediately receives not only mental clarity but also illumination.

* * *

YOUR THOUGHTS DIVINE
ARE IN MY HEART

Your thoughts divine are in my heart;
In Your Heart, my pangs and my sufferings.
In my life is Your Dream;
In Your Life I am the constant torture.
I am the tiniest drop of Your Compassion.
O Nectar-Ocean of Infinity, come, come
    Into my dark room
And bind me with Your cord of Liberation.

* * *

THE GURU

THE GURU

The man-Guru shows you the Throne of the Infinite.
The God-Guru makes you sit on the Throne.

The Guru is at once the sigh of unaspiring disciples
and the ecstasy of aspiring disciples.

A real Guru is the selfless, dedicated and eternal beggar who begs Omnipotence and Omnipresence from
God to feed his unconsciously hungry and consciously
aspiring disciples, in perfect conformity with their souls'
needs.

The Guru has only one compassionate weapon: forgiveness. The disciple has three naked swords: limitation, weakness and ignorance. Nevertheless, the Guru
wins with great ease.

A man may have hundreds of companions. But a
spiritual seeker has only one companion: his Preceptor.

The Guru is the one who closes the door at the Will of
God and opens it to the tears of the disciple.

The Guru and the disciple must test each other
sweetly, seriously and perfectly before their mutual acceptance. Otherwise, if they are wrong in their selection,

the Guru will have to dance with failure and the disciple with perdition.

Who can show a disciple his true Motherland? The Guru. What is the name of that Motherland? Consciousness: Consciousness infinite, Consciousness all-pervading.

When you go to a doctor, you must tell him all about the disease you have been suffering from. Otherwise he will not be able to help you fully. Likewise, you must make a clean breast of your errors and misdeeds to your Guru. Mere acceptance of a Guru, while you secretly move and act at your sweet will, can be of no avail.

The Guru is not the body. The Guru is the revelation and manifestation of a divine Power here on earth.

There is no better way for a disciple to serve his Guru than to listen to his advice. The Guru is at once the source of his disciple's achievements and a most faithful servant of his disciple's love.

The Guru is the consolation for the disciple's despair. Also he is the compensation for the disciple's loss, if there be any, during the seeker's endless journey toward the all-fulfilling Goal.

The Guru's love for his disciple is his strength. The disciple's surrender toward his Guru is his strength.

The Mother aspect of the Guru is sacrifice.

The Father aspect of the Guru is compassion.

The real work of a Guru is to show the world that his deeds are in perfect harmony with his teachings.

* * *

Question: Do you think that an aspirant needs a living Guru in order to realise God?

Sri Chinmoy: A living Guru is not absolutely indispensable in order to realise God. The first person on earth who realised God, the very first realised soul, had no human Guru. He had only God as his Guru.

If you have a Guru, however, it facilitates your inner spiritual progress. A Guru is your private tutor in the spiritual life. There is a big difference between a private tutor and an ordinary teacher. An ordinary teacher will look at a student's paper and then give him a mark. He will examine the student and then pass him or fail him. But the private tutor is not like that. He encourages and inspires the student at home so that he can pass his examination. At every moment in life's journey, ignorance tries to test you, examine you and torture you, but this private tutor will teach you how to pass the examination most easily. It is the business of the spiritual teacher to inspire the seeker and increase his aspiration so that he can realise the Highest at God's choice Hour.

In order to learn anything in this world we need a teacher in the beginning. To learn the ABC's we need a teacher. To learn higher mathematics we need a teacher. The teacher may be necessary for a second or for a year or for many years. It is absurd to feel that for everything else in life we need a teacher, but not for God-realisation. As we need teachers for our outer knowledge, to illumine our outer being, so also we need a spiritual Master to help and guide us in our inner life, especially in the beginning. Otherwise, our progress will be very slow and uncertain. We may become terribly confused. We may get high, elevating experiences, but we will not understand them or believe in them. Doubt may eclipse our minds and we will say, "I am just an ordinary person, so how can I have this kind of experience? Perhaps I am deluding myself." Or we will tell our friends, and they will say, "It is all mental hallucination. Forget about the spiritual life." But if there is someone who knows what the Reality is, he will say, "Don't act like a fool. The experiences which you have had are absolutely real." He encourages the seeker, inspires him, and gives him the proper explanations of his experiences. Or, if the seeker is doing something wrong in his meditation, the Guru will be in a position to correct him.

A soul enters into a human body and the human being completes his first year of existence, his second year and so on. During this time his parents teach him how to speak, how to eat, how to dress, how to behave. The child learns everything from his parents. The parents play their part in the formative years. Similarly, in the spiritual life, the Master teaches the student how to pray, how to meditate, how to contemplate. Then, when the student learns to go deep within, he can do all this by himself.

Why does one go to the university when one can study at home? It is because he knows that he will get expert instruction from people who know the subject well. Now you know that there have been a few—very, very few— real men of knowledge who did not go to any university. Yes, there are exceptions. Every rule admits of exceptions. God is in everybody, and if a seeker feels that he does not need human help, he is most welcome to try his capacity alone. But if someone is wise enough and wants to run toward his Goal instead of stumbling or merely walking, then certainly the help of a Guru can be considerable.

Right now I am in London. I know that New York exists and that I have to go back there. What do I need to get me there? An airplane and a pilot. In spite of the fact that I know that New York exists, I cannot get there alone. Similarly, you know that God exists. You want to reach God, but someone has to take you there. As the airplane takes me to New York, someone has to carry you to the Consciousness of God which is deep within you. Someone has to show you how to enter into your own divinity, which is God.

A spiritual Master comes to you with a boat. He says, "Come. If you want to go to the Golden Shore, I will take you. Moreover, once you get into my boat, you can sing on the boat, you can dance, you can even sleep; but I will bring you safely to the Goal." If you say that you do not need anybody's help, if you want to swim across the sea of ignorance alone, then it is up to you. But how many years, how many incarnations will it take you? And again, after swimming for some time you may become totally exhausted and then you may drown.

If someone becomes a true disciple of a Master, he does not feel that he and his Guru are two totally different beings. He does not feel that his Guru is at the top of the tree and he is at the foot of the tree, all the time washing the feet of the Guru. No! He feels that the Guru is his own highest part. He feels that he and the Guru are one, that the Guru is his own highest and most developed part. Therefore, a true disciple does not find any difficulty in surrendering his lowest part to his highest part. It is not beneath his dignity to be a devoted disciple, because he knows that both the highest and the lowest are his very own.

* * *

WHO IS MORE IMPORTANT— GURU OR GOD?

One day a spiritual Master happened to see two of his disciples having a quarrel. They were almost fighting. So the Master approached them and said, "What is the matter? Why are you quarrelling and fighting?"

Both of them cried out, "Master, Master, help us! We need your guidance. We need your light."

The Master said, "If both of you speak at once, I cannot do any justice to you. So tell me, one of you, what is actually bothering you."

One of them said, "Master, the bone of contention is you and nobody else."

"What?"

The disciple continued, "He says that the Guru is more important than God. I say, impossible, God is more important. He says that the Guru is more important because the Guru shows and paves the way, and then takes the disciple to God. He also says that although God cares for everyone, even the sleeping and the unaspiring, if one wants immediate concern and blessing from God, it is through the Guru that one can have it. That is why the Guru is more important.

"But I say, no. It is God who has given this kind of love and compassion to the Guru; it is God who has made the Guru an instrument to help mankind. So to me, God is more important.

"He says that there is a Goal, but if somebody doesn't take him to that Goal— that somebody being his Guru — then God will always remain a far cry. He says, 'The Goal may be there, but who is taking me to the Goal? I can't go alone; I don't know the road. So my Guru is more important, because the Goal will not come to me.'

"I say, no. The Goal is God. If your Guru takes you to God, and then God does not care for you, what is the importance of the messenger? The Guru can take someone to the Goal; but if the Goal doesn't care for that person, then naturally the journey is useless. A human being can take somebody to a Master, but if the Master is not pleased with the person he has brought, then the case is hopeless. The most important thing is not who has *taken* the disciple, but who is *pleased* with the disciple. If God is pleased with someone, then that is more than enough.

"He says that if the Guru accepts someone as his dearest disciple, then he takes on his shoulders the disciple's karma. When the father knows that his son has done something wrong and the father wants to save the son, he takes the punishment on himself. This is what the Guru does. But God is the Universal Father and He deals with His cosmic Law. If we do something wrong, God will give us the consequences; we shall be punished. So he feels that the Guru is more important, because the Guru takes on his own shoulders the punishment that the disciple deserves, whereas God will always follow His cosmic Law.

"But I say, no: God is not punishing us. God is only giving us experience. Who is punishing whom? God is having His own experience in us and through us. So we are not getting any punishment, but rather, God is enjoying or suffering through us and in us.

"Moreover, God existed before the Guru came into the manifestation, and God will continue to be God long after the Guru leaves the field of manifestation. The Guru came from God and he will return to God, his Source. But God is infinite and eternal. Never will He cease to exist. God is the All; the Guru is His temporary embodiment.

"Guru, I have the utmost devotion to you. Although he is saying that you are more important than God and I am saying that God is more important, I do have the utmost faith in you. Would you please illumine us in this matter?"

The Guru said, "Look, if you think that the Guru is the body, then the Guru is not at all important. If you think that the Guru is the soul, then the Guru and God are equally important; they are one and the same. But if you feel that the Guru is the infinite Self, the transcendental Self, then you have to feel that it is neither the body of the Guru nor the soul of the Guru, but the Supreme in him, who is of paramount importance. The Supreme is the real Guru, everybody's Guru. If you want to separate the physical, the soul and the transcendental Self into three different parts, then you will never be able to realise the highest Truth. In order to realise the highest Truth, you should serve the physical aspect of the Master, love the soul of the Master and adore the transcendental Self of the Master. The most important thing is to see in the physical the boundless light of the Master; in the soul, the consciousness of his inseparable oneness with the Highest; and in the Self, the eternal Liberation. Then only, the Master and God can become one.

"God and the Guru are equally important in the eternal Game, the divine Drama."

* * *

YOUR REAL TEACHER

He who inspires you
　　Is your real teacher.

He who loves you
　　Is your real teacher.

He who forces you
　　Is your real teacher.

He who perfects you
　　Is your real teacher.

He who treasures you
　　Is your real teacher.

* * *

Question: When you are meditating on us and I am looking at you, I think perhaps I should try to be as humble, pure and receptive as possible. Is that right, or should I just forget about all this and keep my mind open?

Sri Chinmoy: It depends on the individual. If the

individual is a student of mine or a disciple of mine—that is to say, someone who has consciously given the responsibility for his spiritual life to me—if he becomes humble to me, if he becomes polite and very devoted, then he will get the utmost from me. If he is arrogant, stubborn and haughty, naturally he will not be able to receive anything from me.

Right now you are coming to the New York Centre, so you can consider yourself a student of mine. In your case, when you offer your humility, please feel that this humility is not touching my human personality. Feel that this humility is entering into the Supreme in me, who deserves everything from you. I am not anybody's Guru. Your Guru, your Master, is God. Your real Master is inside me. My Master, my real Master, is inside you. Just because I have the inner light and inner wisdom, when you approach me with humility and purity, I bring your aspiring soul to the fore. When you have a devoted feeling toward me, you can more easily receive the inner peace, the inner light, the inner wisdom that I have gained.

In the beginning, when you are a student, it is better always to enter into the teacher's heart consciously and with humility. This humility is not humiliation. When somebody is humiliated, he is crushed; but humility is a feeling of total oneness. You feel that you are absolutely one with me because God is the Lord of everything, the Cause of all. I am not superior and you are not inferior. With humility you can establish your oneness with me with the utmost sweetness. Try with your humility, softness, sweetness, divine love, to enter into me and feel your existence inside me. Once you enter into me, then it is my problem, my duty, my responsibility, to give you what you need by the Grace of the Supreme.

Some individuals come here just to get inner peace or inner joy. They are not my students; they have not given me the responsibility for their lives, and I have not taken the responsibility. In their case, what they should do when they look at me is forget about everything and make their mind absolutely calm, quiet and vacant — like an empty vessel — and not allow anything to enter into it during meditation. If they keep in their mind-vessel fears, worries, doubts and so forth, the vessel will be full. Then what can I do? The vessel has to be emptied so that I can fill it with divine peace, love, joy and harmony.

When the vessel is empty, divine thoughts can enter into the individual aspirant and grow. When the vessel is full to the brim with divine thoughts, ultimately it will open the door to divine Peace and Light.

This is to be done by those who are not my disciples, who just come here once a week and who want to have a little peace and nothing else. But those who want to have infinite Peace, infinite Light and infinite Bliss, whose who really want to realise the Highest on earth, have to follow a spiritual path. I have a path; so do other spiritual Masters. Each Master has a path of his own, and ultimately, each path leads to the same goal. All roads may lead to Rome, but one has to follow *one* road. Those meditating here who are not my students, eventually will feel the necessity for a spiritual Master. I am giving them inspiration. Then, when they are inspired, when they want to go to the end of the road, to the ultimate Goal, they will try to get a teacher of their own. At that time, their spiritual Master will tell them what they should and should not do.

* * *

MOTHER, YOU RESPOND TO MY SONG

Mother, You respond to my song;
Therefore I sing.
Your Affection is boundless, Mother, I know.
Even when I forget You through my sulking,
Your infinite Compassion and Peace
   draw me toward You.
You are my ocean, Mother; I am Your tiniest drop.
The stars, the moon and the sun
   are all eternal companions
In Your cosmic Game.

* * *

O YOGI OF THE HIGHEST MAGNITUDE, NOW IT IS MY TURN

O Yogi of the highest magnitude, now it is my turn.
Now accept the garland of my total surrender.
In the forest of my heart I am lost totally,
But there I see the smile of your Pole-Star.
Come, come. Without you the vina of my heart
Will never offer its music, I know, I know.
Therefore I draw you into my bosom.
O Yogi of the highest magnitude, now it is my turn.

* * *

THE MIRACLE-MAKER

His is the life of a miracle-maker.
He started with himself.
Himself he loved,
Himself he caught,
Himself he taught.

He has started teaching.
Nobody passes through him unchanged.
His life is a constant movement
   Upward and inward.
Doctrine he has none.

His heavenly beauty and God
Live under the same roof.
His earthly duty and God
Live in the same room.

* * *

THE GOAL OF GOALS: REALISATION, MANIFESTATION AND PERFECTION

REALISATION

ILLUMINATION

In this world there is only one thing worth having, and that is illumination. In order to have illumination, we must have sincerity and humility. Unfortunately, in this world sincerity is long dead and humility is yet to be born. Let us try to revive our sincerity and let us try, on the strength of our aspiration, to expedite the birth of our humility. Then only will we be able to realise God.

Illumination is not something very far away. It is very close; it is just inside us. At every moment we can consciously grow into illumination through our inner progress. Inner progress is made through constant sacrifice. Sacrifice of what? Sacrifice of wrong, evil thoughts and a wrong understanding of Truth. Sacrifice and renunciation go together. What are we going to renounce? The physical body, family, friends, relatives, our country, the world? No! We have to renounce our own ignorance, our own false ideas of God and Truth. Also, we have to sacrifice to God the result of each action. The divine vision no longer remains a far cry when we offer the result of our actions to the Inner Pilot.

In our day-to-day life we very often speak of our bondage and freedom. But realisation says that there is no such thing as bondage and freedom. What actually exists is consciousness — consciousness on various levels, consciousness enjoying itself in its various manifestations. In the field of manifestation, consciousness has different grades. Why do we pray? We pray because our prayer leads us from a lower degree of illumination to a higher degree. We pray because our prayer brings us closer to something pure, beautiful, inspiring and fulfilling. The highest illumination is God-realisation. This illumination must take place not only in the soul, but also in the heart, mind, vital and body. God-realisation is a conscious, complete and perfect union with God.

We want to love the world; the world wants to love us. We want to fulfil the world; the world wants to fulfil us. But there is no connecting link between us and the world. We feel that our existence and the world's existence are two totally different things. We think that the world is something separate from us. But in this we are making a deplorable mistake. What is the proper connecting link between us and the world? God. If we approach God first and see God in the world, then no matter how many millions of mistakes we make, the world will not only indulge our mistakes, but it will soulfully love us as well. Similarly, when we see the defects, weaknesses and imperfections of the world, we will be able to forgive the world and then inspire, energise and illumine the world just because we feel God's Existence there.

If we do not see God in all our activities, frustration will loom large in our day-to-day life. No matter how sincerely we try to please the world, no matter how sincerely the world tries to please us, frustration will be found between our understanding and the world's understanding. The source of frustration is ignorance. Ignorance is the mother of devastating frustration, damaging frustration and strangling frustration. If we go deeper into ignorance, we see it is all a play of inconscience. Frustration can be removed totally from our lives only when we enter into the Source of all existence. When we enter into the Source of our own existence and the world's existence, we are approaching the Reality. This Reality is our constant Delight, the Delight of the Breath of God.

The world is neither mine nor yours nor anyone's. Never! It belongs to God, and God alone. So we have to be really wise. We have to go to the Possessor first, and not to the possession. The possession is helpless; it can do nothing on its own. It is the Possessor that can do what He wants to do with His possession. So first we have to become one with God, and then we shall automatically become one with God's possessions. When we become one with God and with His possessions, we can certainly and unmistakably feel that the world is ours and we are the world's.

Ignorance and illumination are like night and day. We have to enter into illumination first, and then bring illumination into ignorance-night. Otherwise, the transformation of ignorance will be difficult, slow and uncertain. To enter into the field of ignorance without achieving illumination first is to take a negative path. If we pursue the path of darkness and try to find light in darkness, we are taking the negative path. The best way, the positive way to find light is to follow the path of light, more light, abundant light, infinite Light. If we follow the path of light, then illumination will assuredly dawn in us.

Let us look up and bring down the Light from above. The moment we look up, God's Grace descends. The very nature of God's Grace is to descend upon each individual on earth. When we want to go up to God with ignorance, it is like climbing up a mountain with a heavy bundle on our shoulders. Naturally it is a difficult task. Instead of doing that, we can remain at the foot of the mountain and cry for God's Grace, which is ready and eager to come down to us from the Highest. Needless to say, for God to come down into our ignorance is infinitely easier than for us to carry our ignorance up to God.

Illumination is the conscious awareness of the soul. Illumination is the conscious vision of the Reality that is going to be manifested. Illumination is possibility transformed into practicality. Illumination is like God's divine magic wand. An ordinary magician in this world uses his wand to make one thing turn into another. When God uses illumination in the world, immediately the finite consciousness of earth enters into the Infinite and becomes the Infinite.

Illumination is humanity's first realisation of God's omnipotent Power, boundless Compassion, infinite Light and perfect Perfection. It is our illumination that makes us feel what God really is. Before illumination, God is theoretical; after illumination, God becomes practical. So illumination is the divine magic power that makes us see the Reality which was once upon a time imagination. When illumination dawns in a human being, God is no longer just a promise, but an actual achievement.

Illumination is in the mind and in the heart. When the mind is illumined, we become God's Choice. When the heart is illumined, we become God's Voice. Here in the physical world the mind has evolved considerably. Because man has developed his intellectual mind, he has become superior to the animals, for the standard of the mind is higher than the standard of the physical or the vital. Man has cultivated the capacity of the mind, but he has not cultivated the capacity of the heart. When we cultivate the heart, we will see that its capacity is far greater than we had imagined. When we cultivate the unique sense in our heart that we are of God's highest Vision and we are for God's perfect Manifestation, then illumination will take place.

* * *

Question: Do we have to remove all materialistic goals in order to realise God?

Sri Chinmoy: How we utilise the material life is what is of paramount importance. Matter, as such, has not done anything wrong to God; it is not anti-divine. It is we who use the material things in a wrong way. We must enter into the material life with our soul's light. We can use a knife to stab someone or we can use it to cut a fruit to share with others. With fire we can cook and with fire we can also burn ourselves or set fire to someone's house.

We have to feel that matter and spirit go together. Matter has to be the conscious expression of our spirit. If you say that matter is everything, that there is no spirit, no higher life, no inner reality, then I have to tell you that you are mistaken. There is an inner reality, there is an infinite Truth that wants to express itself in and through matter. Matter is asleep, and it has to be aroused. The material life has to be guided and moulded by the spirit.

But first we have to understand what the material life is for. If by material life we mean lower vital enjoyment and the fulfilment of gross desires, then it is useless to try to accept the spiritual life simultaneously. But if the material life means the life of expansion—the expansion of the heart, the expansion of love—then matter and spirit can easily go together. In this material life we have to see Peace, Light and Bliss. What we see right now in the mind is jealousy, fear, doubt and all undivine things. But in this very mind we can and we must feel harmony, peace, love and other divine qualities. If we want these divine qualities from the material life, then the material life can go perfectly well with the spiritual life.

The true material life is not just eating, sleeping and breathing. The material life is a significant life, and it eventually has to become a life of dedication. Right now in the physical we are trying to possess people and things. But the material life will have meaning only when we stop trying to possess and start trying to dedicate. When we dedicate ourselves to the Supreme, to the unparalleled Goal of realising God, only then will life reveal itself to us as the message of Truth, the message of Infinity, Eternity and Immortality.

Question: When I think of all the failings and undivine qualities in myself and my fellow disciples, illumination seems a million miles away.

Sri Chinmoy: When one is really illumined, one will not see others as imperfect or hopeless human beings. The moment one is illumined, he will feel his real oneness with others and he will see the so-called imperfections in others as an experience God is having in and through them.

Since you are my disciple, I wish to tell you that you see more imperfection, more limitation, more teeming night inside yourself than I can ever imagine. To me you are absolutely natural and normal; you are God's child, and you have every opportunity and capacity to realise, manifest and fulfil the Divine here on earth. Illumination is something which you had, but which you have now forgotten; it is not something totally new.

One who really cares for illumination has to feel that he is growing from light to more light to abundant light. If a seeker always feels that he is deep in the sea of ignorance, then I wish to say that he will never, never come out of ignorance, for there is no end to the ignorance-sea. But if one feels that he is growing from an iota of light into the all-pervading, highest Light, then illumination immediately seems easier and more spontaneous.

Question: Can we actually feel our realisation coming, or does it appear spontaneously and unexpectedly?

Sri Chinmoy: Real realisation cannot dawn unexpectedly. Gradually, gradually we come to the point where we realise God. If one is on the verge of realisation, he will know that it is a matter of days or months or years. Realisation is complete conscious oneness with God. Now, if one does not have a *limited* conscious oneness with God, how can he attain an *unlimited* conscious oneness with God all at once? It is true that God can do everything, that He can grant realisation without asking anything of the seeker. But if God gave you realisation without your meditating and practising the spiritual life, then everybody would expect it.

Some people get realisation after only four or five years of meditation, whereas others who have been meditating for thirty, forty or fifty years are nowhere near realisation. But you have to know that in the case of the person who realises God after having meditated for only four or five years, this is not his first incarnation as a seeker. He started his conscious journey long before you may ever have thought of God. Now he is completing his journey to God-realisation, while you perhaps have just started yours. Again, we have to know that even though we have meditated for many incarnations in the past and for a few years in this incarnation, it does not actually mean that we deserve God. It was God's Grace that operated in our previous incarnations and it is God's Grace that is helping us realise Him in this incarnation as well.

From your constant, lifelong meditation you can expect realisation, but only at God's choice Hour. You may want it immediately, but God may know that if you realise Him right now, you will be more harmful than helpful to mankind. So God has His own Hour for your realisation, and when that Hour nears, you will be aware of it.

Question: What does God-realisation really mean?

Sri Chinmoy: God-realisation, or *siddhi*, means Self-discovery in the highest sense of the term. One consciously realises his oneness with God. As long as the seeker remains in ignorance, he will feel that God is somebody else who has infinite Power, while he, the seeker, is the feeblest person on earth. But the moment he realises God, he comes to know that he and God are absolutely one in both the inner and the outer life. God-realisation means one's identification with one's absolute highest Self. When one can identify with one's highest Self and remain in that consciousness forever, when one can reveal and manifest it at one's own command, that is God-realisation.

Now, you have studied books on God, and people have told you that God is in everybody. But you have not realised God in your conscious life. For you this is all mental speculation. But when one is God-realised, one consciously knows what God is, what He looks like, what He wills. When one achieves Self-realisation, one remains in God's Consciousness and speaks to God face to face. He sees God both in the finite and in the Infinite; he sees God as both personal and impersonal. And in his case, this is not mental hallucination or imagination; it is direct reality. This reality is more authentic than my seeing you right here in front of me. When one speaks to a human being, there is always a veil of ignorance — darkness, imperfection, misunderstanding. But between God and the inner being of one who has realised Him, there can be no ignorance, no veil. At that time one can speak to God more clearly, more convincingly, more openly than to a human being.

As ordinary human beings, we feel that infinite Peace, infinite Light, infinite Bliss and infinite divine Power are all sheer imagination. We are victims to doubt, fear and negative forces which we feel are quite normal and natural. We cannot love anything purely, not even ourselves. We are in the finite, quarrelling and fighting, and there is no such thing as peace or light or bliss in us. But those who practise meditation go deep within and see that there *is* real peace, light and bliss. They get boundless inner strength and see that doubt and fear *can* be challenged and conquered. When we achieve God-realisation, our inner existence is flooded with Peace, Poise, Equanimity and Light.

Question: There are some paths which speak of the goal as enlightenment, and there are other paths which speak of the goal as God-realisation. What is the difference between enlightenment and God-realisation?

Sri Chinmoy: Sometimes when we speak of enlightenment, we mean that we have been in darkness about a particular subject for many years and now we have inner wisdom, or now that particular place in our consciousness is enlightened. But this is just a spark of the boundless Illumination, and that little spark we cannot call God-realisation.

Full enlightenment, complete and all-illumining enlightenment, is God-realisation. But sometimes, when a seeker is in his highest meditation, he gets a kind of inner illumination or enlightenment, and for half an hour or an hour his whole being, his whole existence, is illumined. But then, after an hour or two, he becomes his same old self; he again becomes a victim to desire and undivine qualities. Enlightenment has taken place, but it is not the transcendental Enlightenment which occurred in the case of the Buddha and other spiritual Masters. That kind of all-fulfilling, all-illumining Enlightenment is equivalent to God-realisation. God-realisation means constant and eternal Enlightenment, transcendental Enlightenment. When we get God-realisation, automatically infinite Illumination takes place in our outer as well as our inner existence.

The enlightenment that is spoken of here in the West and also in Japan is only a temporary burst of light in the aspiring consciousness. After a short while it pales into insignificance, because there is no abiding reality in it. Abiding reality we will get only with constant, eternal and transcendental Illumination, which is God-realisation.

Question: After a person realises God, does he still act like an ordinary human being?

Sri Chinmoy: When we use the term 'realisation', people are very often confused. They feel that a realised person is totally different from an ordinary person, that he behaves in a very unusual way. But I wish to say that a realised person need not and should not behave in an unusual way. What has he realised? The ultimate Truth in God. And who is God? God is someone or something absolutely normal.

When someone realises the Highest, it means he has inner Peace, Light and Bliss in infinite measure. It does not mean that his outer appearance or outer features will be any different, for Peace, Light and Bliss are inside his inner consciousness. If a Master achieves realisation, it does not mean that he will grow two big horns or a long tail, or become in some other way abnormal. No, he is normal. Even after a spiritual Master has realised the Highest, he still eats, sleeps, talks and breathes just as others do. But a spiritual seeker will be able to feel tremendous peace and purity in him.

It is inside the human that the divine exists. We do not have to live in the Himalayan caves to prove our inner divinity; this divinity we can bring forward in our normal day-to-day life. Spirituality is absolutely normal, but unfortunately we have come to feel it is abnormal because we see so few spiritual people in this world of ignorance. But this feeling is a deplorable mistake. Real spirituality is the acceptance of life. First we have to accept life as it is, and then we have to try to divinise and transform the face of the world with our aspiration and with our realisation.

Unspiritual people frequently think that a realised person, if he is truly realised, has to perform miracles at every moment. But miracles and God-realisation need not necessarily go together. When you look at a spiritual Master, what you see is Peace, Light, Bliss and divine Power. Enter into his consciousness and you are bound to feel these things. But if you expect something else from a realised soul, if you come to a spiritual Master thinking that he will fulfil your teeming desires and make you a multimillionaire, then you are totally mistaken. If it is the Will of the Supreme, the Master can easily make someone a multimillionaire overnight. He can bring down material prosperity; but usually this is not the Will of the Supreme. The Will of the Supreme is for inner prosperity, not outer affluence.

Question: Does every person who realises God become a spiritual Master?

Sri Chinmoy: There are hundreds of students every year who get their Master's degree from a university. Some then enter into an office or business, while others begin to teach. Similarly, in the spiritual life, some people who have realised God teach others how to realise God, and some do not. Those who do not teach the world are God-realised nevertheless. We cannot deny it. But it has taken them many incarnations to cross the barriers of ignorance, and they are now really tired. It is not an easy thing to realise God, and they feel that they have acted like real divine heroes in the battlefield of life. They have fought against fear, doubt, anxieties, worries, imperfections, limitations and bondage and conquered these forces. Now they feel that they have every right to withdraw from the battlefield and take rest. Their souls speak to God, and if God says they do not have to take conscious part in the cosmic Game any more, and may just observe, then they withdraw. If they have God's permission, naturally they can remain passive.

But the souls who do take part in God's manifestation are also doing something very great. They may not take an active part in the world, they may not go from one place to another to teach or open spiritual centres and accept disciples, but in their meditation they try to offer illumination inwardly by offering their conscious good will to mankind. How many people offer their good will to mankind? Ordinary human beings quarrel, fight and consciously or unconsciously do many undivine things against God's Will. But in the case of these realised souls, they do not enter into any kind of conflict with God's Will; their will has become one with God's Will.

We cannot say that he who works outwardly for mankind is greater than he who helps inwardly. What is of paramount importance is to listen to God's Will. We cannot say that one who is crying for mankind and trying to help is greater than one who withdraws. He alone is great who listens to God's Will. If God tells one illumined soul, "I do not need you to move around from place to place. You just give your Light inwardly," then that person is great by offering his Light inwardly. And if God tells another soul, "I want you to go into the world and offer humanity the Light you have," then he becomes great by helping humanity. Everything depends on what God wants from a particular soul.

Question: Once you said that when a seeker reaches the highest realisation, automatically spiritual manifestation comes. Would you explain to me what you mean by that kind of manifestation?

Sri Chinmoy: When one gets realisation, if he remains in the world, automatically manifestation starts. When you stand in front of a liberated, fully realised soul, what happens? Immediately you see the vast difference between yourself and that person. The first thing you see in him is Peace; in his eyes you will see infinite Peace. From his body you will get a sense of Purity, a Purity which you have never felt before in your life or in anybody else's life. How is it that he is emanating Purity, Light and divine Power, while somebody else is not? It is just because he is fully realised. He is not talking to you, he is not saying anything to you, but from his very presence you get infinite Peace, infinite Bliss, infinite Light. So realisation automatically shows its own capacity, which is manifestation. The inner realisation of the Master is being manifested through his outer form, which is the body.

There is another kind of manifestation, which we find more on the physical plane: it is the manifestation of divinity on earth. This manifestation takes place when a spiritual Master deliberately tries to awaken spiritually hungry individuals. There are many people on earth who are spiritually hungry, but they do not have a Master or a spiritual path. So the Master tries to inspire them and kindle the flame of conscious aspiration in them and put them on a spiritual path.

When a spiritual Master, with the help of his dearest disciples, tries to manifest divinity on earth, sometimes people misunderstand him. They think he wants to convert everyone. But the Master's motive is not that of a missionary. Christian missionaries went to India, and all over the world, saying, "There is only one saviour, the Christ." But if the Christ is the only saviour, then where does the Buddha stand? Where does Sri Krishna stand? Where are Sri Ramakrishna and all the other great Masters? Each genuine spiritual Master is a saviour, needless to say; but to say that he is the *only* saviour, or that his path is the *only* path, is foolishness. If I say that my path is the only path, that if you do not accept me you will go to hell, then there is no more stupid person on earth than I.

On our path we do not want to convert anybody; we want to inspire. Many of you here are not my disciples and are not going to be my disciples. But I am most glad that you have come, and most grateful to you for your presence here. I have the capacity, through God's Grace, to inspire you. You may take my inspiration and then go to whatever path you need or want. I have played my part by inspiring you.

A realised Master never, never tries to convert; he only offers his realisation in the form of inspiration to aspiring souls. That is why the Master has to act like a normal human being. If he does not act like a human being, if he does not eat and take rest and talk in a human way, then people will say, "Oh, you have gone so far beyond us! It is simply impossible for us ever to be like you." But the spiritual Master says, "No, I do everything you do. If I can eat the same food, if I can mix with you the way you mix with others and, at the same time, not lose my highest consciousness, then how is it that you also cannot enter into the life of the Highest?" This is how the Master inspires his disciples.

When there is realisation, inside the realisation you will see manifestation. Manifestation is the outer form of realisation, and one who is really spiritual will immediately feel the manifestation in the realisation itself. For ordinary people, for humanity, it takes time. If I have realised something and manifested it in the outer world, the heart of humanity feels it, but the physical mind may take a little time to perceive and understand the manifestation. In the field of manifestation, the Master is dealing with ignorant, unaspiring people or emotionally bound people who will not see the Master's full Light. But a great aspirant sees the realisation and cannot separate the realisation from the manifestation.

Question: Is there any difference between liberation and realisation, or are they absolutely identical?

Sri Chinmoy: There is a great difference between liberation and realisation. Liberation is much inferior to realisation. One can reach liberation in one incarnation, and realisation in some later incarnation. Or one can become liberated and realised in the same incarnation. But it is not possible to be realised without first being fortunate, will bring down with him a few really liberated souls to help him in his manifestation. Sri Ramakrishna, for example, brought down Vivekananda and Brahmananda. Some of these liberated souls who enter into the earth scene with the great Masters don't care for realisation. They just come to help. Others, like Vivekananda, want realisation also.

A liberated soul is liberated from ignorance, from worldly, undivine qualities. A liberated soul will inspire others with his presence. He will inspire them to be pure, simple, kind-hearted and loving. Tremendous purity and serenity will flow from him, and others will want to touch him, speak to him, look at his face. You can say that he is much more than a saint. True, worldly obscurities, impurities and other things will not enter into the liberated soul, for he will be all the time cautious so as not to allow them to enter into him. But a realised soul is much higher. He is consciously part and parcel of God.

A liberated soul knows that there is a special room where he stays and has his shrine. He knows that there is also a kitchen, which is all dirty and full of impurities. Ordinary human beings have no special room, no shrine at all. They are all the time locked in the kitchen, and naturally they cannot come into the room where the living deity is. The liberated soul is able to live in the room with the shrine, but he is afraid that if he enters into the kitchen to help others, the undivine things there may attack him, and he will again become their victim as he was before his liberation.

But realised souls are extremely powerful. They know what they are and where they have come from. On the strength of their universal and transcendental consciousness, they can enter into the ignorance of humanity, into the earth-consciousness as such, and illumine it with their torch-light. They do so only because of their infinite compassion, not because they still have some temptations or wrong forces in them. No! They enter into ignorance deliberately so that humanity can be radically transformed. But only realised souls of a high order accept this bold challenge.

A liberated soul is like a child, so beautiful and pure. But how long can you stay with a child? With his capacity you cannot go very far, or reach the Highest. But a realised soul is like a mature person, who can offer you tremendous aspiration, light, wisdom and the living reality. A liberated soul will inspire you to walk along the path, but a realised soul will not only inspire you but also guide you and lead you to your destination.

A realised soul is not only the guide, not only the way, but the Goal itself. First he pretends he is not even the guide, but just someone to inspire the seeker. Then he comes and tells the seeker that he is the guide, but not the road. Gradually, however, he shows that he himself is also the road. And finally he makes the seeker feel his infinite Compassion and shows him that he is not only the guide and the road, but the Goal as well, the seeker's own Goal.

A realised soul can touch the foot of the realisation-tree or can climb up to the topmost branch and bring down the fruit to share with humanity waiting below. That is realisation. But even the one who only touches the realisation-tree and sits at the foot of the tree without climbing up or bringing anything down is far superior to the liberated soul.

But again, to reach liberation is no easy matter. It is very, very difficult to become free from ignorance. Out of the millions and billions of human beings on earth, there may be ten or twenty or even a hundred liberated souls. But God alone knows how few realised souls exist. To realise the highest Absolute as one's very own and to constantly feel this realisation is not something you have actually achieved, but something you eternally are—that is called realisation.

* * *

A liberated soul usually does not care for God-manifestation on earth. He feels that once he is liberated, his role in the cosmic Drama is ended. A realised soul cries for God-manifestation. He feels that once he is realised, his role in the cosmic Drama has properly begun.

A liberated soul is freed from the meshes of ignorance and, at the same time, is extremely careful of wild ignorance. A realised soul has discovered his own inner divinity, which is flooded with God's all-seeing Vision and all-fulfilling Reality.

A liberated soul usually uses God according to his own capacity. A realised soul uses God only when asked by God Himself.

The human and the unreal in us cease in liberation.
The divine and the real in us begin in realisation.

* * *

HIDE-AND-SEEK

Every minute inspires me
   To attempt.
Every hour perfects me
   To ascend.
Every day illumines me
   To reach.

   In my attempt
I have come to learn what I can be.
   In my ascension
I have come to learn who I eternally am.
   On my arrival
God and I shall stop playing our age-long game:
   Hide-and-seek.

* * *

MANIFESTATION AND PERFECTION

What is meant by spiritual perfection? It is the constant capacity to live in God and to reveal Him in one's every movement.

* * *

SPIRITUAL PERFECTION

To perfect our human life, by far the greatest necessity is our soul's delight. When we live in the physical, the teeming clouds of desire are natural, necessary and inevitable. When we live in the soul, the ever-mounting flames of aspiration are natural, necessary and inevitable.

When we live in the soul, we spontaneously cultivate God. His Peace, Bliss and Power become ours, absolutely ours and we grow into spiritual perfection. This perfection is at once our divine heritage in a human body and our heavenly birthright on earthly soil.

The human in us must live under the sheltering wings

of the soul. The divine in us must soar into the Beyond with the flying wings of the soul. The human in us must eventually need transformation. The divine in us must eventually need manifestation.

Perfection is what I have inherited from God in my inner life. Transformation is what I have inherited from God in my outer life.

What is perfection? Perfection is realisation. Perfection is manifestation. Perfection in the inner world means realisation. Perfection in the outer world means manifestation. A seeker is a fusion of individuality and personality. When a seeker carries his selfless individuality into the highest vision of Reality and offers his all-loving personality to the Absolute Beyond, he achieves perfection in the world of Infinity's Eternity.

Some people say that perfection exists neither in Heaven nor on earth. I cannot see eye-to-eye with them. Perfection does exist both in Heaven and on earth. The very cry of earth is perfection. The very smile of Heaven is perfection. Earth's soulful cry and Heaven's glowing smile must go together. Then only will satisfaction dawn on God's Face.

When earth cries we must not think that earth is inferior to Heaven, and when Heaven smiles we must not think that Heaven is superior to earth. No, it is not so. It is God, the growing man, who cries in and through earth to realise all that he can eventually be. And it is again God, the fulfilled man, who smiles in and through Heaven in realising what he already is.

Complete and total perfection will come about only when we feel that our perfection is no perfection if the rest of humanity remains imperfect. If we call ourselves children of God, then others are also children of God.

They may be travelling a few miles behind us, or they may be fast asleep. But they must reach the Goal before perfect Perfection can dawn on earth. We will try to conquer our fear, our doubt, our jealousy and other negative forces. But when we go deep within, after we have achieved what we want for ourselves, we will feel that only our limited self has been satisfied. Our larger self, which is humanity entire, is far, far from perfection. So we will try to remove fear, doubt, anxiety, worries and other undivine forces from humanity.

On our path we feel that perfection has to be total and integral. We know that we have imperfection in our nature, and at the same time we have limited perfection. If the imperfection right now looms large, we have to brave that imperfection and transform it into perfection. Through our conscious prayer, meditation, concentration and contemplation, the imperfection of the past can be perfected, and the darkness of yesterday can be transformed into Light.

* * *

Question: What keeps us from attaining perfection?

Sri Chinmoy: What keeps us from attaining perfection? It is our self-indulgence. In self-indulgence we feel that there is something absolutely necessary in our life, and that is pleasure. When we cry for pleasure and want to remain in pleasure, to become pleasure itself, perfection is a far cry. But when we cry for divine Joy, Delight, Bliss, at that time we enter into the ocean of perfection. If we cry continuously, we learn how to swim in the sea of perfection.

When we have an inner cry for Delight, we jump into the sea of perfection. This is the first step. But when this inner cry becomes constant, we swim in the sea of perfection. When we keep Joy and Delight as our goal, perfection automatically grows in us, and slowly, steadily we become the sea of perfection. But what now keeps us from perfection is our fondness for pleasure-life and our indulgence in pleasure-life.

Question: Was God perfect before He created the universe?

Sri Chinmoy: Yes, God was perfect. But just as there is no end to our own perfection, even so there is no end to God's Perfection. We use the term ever-transcending Beyond. God is constantly transcending Himself. God's Perfection means the message of His own Self-transcendence. When you did not know how to play the piano, your goal, which was your idea of perfection, was just to strike the proper notes, and you were exceedingly glad when you knew how to strike the proper notes. After a few years, your perfection was knowing how to play a few pieces properly. Then your perfection was to be able to play some great masterpiece on the piano, and so on. In God's case also, He had the creation in His Vision, and now you see how His evolution is progressing slowly and steadily toward the Highest.

Perfection is like that. When you have something excellent, you think that is perfection. Then you see that what you have can be expanded or improved, and you go farther beyond. The message of progess is perfection. Perfection is constant progress in God's Light.

God was definitely perfect before the creation, but now He has added the message of manifestation to His Perfection. Naturally God's own sense of perfection grows, and He far transcends His previous standard, His previous achievement, His previous Vision. Perfect He was, but now He wants to be perfect in another way, in a higher way, in a more convincing way.

Question: Has the soul always been perfect?

Sri Chinmoy: The soul has always been perfect, but, as I said before about God, we have to know how high the soul is and how much higher it can go. Today's height is perfect for the soul today, but tomorrow the soul can envision a higher height, and it has to climb up. The soul-bird is now on a particular branch, which it thinks is the highest branch. But then it looks up and sees that there is a higher branch, so it jumps up to that branch. Then again it sees something higher and goes there. Each time it casts its glance, it sees something higher. Where the soul stands is perfect for the time being, but then it increases its vision and goes ever higher and higher. There is no end to the height it can achieve.

Again, when it is a matter of manifestation, the soul knows how much it revealed or manifested God's Light in its previous incarnations and how much it can manifest in future incarnations. In a previous incarnation it was just a little, in the present incarnation it was a little more, and in future incarnations it will perhaps be much more.

Question: Will God's Reality ever be found on earth?

Sri Chinmoy: God has two names: one is Dream, the other is Reality. With His Dream He is entering into the world of His fulfilment, which we call constant manifestation of reality. The highest Reality is the transformation of human nature, which is right now half animal and half divine. The highest Reality can be manifested here on earth, but it will take quite a few centuries, perhaps much longer. That doesn't mean that we have to remain silent and inactive—far from it! Each day we shall try to sail in God's Dream-Boat and see where the Boat is taking us. If we are consciously and constantly seated in God's Dream-Boat, then slowly, steadily and unerringly this Dream-Boat will take us to God's Reality-Shore. This Shore of Reality is not somewhere in Heaven; it is here in our day-to-day life, in our thoughts, in our actions, in our very existence on earth.

All worlds are real. But this world, this planet, is more significant than other planets because God has decreed that it is only on this planet that realisation can and will take place. What is realisation? It is conscious oneness with God the Infinite. Only in this world can an aspirant consciously become one with God the Infinite.

Here on earth we can gain constant oneness with the infinite Light and infinite Truth, because Reality is more vivid, more manifest here. Let us not think of Heaven or hell. Our human understanding of Heaven and hell is all deception. Other worlds do exist; we can go to them during our sleep, or during meditation. But if we truly want to be totally one with God, then this earth is the only place where we can see the Real in ourselves, in humanity and in God Himself.

* * *

TRANSFORMATION AND PERFECTION
OF THE PHYSICAL NATURE

Neither an individual effort nor an individual abnegation can bring about the transformation of your consciousness. This transformation is possible only by the descent of a higher Light.

To think of physical transformation without having some kind of realisation is to count your chickens before they are hatched.

Surrender has to look up with folded hands. Transformation has to look down with palms facing the earth-consciousness.

The transformation of human nature in its completeness must unavoidably progress at the speed of a tortoise.

Both the descent of Truth into the lower nature and the ascent of the lower nature into the higher Truth are capable of solving the problem of problems, the illumination of human consciousness. They are equally effective and have an equal speed.

* * *

ABOVE ALL

Man above all:
This is the height
Of my animal realisation.

Love above all:
This is the height
Of my human realisation.

Oneness above all:
This is the height
Of my divine realisation.

God-manifestation above all:
This is the height
Of my absolute Perfection.

* * *

TWO DIFFERENT THINGS

Love is one thing,
   Possession is another.

Possession is one thing,
   Happiness is another.

Happiness is one thing,
   Accomplishment is another.

Accomplishment is one thing,
   Perfection is another.

* * *

Question: God could have made man perfect to begin with. What was His reason for putting us to all the trouble that we are going through to attain perfection?

Sri Chinmoy: God could have started His creation with perfection. But, fortunately or unfortunately, that was not His intention. What God wanted was to go through ignorance to Knowledge, through limitation to Plenitude, through death to Immortality.

In the outer world we see limitation, imperfection, doubt, fear and death. But in the inner world we see Light, Peace, Bliss and Perfection. When we live in God's Consciousness, there is no imperfection. It is all Perfection. When we consciously identify ourselves with God's Consciousness we observe that there is no imperfection, because God is perfect Perfection. But if we do not live in the divine Consciousness, naturally we will be yoked to the imperfection of the outer world.

God is a divine Player. He is playing His divine Game, and He knows the ultimate end. At each moment He is revealing Himself in us and through us, in spite of the fact that we see, nay create, a vast gulf between ourselves and God. In the physical world the miseries, troubles, frustrations and despair that we are going through are nothing but experiences on our way to the ultimate Goal. But who, after all, is having all these experiences? It is God and God alone. What actually is happening is the self-revelation of God in His manifested creation. A seeker of the Supreme, living in the Supreme, being one with the Consciousness of the Supreme, sees and feels that his life, both inner and outer, is a projection of God's ever-transcending Perfection growing into perfect Perfection.

Question: Will the process of striving for perfection ever come to an end?

Sri Chinmoy: It will never come to an end, because God Himself does not want to end His cosmic Game. Today what we feel is the ultimate perfection, tomorrow will be just the starting point of our journey. This is because our consciousness is evolving. When the consciousness evolves to a higher level, our sense of perfection simultaneously goes higher. Let us take perfection as an achievement. When we are a kindergarten student, our achievement of perfection may be very good for that stage. But from kindergarten we go to primary school, high school, college and university. When we get our Master's degree in perfection our achievement is much greater than what it was when we were in kindergarten. But even then we may feel that there are many things more that we have to learn. Then we will study further and enlarge our consciousness still more.

If the child thinks that the Master's degree will always remain unattainable, then he is mistaken. The spiritual ladder has quite a few rungs. If we do not step onto the first rung, then how can we climb up to the ultimate rung of the ladder?

* * *

PERFECTION-GOAL

Perfection is the seeker's fulfilling realisation and fulfilled manifestation. Everything else has dawned on earth save perfection, perfect Perfection.

Perfection is the tree.

Perfect Perfection is the fruit.

Man's speculation about perfection is his ignorance. Man's concentration on perfection is his knowledge. Man's meditation on perfection is his wisdom. Man's contemplation of perfection is his world-illumining, world-transforming inner eye.

God's Message is Perfection.
Man's message is temptation.

God's Message is Perfection.
Man's message is frustration.

God's Message is Perfection.
Man's message is destruction.

Perfection-Goal and the freedom-soul go together. He who reaches the state of freedom-soul has conquered his outer life and immortalised his inner life. He is the chosen instrument of God. He is the direct channel of God. He is the representative of God here on earth.

Cry and try.

When we cry to see the transcendental Light and when we try to perfect our outer nature, our perfection does not remain a far cry. Perfection is ours.

Exert and control.

When we exert the divine in us and control the animal in us, perfection begins to dawn within us. The flower of perfection blooms.

See and be.

When we try to see the truth with the Eye of God, not with our own eyes, and when we consciously try to be the surrendered instrument of God, perfection in no time dawns. The Golden All of perfection beckons our aspiring hearts.

When we use the term 'Heaven', we feel that Heaven is all Light, Delight and Perfection. But where is that Heaven? It is deep within us, in the inmost recesses of our hearts. High Heaven, higher Heaven and the highest Heaven are all within us.

When we offer our soulful thoughts to our brothers and sisters, we live in high Heaven.

When we offer the results of our soulful actions to mankind, we live in higher Heaven.

Finally, when we offer our soulful existence to humanity at large, unreservedly and unconditionally, we live in the highest Heaven.

We have to start our journey with inspiration. We have to feel every day deep within us in all our activities the necessity of inspiration. Without inspiration there can be no proper achievement. Then we have to go one step farther. After inspiration we have to feel the momentous necessity of aspiration. We have to aspire to reach the Golden All, to see the Golden Shore of the Beyond, the ever-transcending Beyond. This is what we expect from aspiration, the mounting flame within us.

But aspiration is not enough either. We have to meditate. Aspiration needs meditation. When we meditate, we have to feel that we are entering into Infinity, Eternity and Immortality. These are not vague terms, but our true possessions. Someday we shall all enter into our divine possessions — Infinity, Eternity and Immortality. This is our birthright.

Then, when we become advanced in our meditation, when meditation starts offering us its fruits, we enter the realm of realisation. We realise the highest Truth in this body, here on earth. We do not have to go elsewhere to realise God. We do not have to enter a Himalayan cave or sit on a snow-capped mountain in order to realise God. No. Here on earth we have to realise the highest Truth.

But even realisation is not enough. After realisation we have to reveal our realisation. If we do not reveal our realisation, we act like a miser, hoarding our treasure. This is not right. We have to offer our realisation in the form of revelation to mankind.

Yet revelation is not enough, either. We have to enter into the domain of manifestation. If we do not manifest what we have realised here on earth, if Mother Earth does not receive the fruit of our realisation, and if she does not have it for good, we can never be truly fulfilled. Here on earth the manifestation of realisation has to take place; and when manifestation takes place, perfection is bound to dawn. Perfect Perfection is nothing other than the absolute manifestation of God's Transcendental Will here on earth.

We are all seekers of the infinite Truth. It is our bounden duty to rise high, higher, highest. Each human being has come into the world with the message of perfection. No human being on earth will remain unrealised. No human being on earth will remain unfulfilled. No human being on earth will remain imperfect.

Realisation, fulfilment and perfection: these are three

brothers. Realisation is the youngest, fulfilment is the middle and perfect Perfection is the eldest in the family. These three brothers must go together. They have to walk along the road of aspiration. They have to swim in the sea of meditation. They have to fly in the sky of contemplation.

God-realisation, God-revelation and God-manifestation can take place only when man feels that he has to transcend himself. His goal of today is not the ultimate Goal. Today's goal has to be transcended tomorrow. If we transcend ourselves at every moment, deep within us we shall find and manifest the message of perfection.

* * *

THEY ARE KNOWN

By the servant's submissiveness,
    The master is known.

By the lover's oneness,
    The beloved is known.

By the wife's unhappiness,
    The husband is known.

By the disciple's aspiration,
    The Guru is known.

By man's perfection,
    God is known.

* * *

THEY ALL DISAPPEAR

Darkness disappears
  When dawn appears.

Hate disappears
  When love appears.

Ego disappers
  When oneness appears.

Ignorance disappears
  When perfection appears.

* * *

*Question: If all creation and all interplay between
man and his environment are nothing but the manifestation of God, then the whole universe is, in truth,
divine. If this is so, then what about the problem of evil?*

Sri Chinmoy: Here we are making a mistake. God is
in everything. The universe is God's manifestation, but
it is not yet God's Perfection. In the case of mankind,
God is proceeding toward His Self-perfection through
the process of evolution. Perfection has not yet taken
place. The harmony is not yet perfect; nothing is
perfect yet. God is acting, He is moving, He is doing
everything; but perfection, divine perfection, has not
yet taken place. Divine perfection is the gradual transformation of our entire being, of our entire consciousness. Transformation, perfection and Immortality:

these three go together. God is revealing Himself in and through His manifestation. He has descended into matter; the Spirit has descended into matter. Now, with aspiration, the Spirit has to return to its highest sphere. When it goes to its highest sphere and brings down infinite Light, Peace and Bliss into the physical, then a transformation can take place. And when this transformation takes place, perfection is bound to dawn on humanity and the universe.

* * *

FROM GLORY TO GLORY

My awakened body
Is walking from glory to glory.

My transformed vital
Is marching from glory to glory.

My illumined mind
Is running from glory to glory.

My liberated heart
Is flying from glory to glory.

My fulfilled soul
Is dancing from glory to glory.

* * *

ABOUT SRI CHINMOY

Sri Chinmoy is a fully realised spiritual Master dedicated to inspiring and serving those seeking a deeper meaning in life. Through his teaching of meditation, lectures and writings, and through his own life of dedicated service to humanity, he tries to show others how to find inner peace and fulfilment.

Born in Bengal in 1931, Sri Chinmoy entered an ashram (spiritual community) at the age of 12. His life of intense spiritual practice included meditating for up to 14 hours a day, together with writing poetry, essays and devotional songs, doing selfless service and practising athletics. While still in his early teens, he had many profound inner experiences and attained spiritual realisation. He remained in the ashram for 20 years, deepening and expanding his realisation, and in 1964 came to New York City to share his inner wealth with sincere seekers.

Today, Sri Chinmoy serves as a spiritual guide to disciples in some 80 centres around the world. He teaches the "Path of the Heart," which he feels is the simplest way to make rapid spiritual progress. By meditating on the spiritual heart, he teaches, the seeker can discover his own inner treasures of peace, joy, light and love. The role of a spiritual Master, according to Sri Chinmoy, is to help the seeker live so that these inner riches can illumine his life. Sri Chinmoy lovingly instructs his disciples in the inner life and elevates their consciousness not only beyond their expectation, but even beyond their imagination. In return he asks his students to meditate regularly and to try to nurture the inner qualities he brings to the fore in them.

Sri Chinmoy teaches that love is the most direct way for a seeker to approach the Supreme. When a child feels love for his father, it does not matter how great the father is in the world's eye; through his love the child feels only his oneness with his father and his father's possessions. This same approach, applied to the Supreme, permits the seeker to feel that the Supreme and His own Eternity, Infinity and Immortality are the seeker's own. This philosophy of love, Sri Chinmoy feels, expresses the deepest bond between man and God, who are aspects of the same unified consciousness. In the life-game, man fulfils himself in the Supreme by realising that God is man's own highest self. The Supreme reveals Himself through man, who serves as His instrument for world transformation and perfection.

Sri Chinmoy's path does not end with realisation. Once we realise the highest, it is still necessary to manifest this reality in the world around us. In Sri Chinmoy's words, "To climb up the mango tree is great, but it is not enough. We have to climb down again to distribute the mangoes and make the world aware of their significance. Until we do this, our role is not complete and God will not be satisfied or fulfilled."

In the traditional Indian fashion, Sri Chinmoy does not charge a fee for his spiritual guidance, nor does he charge for his frequent lectures, concerts or public meditations. His only fee, he says, is the seeker's sincere inner cry. Sri Chinmoy takes a personal interest in each of his students, and when he accepts a disciple, he takes full responsibility for that seeker's inner progress. In New York, Sri Chinmoy meditates in person with his disciples several times a week and offers a regular Wednesday evening meditation session for the general public. Students living outside New York see Sri Chinmoy during worldwide gatherings that take place three times a year, during visits to New York, or during the Master's frequent trips to their cities. They find that the inner bond between Master and disciple transcends physical separation.

As part of his selfless offering to humanity, Sri Chinmoy conducts peace meditations twice each week for ambassadors and staff at United Nations Headquarters in New York. He also conducts peace meditations for government officials at the United States Congress in Washington, D.C., and recently he was invited to inaugurate a regular series of meditations at the British Parliament.

In addition, Sri Chinmoy leads an active life, demonstrating most vividly that spirituality is not an escape from the world, but a means of transforming it. He has written more than 700 books, which include plays, poems, stories, essays, commentaries and answers to questions on spirituality. He has painted some 140,000 widely exhibited mystical paintings and composed more than 5,000 devotional songs.

Sri Chinmoy accepts students at all levels of development, from beginners to advanced seekers, and lovingly guides them inwardly and outwardly according to their individual needs. For further information, please write to:

Aum Publications
86-24 Parsons Blvd.
Jamaica, N.Y. 11432

BOOKS

Beyond Within: A Philosophy for the Inner Life, $10.95
522 pages

In this book Sri Chinmoy offers profound insight into man's relationship with God and sound advice on how to integrate the highest spiritual aspirations into your daily life. Including essay questions and answers, poetry and parables on: the spiritual journey, the transformation and perfection of the body, meditation, using the soul's will to conquer life's problems, the relationship between the mind and physical illness, the purpose of pain and suffering, overcoming fear of failure, throwing away guilt, the occult and much more.

Meditation: Man-Perfection in God-Satisfaction, $6.95
300 pages

Presented with the simplicity and clarity that have become the hallmark of Sri Chinmoy's writings, this book is easily one of the most comprehensive guides to meditation ever written. Some key topics: proven meditation techniques that anyone can learn, how to still the restless mind, developing the power of concentration, carrying peace with you *always!*, awakening the heart centre to discover the power of your soul, how to effectively pray . . . plus special section in which Sri Chinmoy answers questions on a wide range of experiences often encountered in meditation.

Kundalini: The Mother-Power, $4.95

Enroute to his own spiritual perfection, Sri Chinmoy attained mastery over the Kundalini and occult powers. In this book, he explains the different techniques for awakening the Kundalini and the chakras. He warns of the dangers and pitfalls to be avoided and discusses some of the occult powers that come with the opening of the chakras. Topics include: developing occult power, the significance of the different chakras, concentration and will power, mantras to awaken the Kundalini centres, opening the heart centre and more.

oga and the Spiritual Life, $4.95

This book clearly presents the major concepts of India's mystical adition in a form specifically tailored for Western readers. It pro- des a perfect introduction for the beginner and yet offers much ore to advanced students of Yoga and Eastern mysticism. Of par- cular interest is the section devoted to questions and answers on e soul and the inner life. Some of the topics covered include: derstanding the enigmatic law of karma, reincarnation and evo- tion, using mantra and japa to develop purity, the soul's mission d the synthesis of East and West.

eath and Reincarnation, $4.95

This deeply moving book has brought consolation and under- anding to countless people faced with the death of a loved one or ar of their own mortality. Topics include: how you can overcome ur fear of death, is death painful, postponing the hour of death, e meaning of a violent death, the truth about reincarnation, lping those who are dying, the soul's journey after death and the eaning of Heaven and hell.

he Summits of God-Life: Samadhi and Siddhi, $3.95

This book is Sri Chinmoy's first-hand account of states of con- iousness that only a handful of Masters through the ages have er experienced. Not a philosophical or theoretical work, but a vid and detailed description of the farthest possibilities of human nsciousness — essential reading for all seekers longing to discover eir own spiritual potential.

Child's Heart and a Child's Dreams: Growing Up with iritual Wisdom — A Guide for Parents and Children, $4.95

Sri Chinmoy offers practical advice on a subject that is not only idealist's dream, but a concerned parent's lifeline: fostering ur child's spiritual life, watching him or her grow up with the ve of God and a heart of self-giving. Topics include: insuring ur child's spiritual growth, education and spirituality — their eeting ground, answers to children's questions about God and a ide to meditation.

Astrology, the Supernatural and the Beyond, $4.95

Sri Chinmoy describes the unseen forces that operate in an
around you. You'll learn how to welcome the positive forces whi
protecting yourself from the negative ones. Topics include: propl
esy, occult power, black magic, psychic power, the spirit worlc
mediums, spiritual healing, life on other planets, flying sauce
and hostile forces.

God's Hour: Daily Meditation for Spiritual Living, $4.95

The daily meditations in this book will bring a special glow t
your life. Reading them every morning will open your eyes to ne
possibilities and fill your day with energy and direction. The 36
meditations offer the rare inspiration, wisdom and guidance whic
can only come from a true spiritual Master.

My Lord's Secrets Revealed, $4.95 ($9.95 hardbound)

What does God really feel about you? For starters, He knows a
your thoughts and everything you've ever done . . . or intend
do. This can be pretty scarry. What's more, He's omnipotent. Th
can be downright frightening. But before you decide to forget tl
whole thing and move out of the universe, Sri Chinmoy wants
let you in on some of God's most closely guarded secrets. Secr
number one: God loves you infinitely more than you love yoursel
Secret number two: There's nothing you could ever do to mal
God stop loving you. Secret number three: God wonders why yc
don't talk with Him more and why you seem to be afraid of Him

How, you might ask, did Sri Chinmoy uncover all these secret
He has been blessed with a life of loving oneness with God and,
he describes in this book, God simply told him. A profoundly up
lifting and inspiring book.

Songs of the Soul, $4.95 ($9.95 hardbound)

The soul is the spark of divinity within you, the part of you
nature that is in constant communion with God. If you were awa
of what your soul is telling you, your life's problems would en
You would know what to do all the time and have the courage
do it. Right now, however, it may be difficult to separate the soul
clear message from your thoughts, emotions and desires.

To help you discover your own soul's truth, Sri Chinmoy has di
tilled the essence of his own inner experiences in this rare and ill

nining book. The deep wisdom offered here reveals the inmost mysteries of the soul and serves as an unwavering guide for all on the spiritual path.

Flower-Flames, $9.95
(An anthology selected from the original 100-volume *10,000 Flower-Flames* series)

In 1979 Sri Chinmoy began writing a series of poems that when completed, less than four years later, numbered 10,000. Originally published in 100 volumes, they were called *10,000 Flower-Flames* and have since become an integral part of Sri Chinmoy's teachings on living the spiritual life. Now the Master has chosen 207 of his favourite poems from this series to be published in one volume.

These poems will slip into that centre of stillness which transcends the limits of your mind, there to resonate with your eternal Self. If you learn a few by heart and repeat them over and over, like mantras or prayers, they will reveal their power to calm the mind and awaken your awareness to the divinity within.

TAPES

Flute Music for Meditation, $8.95
While in a state of deep meditation, Sri Chinmoy plays his haunting melodies on the echo flute. It's rich and soothing tones will transport you to the highest realms of inner peace and harmony.

Ecstasy's Trance: Esraj Music for Meditation, $8.95
The esraj, often described as a cross between a sitar and a violin, is Sri Chinmoy's favourite instrument. He seems to draw the music from another dimension. The source of these unforgettable compositions is the silent realm of the deepest and most sublime meditation.

Inner and Outer Peace, $8.95

A tapestry of music, poetry and aphorisms on inner and outer peace. Sri Chinmoy's profoundly inspiring messages are woven into the calm and uplifting music, with the Master chanting and playing the flute, esraj, cello, harpsichord and synthesizer.

Existence, Consciousness, Bliss, $8.95

In 1984 Sri Chinmoy embarked on a Peace Concert tour that took him to major cities in the U.S., Canada, Europe, Japan and Australia. The response to these concerts was overwhelming, as thousands turned out to hear the Master's musical call for peace. This powerful tape captures some of the most stirring moments of these concerts. Sri Chinmoy sings and plays the esraj, bamboo flute, echo flute and harmonium.

The Dance of Light: Sri Chinmoy Plays the Flute, $9.95

Forty-seven soft and gentle flute melodies that will carry you directly to the source of joy and beauty: your own aspiring heart. Comes with a free booklet on music-meditation.

Please send your order to:
AUM PUBLICATIONS
Dept. BM
86-24 Parsons Blvd.
Jamaica, NY 11432

Shipping: $2.00 for first item, $.50 for each additional item.